QUALITY OF JUSTICE

General Council of the Bar

QUALITY OF JUSTICE
THE BAR's RESPONSE

Published by Butterworths on behalf of The General Council of the Bar
1989

Published by Butterworth & Co (Publishers) Ltd
88 Kingsway, London WC2B 6AB on behalf of

The General Council of the Bar
11 South Square, Gray's Inn, London WC1R 5EL

© 1989 The General Council of the Bar

ISBN 0 406 88899 X

Photoset by Phoenix Photosetting, Chatham
Printed and bound in Great Britain by
Mackays of Chatham PLC, Chatham, Kent

Contents

Chapter 1   **Introduction**   1
The Aims of the Bar Council   1
Change   3
Time for Response   3
The Burden of Proof   4
The Scheme of this Book   4

Chapter 2   **Summary of Bar Council's Response**   6
The Starting Point   6
A Career at the Bar   7
Structure of the Bar   8
Access to Justice for All   10
The Government's Main Proposals are
    fundamentally flawed   12
Rights of Audience   13
Direct Lay Access to Counsel   15
Attendance on Counsel   15
Crown Prosecution Service   15
Independence of the Judges and the Legal
    Profession   16
Partnerships, Incorporation and Multi-
    Disciplinary Practices (MDPs)   16
Appointment of the Judiciary   17
Queen's Counsel   18
Professional Standards   18
Legal Education Committee   19
The Foreign Dimension: The EEC, the
    U.S.A. and the Commonwealth   19
Probate   20
Conveyancing   21
Contingency Fees   21
Ethnic Minorities   22

	Professional Bodies in the Legal Professions	22
	Epilogue	23
Chapter 3	**The Context of The Green Papers**	24
	The Royal Commission on Legal Services	24
	The Government's Response to the Commission Report	25
	Independence and Self-Regulation	26
	Fusion of the Profession	26
	Rights of Audience	28
	The Marre Commitee	29
	The Government's Approach in the Green Papers	31
	Proposals not thought through	34
	The present Context	34
Chapter 4	**Legal Professions**	36
Chapter 5	**Solicitors' and Barristers' Practices**	39
	Solicitors	41
	Barristers	42
	Transfer between the Bar and Solicitors	43
Chapter 6	**The Bar**	47
	Independence and the "Cab-Rank" Rule	47
	Barristers as Consultants	49
	The Bar today	50
Chapter 7	**The Judges**	56
Chapter 8	**Accountants' Firms**	61
Chapter 9	**Access to Justice for All**	64
	What does this mean?	64
	Lack of Access to Justice	64
	Legal Aid	65
	Legal Aid for Representation in Civil Proceedings	66
	Legal Advice and Assistance (the Green Form Scheme)	66
	Fair and Reasonable Remuneration	68
	Deficiences in the Legal Aid System	68
	What can the Bar do?	71
	The duty of the Bar to do Legal Aid work	71
	Free Representation by the Bar	72
	The Further Development of FRU	72
	Tribunals before which Legal Aid is not available	72

	Advice to Charities	74
	Preliminary proposals for FRU	75
	Citizens Advice Bureaux and other Agencies	76
	Law Centres	77
	Agencies generally	78
	Conciliation and out-of-court settlement	78
	Simplification of Court and Tribunal Procedures	80
	Administration of Courts and Tribunals	80
	Contingency Fees	83
Chapter 10	**Fundamental Flaws in the Green Papers**	84
	A little History	86
	The Practical Consequences of the Government's Proposals	88
	Solicitors and Barristers in the same Practices	89
	Conflict of Interest	91
	Accountants and other Professionals in practice with Solicitors and Barristers	93
	Medium-sized Solicitor Firms	94
	Small Solicitor Firms	99
	The Threat to Small Solicitor Firms	99
	The Independent Bar	103
	Ending of Separation of Legal Professions	106
	The Royal Commission	106
	Separate Legal Professions	107
	Rights of Audience in the Higher Courts	111
	Multi-Disciplinary Practices (MDPs) and Partnerships at the Bar	113
	Conveyancing	115
	Lay Direct Access to Barristers	115
	The Next Stage after the Royal Commission	116
Chapter 11	**Competition – Choice – Access – Quality – Cost**	117
	The Present Position	117
	Competition and Choice	120
	Monopolies	123
	Access	123
	Quality	125
	Cost	125
Chapter 12	**Rights of Audience – Direct Access to Counsel – Attendance on Counsel**	128
	Rights of Audience	128
	Control by the Judges, not the Government	131
	Audience in the Higher Courts	132
	Certification	134

Pleas of Guilty in Crown Court 136
Education and Training 137
Advisory Committee 137
Employed Barristers and Solicitors 137
Crown Prosecution Service 138
Lay Advocacy 138
Advocacy by Government Departments 139
Transitional Arrangements 139
Direct Access to Counsel 140
Lay Access 140
Professional Access 142
Attendance on Counsel 143

Chapter 13 The Crown Prosecution Service 146
Scotland and the Office of Procurator Fiscal 152
Treasury Counsel 155
The Main Danger, and how it is now avoided 155
The Green Papers 157
The Way Ahead: the Bar Council's Proposals 161
Crown Courts 162

**Chapter 14 Independence of the Judges and the
Legal Profession** 163

**Chapter 15 Partnerships, Incorporation and Multi-
Disciplinary Practices** 170
The Templeman Committee 170
Royal Commission on Legal Services 171
Director-General of Fair Trading 171
Less Choice 171
Reduced Access 172
Less Competition 173
Decline in Standards 173
Increased Cost 174
Incorporation 177
Overseas Practice 177
Purse-Sharing 177
Multi-Disciplinary Practices (MDPs) 178
The EEC and Foreign Dimensions 181

Chapter 16 Appointment of the Judiciary 183
Ex-Barrister Judges 183
Ex-Solicitor Judges 185
Qualifications for Promotion to the Bench 185
Who should appoint the Judges 186

Chapter 17 Queen's Counsel 188

Chapter 18   Professional Standards   191
           The Bar   191
           Codes of Conduct   193
           Advisory Committee   195
           Legal Services Ombudsman   196
           Liability for Costs   196

Chapter 19   Legal Education, Training, and Specialisation   198
           Legal Education and Training   198
           Academic Stage   198
           Funding of University and Polytechnic Law
              Schools   1998
           Vocational Stage   200
           Common Vocational Training   201
           Students Grants and other Funding   202
           Pupillage: the Practical Stage   203
           Finance in Pupillage   205
           Pupillage with Employed Barristers   205
           Continuing Education   206
           Specialisation   206
           Lord Chancellor's Advisory Committee   207
           A Legal Education Committee   208

Chapter 20   Barristers Practices and Advertising   209
           Recruitment   209
           Pupillages   210
           Allocation of Pupillages   210
           Financing of Pupils   211
           Estabilishment in Practice at the Bar   212
           Tenancies   212
           Chambers   212
           Other Means of Establishment   214
           A Library System   215
           Employment of Others   216
           Financing of Barristers in Early Years of
              Practice   216
           Management of Chambers   217
           Circuits   217
           Other Restrictions   218
           Overseas Practice   218
           Advertising   219
           Advertising and Publicity in the Future   220
           Contracts for Fees   220

**Chapter 21   The Foreign Dimension: The EEC, U.S.A.
           and Commonwealth**   220
           Work of English Barristers in Europe   221

European Community: Potential Problems 223
Multi-Disciplinary Practices (MDPs) 226
Multi-National Practices (MNPs) 227
Contingency Fees 227
Conveyancing 227
Pause for Thought 228
The United States of America 228
U.S. and District Attorneys 231
Lessons to be learned from the
   Commonwealth 232
New Zealand 232
Australia 235
Canada 239

Chapter 22   Probate 242
Fraud 243
Incompetence 243
Who should do Probate Work for Reward? 244
Extension of Section 23 244
The Oath 244
Charges 245
Share Capital of Trust Corporations 246

Chapter 23   Conveyancing 247
The Average House-Buyer 248
The "One-Stop-Shop" 249
The Royal Commission on Legal Services 250
Adequate Safeguards? 251
Inconsistency with Consumer Credit
   Protection 254
Social Needs 256
Conclusion 257

Chapter 24   Contingency Fees 258
The Speculative Basis 258
The Revised Speculative Basis 261
The Restricted and Unrestricted Award-
   Sharing Bases 262
Contingency Legal Aid Fund 263
The Balance of Benefit and Detriment 264
Excluded Proceedings 265

Chapter 25   Ethnic Minorities 267

Chapter 26   Professional Bodies 270
The Bar 270
Solicitors 272

Chapter 27   Epilogue 274

Annexes

(These Annexes are separate from this book)

Annex 1 Fusion of the Legal Profession? Article by Dr. F. A. Mann C.B.E. F.B.A. in (1977) 93 L.Q.R. 367–377

Annex 2 Evidence of the High Court Judges and the Circuit Judges to the Royal Commission on Legal Services

Annex 3 Report by Professor Yamey C.B.E. F.B.A. April 1989

Annex 4 Report by Working Party of the General Council of the Bar on Contingency Fees (Chairman: Francis Ferris Q.C.) January 1989

Annex 5 Report dated 17 January 1989 of the Accommodation Committee of the Bar Council (Chairman: the Hon Mr. Justice Hirst)

1

Introduction

1.1 The General Council of the Bar of England and Wales publishes this book in response to the Government's three Green Papers of January 1989 on some aspects of the system of justice in England and Wales, entitled (1) The Work and Organisation of the Legal Profession; (2) Contingency Fees; and (3) Conveyancing by Authorised Practitioners, referred to hereafter as the "main Green Paper", the "Contingency Fees Green Paper" and the "Conveyancing Green Paper". This book has the full support and approval of the members of the Bar Council, of each of the Circuits and of each of the specialist Bar Associations.

THE AIMS OF THE BAR COUNCIL

1.2 This book is directed throughout to the interests of the public, of every man, woman and child in England and Wales, as "consumers of legal services", to use the wording of the Green Papers. The proposals made by the Bar Council and its criticisms of the Government's proposals are to be judged according to whether they best serve the interests of the public and the administration of justice throughout England and Wales, and *not* according to whether they serve the interests of the Bar.

1.3 The aims of the Bar of England and Wales are to ensure:

(1) *Justice*: that everyone can obtain justice in the Courts within a reasonable time and at reasonable expense;

(2) *Access*: that everyone has the best possible access to the services of lawyers of the calibre they need, both solicitors and independent and specialist barristers;

(3) *Choice and Competition*: that everyone has the widest possible choice

1

(a) from local solicitors strongly competing with each other
(b) from all the independent and specialist barristers (now about 6,000) strongly competing with each other, the choice of barrister being made with the expert help of a solicitor or other professional;

(4) *"Cab-Rank" Rule*: that barristers are available to represent everyone requiring legal representation whether in criminal or civil proceedings, whoever they may be and whatever their cause;

(5) *Quality and Standards*: that the services provided by independent solicitors and by barristers are of high quality and appropriate to the needs of each client; that the same high quality and standards of service are available to each client, whether poor or rich, and are maintained by strong competition and by the training, ethos and disciplines of the profession exercised both informally and formally;

(6) *Fair and Reasonable Price*: that solicitors and barristers are paid no more and no less than a fair and reasonable price for their services provided in competition;

(7) *Advocacy*: that independent barristers (who develop and maintain their skills and integrity by constant practice in Court and by not being involved in the investigation and assembling of evidence) represent their clients (a) fearlessly, (b) independently of all pressures and conflicting interests whether of Government or otherwise, (c) irrespective of the popularity or unpopularity of the client or the client's cause, and (d) with proper regard to the requirements of the administration of justice;

(8) *Legal Advice*: that objective advice of high quality is available from solicitors and through solicitors and other professionals from an independent Bar;

(9) *Quality of Judges*: that by strong competition between independent barristers engaged in regular practice in Court, there continues to be a supply (but not an exclusive one) of men and women available for promotion as Judges of the highest quality possible, who have been tested in the Courts for their judicial calibre and assessed as suitable for promotion by the Judges.

1.4 These aims include the aims stated in the Government's main Green Paper. But they go beyond the Government's aims, particularly in requiring access to the same quality of justice for poor as well as rich, and access to justice throughout the country through the availability of local solicitors and of all members of the Bar on a consultant basis.

CHANGE

1.5   The Bar Council and its members fully support evolutionary change of the legal system and of the legal profession to meet the changing needs of the public and of the administration of justice in the public interest. By "evolutionary change" is meant change to improve the system and the profession, and to remedy known defects, not change for change's sake.

1.6   The Green Papers were issued at a time when the barrister profession was already undergoing radical changes, for example in the education and training of barristers, with the full support of successive Lord Chancellors. Some of these changes as already made or already in train are outlined in Chapter 6 below. Others form part of the Bar Council's proposals, set out in this book.

1.7   The Bar Council has taken the opportunity given by the debate on the Green Papers to initiate further profound changes in the structure and practices of the profession. These changes are summarised in Chapter 2 and dealt with more fully in later Chapters, especially Chapters 19 and 20. In many respects they go beyond what the Government is proposing.

TIME FOR RESPONSE

1.8   The changes proposed by the Bar Council are not in complete form, and the response of the Bar Council to the Government's proposals is not complete. The time allowed for responding, 3 months, is far too short to allow a fully considered response to proposed far-reaching changes which if implemented would be adverse to the interests of the public and to the good administration of justice in many respects. To assemble the evidence required to back up the Bar Council's response will take longer than 3 months. So the Bar Council will continue to add to its response and to refine it after 2 May 1989.

1.9   Not merely is the time for responding too short, but also the Green Papers were conceived in haste, in a period of only 3 months. There were no studies of the merits or defects of the present structure, no examination of the consequences of the Government's proposals, no assessment whether they would in fact remedy any defects in the present structure, or whether they would in turn cause damage to the public interest, and if so whether that damage would or would not outweigh any present defects. No calculation of the costs to the taxpayer was made: see the Lord Chancellor's written answer in the House of Lords on 4 April 1989. The evidence reaching the Bar Council, and in particular from solicitors practising in firms other than the largest firms, of whom some 1400 have written to the Bar Council, indicates that the public would be substantially worse off if the Government proposals went through, in terms of less choice, less competition, reduced access, lower quality and increased cost. So the failure of the Government to carry out any of this necessary preparatory work, combined with the failure to allow a sufficient period for consultation, gives rise to all the more concern.

1.10   The Bar Council has not asked for more time so as to be able to respond with detailed evidence, because it is clear that if the Bar Council did so that would be used as a basis for criticism of the profession.

THE BURDEN OF PROOF

1.11   The Government has formulated in the Green Papers a large number of complex proposals with complex inter-relationships between them. The Government has then effectively put the Bar to proof that (1) the structure of the legal profession is in the public interest; and (2) that the Government's proposals are not in the public interest. The Bar is given 3 months to do this. Naturally it is not possible to assemble all the evidence to prove both the merits of the present system and the demerits of the Government's proposals in 3 months.

1.12   But the Government ignores the fact that there has been a recent and comprehensive review of every aspect of the legal profession and the provisions of legal services by the Royal Commission on Legal Services (in England and Wales) and a similar Royal Commission in Scotland. The work of the Royal Commission and its long report provides the clearest statement of the relevant evidence on all matters covered by the Green Papers. So in this book there will be found many references to the evidence placed before the Royal Commission and to the conclusions reached on that evidence. Reference will also be made to the subsequent report by the Marre Committee. Where it has been possible in the time allowed, reference is made to the further evidence now available to the Bar Council.

THE SCHEME OF THIS BOOK

1.13   Chapter 2 contains a brief summary of the Bar Council's positive proposals and some of the main points of criticism of the Government's proposals in the 3 Green Papers.

Chapter 3 sets the Government's proposals in context.

Chapters 4 to 8 contain brief statements of facts relating to the barristers and solicitors professions, the Judiciary and the accountants profession, as background to the remaining Chapters.

Chapters 9 to 27 contain the details of the Bar's positive proposals and of the criticisms of the Government's proposals.

1.14 The Annexes are in a separate volume.

2

Summary of Bar Council's Response

2.1 This summary contains a brief outline of the Bar Council's Response to the Green Papers with the Bar Council's main proposals and its principal criticisms of the Government's proposals.

THE STARTING POINT

2.2 The Bar Council's starting point is that the public will be best served by continuance of the independent barristers' and solicitors' professions with their separate and specialised functions. Amalgamation or fusion of the two professions whether by law or in practice would be contrary to the public's needs as the Royal Commission, the Marre Committee, the Director General of Fair Trading and Lord Mackay himself have stated. The cornerstones of the Bar as a specialist profession are cost-effectiveness and strong competition in "the most competitive business going", as the Lord Chancellor has described the Bar.

2.3 The strength of the Bar lies in its independence, in the "cab-rank" rule made possible by the independence of barristers in private practice as sole practitioners, and in its being a consultant profession acting on referral from solicitors and other professionals. The "cab-rank" rule requires a barrister to represent fearlessly any client without regard to the character, reputation or cause of the client. This rule has been described by Lord Mackay as an "important constitutional guarantee" (para. 6.1(2) below).

2.4 Only those rules of the Bar which are necessary for the maintenance of its independence, the "cab-rank" rule and the consultant nature of the profession should be maintained. Rules which are not necessary to ensure this will be removed. The Bar Council will move to change its rules with despatch, taking full account of the interests of the public which must be paramount.

A CAREER AT THE BAR

2.5   Academic Stage of Education (Chapter 19)

(1) The entry requirements (a first or second class honours degree, and qualification in some core law subjects) should be maintained (para. 19.2).

(2) The core subjects should be kept to a minimum (para. 19.3).

(3) The laws of the European Community and the European Convention on Human Rights should be studied at the Academic stage or the Vocational stage (para. 19.4).

(4) The teaching of foreign languages in schools, universities, polytechnics and vocational courses requires urgent upgrading. The Bar Council will offer language courses as part of its continuing education and training (para. 19.5).

(5) Close collaboration has been established by the Bar Council and the Council of Legal Education, which runs the Inns of Court School of Law (ICSL), with the Chairmen of the Committees of Heads of Law Schools at the Universities and Polytechnics. This will be maintained and broadened (para. 19.6).

(6) Funding of the Law Schools at the Universities and Polytechnics needs to be improved if standards are to be maintained and adequate numbers of future barristers and solicitors are to be taught at the Law Schools (para. 19.7).

2.6   Vocational Stage of Training (Chapter 19)

(1) The new ICSL course will be the only full course wholly devoted to the teaching of advocacy, negotiation and communication skills and professional ethics and conduct. Any student wishing to aim for a career in advocacy in the higher Courts will need to come to the ICSL for the foreseeable future whatever changes the Government may propose (para. 19.8).

(2) The Government needs to ensure that local education authority (LEA) grants for students during the vocational stage are provided according to established criteria, rather than the present arbitrary basis (paras. 19.14, 19.15, 20.4).

(3) Common training for Bar and solicitor students appears to be impractical (paras. 19.10 to 19.13).

(4) The Bar Council with the Inns of Court will continue to do all that it can to ensure that students are fully aware of what is involved in a career at the Bar (paras. 19.11 to 19.12). The Bar Council is committed to its existing policy for easy transfer, in either direction, between the Bar and the Solicitor profession (para. 5.20).

(5) It is the Bar Council's policy that scholarship funds of the Inns should be devoted primarily to helping students on the vocational

course (paras. 19.15 and 20.4). The aim is to ensure that with the help of LEA grants, Inns scholarships and some help from Chambers, each of the Bar students will be adequately financed during the vocational year so as to avoid the build-up of an undue burden of loans.

(6) The mix of students coming to the ICSL for the vocational stage is wide and growing wider (paras. 6.6 and 19.15).

2.7 Pupillage: the Practical Stage of Training (Chapters 19 and 20)

(1) One year's pupillage (with the pupil engaging in some advocacy during the second six months) is a vital part of the training of an advocate, and should always be with an experienced and approved pupil-master (paras 19.16 to 19.18).

(2) The Bar Council and the Inns will maintain and improve the scheme for the registration of pupil masters and for the content of pupillage training (paras. 19.16 and 20.10).

(3) Pupillages at the employed Bar will continue to be developed in cooperation with the Bar Association for Commerce, Finance and Industry, the Government Legal Service, the Crown Prosecution Service, Local Government and others (paras. 19.21 and 20.12).

(4) The Bar Council recognises that it is the obligation of the profession to ensure that all properly qualified pupils are adequately remunerated, and has resolved to set a level of minimum income for pupils annually, so that each pupil will be in receipt during the 12 months of pupillage of that minimum income, and that it will be the professional obligation of all members of the Bar to ensure that this requirement is met. A working party is to report by 20 May 1989 with detailed proposals for a scheme which could be implemented by the Bar to make this provision for finance for pupils (paras. 19.19 and 20.13).

(5) This should be achieved without causing any major reduction in the number of pupils (paras. 19.20 and 20.14).

(6) A Pupillage and Tenancy Recruitment Information Centre (PATRIC) is to be in place by the summer of 1989 to help with the allocation of pupillages. From 1990 it is intended that the use of PATRIC will be mandatory (para. 20.9).

(7) Steps will be taken with the help of the Bar Council's Race Relations Committee to ensure that students from ethnic minorities continue to obtain their fair share of pupillages (para. 20.11 and Chapter 25).

STRUCTURE OF THE BAR (Chapter 20)

2.8 At present the only way to become established at the Bar is by finding a tenancy in chambers. The Bar Council intends to ensure other means of establishment through a "Library System" modelled on those in Scotland and Ireland in which barristers will be able to practise individually and not within Chambers.

2.9   The Bar Council will use PATRIC as an information centre to help with the allocation of tenancies in Chambers. It is intended that use of PATRIC by Chambers when considering applicants for tenancies will be made compulsory (pars. 20.15 and 20.16).

2.10   No consent will be required for the opening of Chambers (para. 20.18). It is not necessary now to have a clerk and any remaining restrictions based on employment of a clerk will be removed (paras. 20.36 to 20.38). Chambers will have to be registered with the Bar Council and competently and efficiently managed (para. 20.18).

2.11   Steps will continue to be taken in collaboration with the Inns to secure further accommodation, provided that the Government's main proposals which would lead to a substantial contraction of the Bar are not implemented (para. 20.19).

2.12   The Bar Council wishes to work with the Lord Chancellor to ensure adequate library facilities in each of the main Court centres outside London (paras. 20.20 and 20.21).

2.13   Chambers will be encouraged to help those pupils to whom a tenancy is not offered to find a tenancy in other chambers, or to become established in the Library System, or to find another career, and until the pupils' future career is arranged to keep the pupils in Chambers (paras. 20.24 and 20.25).

2.14   The Bar Council will carry out a detailed study of how a Library System could be set up in London, with the intention of starting such a system (in collaboration with Chambers) in 1990 (paras. 20.26 to 20.29).

2.15   The Bar Council recognises the importance of ensuring that young barristers embarking on a career at the Bar have a guaranteed income until their receipts of fees reach a minimum level. The working party referred to in para. 2.7(4) above is to report by 20 May 1989 with detailed proposals for achieving this (paras. 20.31 to 20.36).

2.16   Membership of a Circuit will be strongly encouraged for barristers who practise regularly on a Circuit so as to maintain the collegiate life, the ethos and the discipline of the Circuit (para. 20.39).

2.17 Advertising The limited restrictions now in force will be removed or relaxed, and will be brought into line with those for overseas practice as the minimal restrictions necessary for a consultant profession (paras. 20.43 to 20.47).

2.18 Contracts The Bar Council will welcome a change in the law to enable barristers to contract for their fees and other matters (para. 20.48).

2.19 The Bar Council is already reviewing its rules of practice as set out in the Code of Conduct. It will remove or relax all restrictions contained in its rules in so far as they are not necessary for the maintenance of the quality and standards of the Bar as a consultant profession of independent practitioners operating under the "cab-rank" rule (paras. 20.40 and 20.41).

ACCESS TO JUSTICE FOR ALL (Chapter 9)

2.20 Access to justice for those of small means can be ensured only through (1) adequate Legal Aid, and (2) free legal advice and representation (paras. 9.1 to 9.8).

2.21 The Government has for 10 years reduced the availability of Legal Aid and thus greatly increased the number of those with small means who cannot afford necessary legal advice and representation (paras 9.1 to 9.18).

2.22 Legal aid work is becoming to a major extent unremunerative for solicitors (para. 9.19).

2.23 Legal aid is not available for tribunals deciding points of major importance to those whose cases come before the tribunals (para. 9.15).

2.24 The Legal Aid Scheme requires proper organisation so that it provides the necessary help to those who need it. Efficiency in the management of the social security system and in the Courts and tribunals would save money which could be spent on providing legal aid (pars. 9.20 and 9.51 to 9.58).

2.25 The Bar Council reaffirms the duty of each barrister in independent practice to comply with the "cab-rank" rule, and to represent any client, whether legally aided or not, in cases within each barrister's field of practice. The Bar Council regards it as wrong that instructions of any kind should be refused on the ground that the barrister does not accept legally aided work. The Bar Council will revise the terms in which the "cab-rank" rule is drafted so as to make absolutely clear that it applies (1) to instructions of any kind, and (2) to all work whether legally aided or not. The Bar Council will deal with any case of a barrister failing to abide by the "cab-rank" rule through the Bar's disciplinary procedures. The Bar Council calls on the Government to respond by paying reasonable fees promptly and without the present serious delays (para. 9.22).

2.26 The Bar Council will encourage barristers to undertake "pro bono" work, and will encourage the Free Representation Unit to expand both in London and in other major centres for this purpose (paras. 9.24 to 9.37).

2.27 The Bar Council warns that the large amount of public service work done by barristers and solicitors as part-time Judges would be likely to diminish if the Government's proposals went through (para. 9.37).

2.28 The Citizens Advice Bureaux, Law Centres and Legal Advice Centres cannot take on more work, or even continue with their current volume of work, without assured funding. They cannot be used as a substitute for a proper system of legal aid (paras. 9.38 to 9.43).

2.29 The Bar's and solicitors' work in conciliation and out- of-court settlement needs to be developed further. Working parties of Judges, barristers and solicitors are needed to lay down effective means for bringing to an early conclusion civil and criminal cases which do not need to be fought at trial (paras 9.44 to 9.50).

2.30 The Bar Council makes proposals for taking forward the work of the Civil Justice Review and the Council on Tribunals in simplifying Court and Tribunal procedures (para. 9.51).

2.31 Concern is expressed at the standard of administration of courts and tribunals by the Government departments involved. The proposed Legal Services Ombudsman should have a power to oversee the work of these Government departments and to examine the way in which complaints are dealt with (paras. 9.53 to 9.58).

2.32 Contingency fees are not acceptable in principle. They would have only a very limited application in any event, and could not be a substitute for legal aid (para. 9.59 and Chapter 24 below).

THE GOVERNMENT'S MAIN PROPOSALS ARE FUNDAMENTALLY FLAWED (Chapters 10 and 11)

2.33 In Chapter 10 the Government's main proposals for (1) multi-disciplinary practices involving barristers (2) partnerships between barristers (3) access by lay clients direct to barristers (4) rights of audience in the higher Courts made available to any licensed advocate (5) allowing large finance organisations to do conveyancing and to compete unfairly with solicitors in that field, are considered in the context of

(A) the evidence as to the consequences of these proposals for the public as consumers of legal services
(B) the evidence from the Royal Commission and other bodies that have examined these matters thoroughly.

2.34 The Bar Council regrets that the Government did not consider with more care the nature and consequences of its proposals, and wishes to record the fact that the Government has not allowed adequate time for its proposals to be considered and responded to with detailed evidence (Chapters 1 and 3).

2.35 The practical consequences of the Government's main proposals are considered in Chapter 10. These would include:

(1) Effective fusion of the Bar and the solicitors profession through the introduction of direct access by the lay client to the barrister and the combination of barristers and solicitors in single practices.
(2) Loss of the present system of cross-monitoring which operates to the benefit of the consumer and the Court. At present solicitors monitor barristers for their efficiency as advocates and specialist advisers, and barristers monitor solicitors for thoroughness and integrity towards the Court in their preparation of cases.
(3) A reduction of entrants to the independent Bar, since solicitors or multi-disciplinary practices could offer a career in advocacy without the uncertainties of the Bar.
(4) The immediate loss of some experienced independent barristers to multi-disciplinary practices.
(5) Over a period of years a substantial contraction of the independent Bar, through the developing use of in-house advocates by multi-disciplinary practices.
(6) Loss of many local solicitors' practices through unfair competition of large financial organisations in the field of conveyancing, with the serious loss to the consumer of independent legal advice through such solicitors and the barristers they instruct.
(7) Loss of the work now sent to the independent Bar by these local solicitors, leading to further contraction of the independent Bar.

There is a large and serious body of opinion which considers that the Government's main proposals *will* lead over a period to the loss of the independent Bar and of local Solicitors firms. On any view the *risk* of this loss is substantial. The Green Papers do not show any real advantage to the public which would justify the taking of that risk.

2.36 The consequences of these changes in practical economic terms for the consumer are spelled out in Chapter 11: in particular

(1) reduced competition in the provision of legal services through the loss of independent barristers and the concentration of lawyers in fewer, larger practices, and **not** the greater competition suggested by the Government;
(2) reduced choice for the consumer;
(3) reduced access to legal services for the consumer;
(4) lower quality of advocacy services through lack of constant practice in Court and the peer discipline of independent barristers, leading to lower quality of Judges, and in turn leading to more, longer and more inefficiently conducted trials;
(5) increased cost to the paying consumer through higher prices paid to fewer providers of legal services, and to the taxpayer through the Legal Aid scheme and through the increased number of Courts and Judges required.

RIGHTS OF AUDIENCE (Chapters 12 and 13)

2.37 Rights of audience in the higher courts have long been controlled by the Judges. These rights have been largely confined to barristers in independent practice as sole practitioners with the advantages to the public of (1) the "cab-rank" rule; (2) specialisation by barristers in advocacy and by solicitors in the conduct of case preparation; (3) maximum competition in advocacy; (4) maximum choice of barristers; (5) maximising the constant practice in advocacy needed to develop high standards of competence; and (6) enabling the specialist corps of practitioners in advocacy to develop standards of practice and integrity under firm supervision of the Judges and the influence of "peer group discipline" (paras. 12.3 to 12.5). The Royal Commission in 1979, and the Government in its White Paper in 1983, in Parliamentary statements in 1984 and 1985, and in its White Paper in 1987, concluded that any extension of rights of audience in the higher Courts would be contrary to the public interest.

2.38 Control should be with the Judges, and ultimate control should not be with the Government (paras. 12.10 and 12.11 and Chapter 14). The Bar Council wishes to discuss with the Judges and with the Government the precise boundaries for rights of audience in the different Courts, on the understanding that the basic principles set out in this book would be fully safeguarded in the interests and for the protection of the public.

2.39   If solicitors or others were to be given rights of audience in the higher Courts that should only be on the basis of fair competition on equal terms, e.g. (1) either all advocates should be independent sole practitioners subject to the "cab- rank" rule or none should be; (2) either all advocates should act as consultants or none; (3) barristers and solicitors as advocates in publicly funded work should be paid at the same rates, and not, as at present, at higher rates for solicitors because of their higher overheads (paras. 12.13 and 12.14).

2.40   The Bar Council considers that if other lawyers were to have advocacy rights in the higher Courts, that should only be on the same basis as barristers i.e. independent sole practitioners acting only as consultants and subject to the "cab-rank" rule. The Bar Council would welcome such lawyers as barristers and would ensure that **in practice** there were no barriers to entry to the Bar (see Chapter 20 and paras. 2.8 to 2.19 above), subject to recognition by the Judges (para. 12.14).

2.41   Certification would be an inadequate control of an advocate's ability. The **substance** of selection by solicitors as informed professionals (the present system) is much to be preferred to the proposed **form** of certificates based on the number of "flying hours" in Court, which would encourage litigation and discourage settlement, and would be inappropriate for the specialist nature of many barristers' practices (paras. 12.15 to 12.17).

2.42   The Judges led by the Lord Chancellor as the President of the Supreme Court should be asked to consider carefully and in detail any defects in the present system under which barristers appear in the higher Courts, and any remedies for any defects they may identify (paras. 12.18 and 12.19).

2.43   The decision whether to enter a plea of guilty may well be a difficult matter: in many cases it involves complex points of law or evidence. If less experienced advocates were substituted, that would be likely to lead to fewer sensible pleas of guilty, more Court and Judge time wasted, and greater expense (paras. 12.20 to 12.24).

2.44   Lay advocacy is no substitute for a properly run Legal Aid system or for trained lawyers whether on Legal Aid or not (paras. 12.29 to 12.34).

2.45 The suggested transitional provisions would in any event have to be reconsidered in view of their inappropriateness e.g. for barristers temporarily in employment and for students in training or about to enter training for the Bar (para. 12.36).

DIRECT LAY ACCESS TO COUNSEL (Chapter 12)

2.46 If lay clients were to have direct access to barristers that would turn the Bar into another solicitors profession, with barristers having to deal with lay clients on a continuing basis and to engage in solicitors' specialist work of case preparation. That would be expensive for the public and damaging to the quality of advocacy. It would in serious cases militate against the scrupulous performance of a barrister's duty to the Court, on which our system of justice so much depends. There would be no cross-monitoring (paras. 12.38 to 12.41).

ATTENDANCE ON COUNSEL (Chapter 12)

2.47 Whether Counsel is attended in Court depends on the interests **both** of the lay client **and** of the administration of justice. The Bar already permits barristers to be unattended in Magistrates Courts and the Crown Court where they assess this to be in the interests of both client and public (this is to be extended to the County Court). The power to decide on attendance should continue to be with the barristers but subject to the discretion of the Court either pre-trial or at the trial. The Government's proposal would simply enable the Legal Aid scheme to be run with unattended barristers irrespective of the client's and the public's interests (paras. 12.45 to 12.52).

CROWN PROSECUTION SERVICE (Chapter 13)

2.48 The proposed extension of Crown Prosecutors' rights of audience into cases in the Crown Court

(1) would be contrary to the Government's settled policy since the Crown Court was created (paras. 13.1 to 13.19) including the policy stated in its White Paper as recently as March 1987 (para. 13.17);

(2) would be contrary to the conclusions of two Royal Commissions and the Marre Committee, and previous Lord Chancellors;

(3) The suggestion that such an extension would give a "fillip to morale" of the civil servants in the Crown Prosecution Service (CPS) is no justification for abandoning carefully thought out

policy, and contrary to the Government's general policy to privatise, not to nationalise (paras. 13.20 to 13.24).

(4) The Scottish experience provides little support for the proposed extension (paras. 13.25 to 13.32). The experience in the U.S.A., Canada, Singapore and Hong Kong is against the proposal (paras. 13.20, 13.46, 13.50).

(5) The proposal would be unlikely to achieve cheaper representation, and if it did that would be at the expense of quality (paras. 13.31 and 13.32).

(6) The proposal would cause the loss of the valuable role of prosecuting counsel drawn from barristers in independent practice, and lead to unfortunate "polarisation" between prosecuting and defending lawyers (paras. 13.35 to 13.39 and 13.43 to 13.55).

2.49 The Bar Council puts forward its own constructive proposals to ensure for the CPS the career structure that it wishes to have, without abandoning the Government's policy that prosecuting Counsel drawn from barristers in independent practice should prosecute in the Crown Court (para. 13.56).

INDEPENDENCE OF THE JUDGES AND THE LEGAL PROFESSION (Chapter 14)

2.50 The Government's proposals would be an unfortunate step on the road to Government interference with the independence of Judges and the legal profession, and would in this respect be contrary to the Government's own aims (Chapter 14). The independence of the Bar is essential, because in all criminal cases and in cases such as those involving alleged abuses of power barristers appear for lay clients against the state.

PARTNERSHIPS, INCORPORATION AND MULTI-DISCIPLINARY PRACTICES (MDPs) (Chapter 15)

2.51 If barristers were to be permitted to enter into partnership or incorporated practices or multi-disciplinary practices that would be inconsistent with the basic requirement of independence and would remove the benefit to the public of the "cab-rank" rule.

2.52 Over a period of time barristers would be drawn into such practices and not be available to the general public at the independent Bar. That would have further adverse effects for the public:-

(1) **Choice** of advocate would be reduced (paras. 15.8 and 15.9): otherwise the conflicts of interest would be unacceptable (para. 15.9)
(2) **Access** and **competition** would equally be reduced (paras. 15.10 and 15.11)
(3) **Standards** would tend to fall, as the Templeman Committee advised (para. 15.12)
(4) **Costs** would increase (para. 15.13).

2.53 The proposal is contrary to the advice of (1) the Templeman Committee (2) the Royal Commission (3) the Director General of Fair Trading (4) Lord Mackay when leader of the Scottish Bar (paras. 15.3 to 15.6, para. 10.5(4), para. 15.14).

2.54 The advantage of partnership to barristers would be small, and outweighed by the damage to the public interest (paras. 15.16 to 15.18).

2.55 Incorporation would suffer from the same disadvantages as partnership for barristers (para. 15.19).

2.56 "Purse-sharing" at the Bar has been an unsuccessful experiment and is no support for any argument in favour of partnership. It is to be re-examined by the Bar Council (para. 15.21).

2.57 MDPs involving barristers would be in effect fusion of barristers with other professions and would remove the present benefits of independence and the "cab-rank" rule, as Lord Mackay himself has pointed out (paras. 15.22 to 15.24).

2.58 MDPs involving solicitors would have adverse consequences for the public interest without sufficient countervailing advantage to the public (paras. 15.25 to 15.28).

2.59 EEC and other foreign considerations point to the need for an agreed European Community approach before MDPs involving solicitors were considered for the U.K. (paras. 15.29 to 15.31).

APPOINTMENT OF THE JUDICIARY (Chapter 16)

2.60 The Bar Council supports the eligibility of solicitor Circuit Judges for promotion to the High Court Bench (paras. 16.1 to 16.10).

2.61 The proposed qualifications for the High Court Bench based on "full general advocacy certificates" would have excluded most of the Lords of Appeal and many of the Lords Justice and High Court Judges from promotion to that Bench. In any event that proposal would not be appropriate for the specialised Bar of England and Wales and would have to be re-considered (paras. 16.11 and 16.12).

17

2.62 Solicitors should continue to sit for 3 years as part- time Judges before promotion to the Circuit Bench (para. 16.13).

2.63 Consideration should be given to the appointment of Judges on the recommendation of a Judicial Appointments Board. A committee of Privy Councillors drawn from senior Judges and non-lawyers should be asked to consider this and recommend what changes should be made (paras. 16.14 to 16.19).

QUEEN'S COUNSEL (Chapter 17)

2.64 The title of Queen's Counsel should continue to be used to denote independent sole practitioners adhering to the "cab-rank" rule (para. 17.3 to 17.7).

2.65 The experience in Australia and New Zealand is that this has been a significant factor in maintaining the independent Bars in those countries (para. 17.12).

2.66 The qualifications proposed would (as in the case of the Judges: para 2.61 above) be inappropriate and would need in any event to be reconsidered (para. 17.8).

2.67 Consideration should be given to the appointment of Queen's Counsel on the recommendation of the Judges. The Committee referred to in para. 2.63 above should be asked to consider this and to recommend what changes should be made (paras. 17.9 to 17.11).

PROFESSIONAL STANDARDS (Chapter 18)

2.68 The Bar's Code of Conduct should continue to be supervised by the Judges (paras. 18.5 to 18.9).

2.69 Advisory Committee There should be a Legal Professional Standards Committee advising the Judges on the Codes of Conduct and standards of the Bar and the solicitors with lay representation (paras. 18.10 and 18.11).

2.70 Legal Services Ombudsman There should be such an Ombudsman, provided that

(1) he should examine allegations of maladministration of the Courts and Tribunals by the Government departments concerned and their handling of complaints, since delays in cases,

18

for which solicitors and barristers are often blamed, are not infrequently caused by problems in the administration of the Courts by Government departments (para. 9.58);

(2) in respect of the Bar he should examine only the handling of complaints about barristers by the Bar Council, and should not interfere in the decisions by Judges as Chairmen of Disciplinary Tribunals or on appeals to the Judges as the Visitors (para. 18.12);

(3) any question of payment of compensation by the Bar Council would raise serious practical problems in view of the small size of the profession (para. 18.12).

2.71 Any proposal to empower the Courts to order a barrister to pay personally the costs of an action would require detailed study including the insurance position, otherwise it might prevent barristers practising as independent sole practitioners bound by the "cab-rank" rule (para. 18.13).

LEGAL EDUCATION COMMITTEE (Chapter 19)

2.72 This should advise and guide the Law Schools and the legal professions, not the Lord Chancellor. It should be representative of those responsible for legal education in the Law Schools and the legal professions and should have strong lay representation especially of those experienced in higher education and the training of other professions. It should be separate from the Legal Professional Standards Committee (paras. 19.28 to 19.32).

THE FOREIGN DIMENSION: THE EEC, THE U.S.A. AND THE COMMONWEALTH (Chapter 21)

2.73 The work of English barristers in Europe does not support the Government's hope or expectation, expressed in para. 8.8 of the main Green Paper, that despite its changes a free market in independent advocacy services would flourish (paras. 21.2 to 21.10).

2.74 The European Community The present state of development of EC law relating to the professions, and to legal professions in particular, requires further careful consideration of the potential consequences of the proposed changes, and an agreed and collaborative approach with the other member states before any such changes are made (paras. 21.11 to 21.27). If the Government proceeded now with the changes it proposes, that might have undesirable effects on the competitiveness of English barristers and solicitors in Europe.

2.75   The U.S.A.   The American profession is a clear warning to the Government and the legal profession in the U.K. of the direction in which the proposed changes might take the professions:-

(1) advocacy by inexperienced advocates with the result that cases take longer and are tried less efficiently;
(2) fewer settlements, leading to cases being tried unnecessarily;
(3) the development of mega-firms with emphasis on high charges and concentration on only the most remunerative work;
(4) increased delays in the Court system and increased costs;
(5) the money ethic superseding the ethic of professionalism;
(6) employed prosecutors whose primary interest is in their success rates.

The position in **Canada** is similar to the U.S.A. though the problems are less acute.

2.76   New Zealand and Australia   The circumstances in New Zealand and Australia are different and provide only limited assistance in assessing the effect of the proposed changes. The lessons to be learned are that:-

(1) the appointment of Queen's Counsel and Judges from the ranks of the independent Bar has played a major part in maintaining the independent Bar in existence.
(2) the "mega-firms" of solicitors, particularly in Sydney, would (if they could) seek to include within their litigation departments a range of barrister advocates, both juniors and Queen's Counsel. The proposal to enable them to do this in New South Wales was rejected by the State Government when legislation was enacted in 1987.
(3) the trend in Australia is towards specialisation, and not, as the Government's proposals would be, towards generalist legal practices.
(4) the New South Wales system of employed prosecutors has not worked well, whereas the use of the independent Bar in Victoria as prosecuting Counsel in 70% of the cases has been successful.

PROBATE

2.77   The public need protection in probate matters against those who are fraudulent or incompetent or over-charge (paras. 22.5 to 22.7).

2.78   Those entitled to do probate work for reward should be limited to solicitors, barristers and notaries (as now) with the addition of trust corporations, and the Government's Option A should therefore be followed (paras. 22.4 and 22.8 to 22.10).

2.79 The charges made by trust corporations should be subject to the same control as lawyers' charges (paras. 22.4 and 22.13 to 22.15).

2.80 The requirement to swear an affidavit on oath should be retained so long as it is retained generally for oral and written evidence (paras. 22.4 and 22.12).

2.81 Consideration should be given to extending the protection to any act done for reward as an executor or administrator with suitable exceptions (paras. 23.11).

2.82 Consideration should be given to increasing the minimum paid up share capital of trust corporations: at present the minimum is too low (para. 23.16).

CONVEYANCING (Chapter 24)

2.83 Conveyancing should not be permitted to be carried out by finance organisations as proposed, since that would be contrary to the interests of the public. The Government proposals

(1) would introduce unfair competition against which no "level playing field" safeguards could be effective, as the Building Societies Association has acknowledged;
(2) would be likely to destroy the economic base of many of the 80% of solicitors firms with 4 partners or fewer, causing the serious loss to the public of the independent legal advice available from those solicitors without any commensurate benefit to the public;
(3) would create wholly unacceptable conflicts of interest in the largest and most important transactions undertaken by members of the public, against which conflicts no formal code of conduct could provide any adequate safeguards;
(4) would be directly contrary to the aims and effect of the scheme laid down by Parliament in the Consumer Credit Act 1974 for the protection of the public when borrowing on the security of their houses or flats;
(5) would give monopoly rights to the large financial organisations contrary to the Government's stated aim of increasing competition and would give those organisations the ability to profit at the expense of the ordinary house or flat buyer inexperienced in conveyancing, mortgages, life insurance and similar matters.

CONTINGENCY FEES (Chapter 24)

2.84 The fundamental principle is that a lawyer should have no interest in the result of a case, beyond that of service to his client and to the administration of justice. This principle should not be eroded.

2.85 No form of contingency fee arrangement should be permitted, since

(1) there are strong objections based on public interest both in the protection of the poor, the sick and the inexperienced, and in the administration of justice;
(2) the American experience shows that codes of conduct offer no practical protection;
(3) the "speculative" action in Scotland is little used, and would be of little use to litigants in England and Wales.

2.86 The proposal for a Contingency Legal Aid Fund made by Justice and others, and ignored by the Government, should be tested for its viability by a carefully controlled pilot scheme (para. 24.12).

2.87 Contingency fee arrangements could not be any substitute for a properly funded Legal Aid Scheme.

ETHNIC MINORITIES (Chapter 25)

2.88 The ethnic minorities are better represented in the Bar (as 5% of barristers and 12% of pupils) probably than in any other profession.

2.89 Barristers from the ethnic minorities are in too few Chambers. The Bar Council through its active Race Relations Committee chaired by a High Court Judge is going to introduce policies designed to ensure that barristers from the ethnic minorities find places in a wider spread of Chambers.

2.90 The Government in its Green Papers has failed even to consider the problems of the ethnic minorities.

2.91 The Race Relations Committee has serious fears that the Government's proposals would be likely to have adverse effects on access to justice for the ethnic minorities.

THE PROFESSIONAL BODIES IN THE LEGAL PROFESSIONS (Chapter 26)

2.92 The Bar

(1) The Inns of Court and the Council of Legal Education should continue to train the advocates who aspire to advocacy in the higher Courts, through the Inns of Court School of Law which is

the only school able to teach a full course in advocacy, communication, negotiation and drafting skills and in professional ethics and conduct.
(2) The Inns should continue to exercise discipline over advocates under the supervision of the Judges.
(3) The Inns should continue to provide the centre of collegiate life, and the ethos and peer discipline for those who may appear in the higher Courts.

2.93 Solicitors

(1) The Solicitor profession should be supervised in the same way as the Bar by the Judges led by the Master of the Rolls.
(2) The Bar Council has already taken steps to ensure that transfer from the solicitor profession to the Bar is as easy as possible and is committed to that policy (paras. 5.19 and 5.20).

EPILOGUE

2.94 A letter to the Times from a retired Welsh solicitor states simply and clearly the public interest in the maintenance of a strong and independent Bar.

3

The Context of the Green Papers

3.1 As indicated in Chapter 1, the Government has put the Bar Council to proof of (1) the merits of the legal profession, and (2) the demerits of the Government's proposals. The starting point for the examination of both these matters must lie in the work done in recent years by those given the task of assembling evidence and reporting on the legal profession. It is of the more importance to start with their work because the Government has decided to allow only 3 months for response to the Green Papers, a period which as the Government appreciates is inadequate for assembling the up-to-date evidence which the Government itself has failed to assemble.

THE ROYAL COMMISSION ON LEGAL SERVICES

3.2 On 20 July 1976 the Royal Commission on Legal Services was appointed. Its 15 members covered a very wide range of practical experience, especially in the field of consumer interest. The Chairman was Sir Henry Benson G.B.E. (now Lord Benson), a distinguished Chartered Accountant. Its terms of reference were:

> "to inquire into the law and practice relating to the provision of legal services in England, Wales and Northern Ireland, and to consider whether any, and if so what, changes are desirable in the public interest in the structure, organisation, training, regulation of and entry to the legal profession, including the arrangements for determining its remuneration, whether from private sources or public funds, and in the rules which prevent persons who are neither barristers nor solicitors from undertaking conveyancing and other legal business on behalf of other persons".

3.3 Over a period of 3 1/4 years, the full Commission met 74 times; its committees met formally 67 times and informally on numerous other occasions. Members of the Commission paid a large number of visits to solicitors, barristers, courts, tribunals, the Inns of Court, law and legal advice centres, citizens advice bureaux, building societies, schools of law, polytechnics, colleges, local authorities, the Land Registry and other government offices and prisons.

3.4 The Commission received written evidence from nearly 3,500 persons and organisations, in response to lengthy questionnaires issued by the Commission and to circulars and advertisements inviting evidence. The Commission heard oral evidence from 153 witnesses, including e.g. the Chief Justices of the U.S.A., Australia and New Zealand. The evidence (apart from that withheld from publication for reasons of confidentiality) is contained in 23 boxes of written evidence and 4 boxes of transcripts of the oral evidence.

3.5 The Commission undertook a number of surveys and studies, including the User's Survey carried out on a nationwide basis among a sample of 16,000 adults.

3.6 The Commission reported in October 1979. Its detailed Report was contained in 2 volumes of 864 pages, with 2 further volumes of appendices summarising the results of the surveys and studies. The Commission made a total of 369 recommendations. The total expenditure of the Commission was £1,245,606.

3.7 Apart from some passing references, the evidence to the Commission, the surveys and studies by the Commission, and the conclusions and recommendations of the Commission are completely ignored by the Government in its Green Papers.

THE GOVERNMENT'S RESPONSE TO THE COMMISSION REPORT

3.8 The present Government spent over 4 years in careful and detailed consideration of the Report of the Royal Commission, and published its Response as a White Paper in November 1983.

3.9 The Government divided the 369 recommendations of the Royal Commission into 2 categories: (1) those for which the Government was responsible, and on which it responded; and (2) those which were "properly the responsibility of the legal profession" and not of the Government.

3.10 The Government stated that it had been guided in deciding what action to take on the recommendations for which it was responsible by these principles:-

- legal services should in general be provided by the private sector and as economically and efficiently as possible;
- there should be effective access to the Courts for the resolution of disputes and the defence or enforcement of rights;
- legal aid from public funds should be available in appropriate cases to individuals who have inadequate resources;
- full consideration must always be given to the need to limit public expenditure."

3.11   On the recommendations of the Royal Commission for which it was responsible, the Government fully accepted most of these recommendations. The examples in paras. 3.12, 3.13 and 3.14 below conveniently illustrate this.

INDEPENDENCE AND SELF-REGULATION

3.12   The Royal Commission recommended (R3.2) that when the decisions arising out of its Report had been taken and implemented, the legal profession

"should have a period of orderly development free, so far as possible, from external interventions."

The Government's response to this and other recommendations was:

"The existence, strength and vitality of an independent legal profession, and public confidence in it, are fundamental to our freedom under the law. Responsibility for qualifications and admission, and for conduct and for discipline, properly rests with the profession, in exercising that responsibility, to take steps as occasion demands to secure that its practices and rules properly satisfy public expectations and requirements."

Nevertheless in the Green Papers the Government has taken the opposite course. The Government proposes to remove from the Judges, the Inns of Court and the Bar Council ultimate responsibility for qualifications and conduct, and for the practices and rules of the Bar, and to ensure that the Bar is no longer independent of Government control and pressures.

FUSION OF THE PROFESSION

3.13   The Royal Commission unanimously recommended (R17.1) that the legal profession should continue to be organised in two quite separate branches. The Government accepted this recommendation.
  The Royal Commission reached the conclusion that barristers and solicitors should remain separate, after considering a large body of

evidence both from England and Wales, and from Senior Judges in Australia, New Zealand and the U.S.A. This evidence is referred to more fully below. For example, the evidence of the London Criminal Courts Solicitors' Association was that:

"We have no doubt that in a fused profession the costs of legal services would escalate enormously, the range of choice available would decline and the degree of specialisations possible in the present system would also decline..... The result of fusion would be a general decline in the service offered to the clients at a considerably increased cost".

These factors, i.e. (1) much increased cost; (2) reduced range of choice; and (3) general decline in service both in quality and in specialisation, were factors which the Royal Commission regarded as particularly important. The Royal Commission summarised its conclusions in paras. 17.45 and 17.46, including the following:-

– "We consider it likely that in a fused profession there would be an unacceptable reduction in the number and spread of the small firms of solicitors and an increase in the proportion of large city firms. This would accentuate the present uneven distribution of solicitors and reduce the choice and availability of legal services."
– "Fusion would disperse the specialist service which is now provided by the Bar and we consider that this would operate against the public interest."
– "With regard to the administration of justice, the weight of evidence is strongly to the effect that a two-branch profession is more likely than a fused one to ensure the high quality of advocacy which is indispensable, so long as our system remains in its present form, to secure the proper quality of justice."

Lord Mackay as leader of the Scottish Bar, when responding to the Royal Commission on Legal Services in Scotland, strongly opposed any suggestion that there might be fusion or any similar alteration in the structure of the Scottish legal professions. He stated in the written submissions to the Scottish Royal Commission (page 64) that "fusion would have serious disadvantages from the public point of view, and few, if any, advantages". He pointed out (pages 64-65) that if the distinction between Counsel and Solicitors went,

"this would probably mean that all lawyers would operate from solicitors' offices. While some lawyers in the larger firms might be able to insulate themselves sufficiently from their clients and routine to be able to devote as much time and attention to the preparation and presentation of their cases as advocates are able to do at present, this could not be expected to happen in the smaller firms of which there are many in this country. The result would be a reduction in the number of lawyers specialising in pure advocacy".

"If fusion were to occur it is less likely that as many lawyers as do at present, would be prepared to devote their entire career to litigation. This would be likely to lead to reduction in the number of lawyers available in this country with substantial experience in this type of work. It could in turn also lead to a general lowering of the standard of pleading and presentation, both in the Supreme Court and elsewhere. In cases of a routine nature this might not matter very much, but in more difficult cases the consequences to the litigant could be very serious". (pages 65–66)

"The measure of independence which is enjoyed by the advocate as compared with the solicitor is a valuable safeguard in such matters, especially in the conduct of litigation in the Supreme Courts. The advocate, with his more intimate knowledge of the judges, is also better placed to offer to the client a detached appraisal of the merits of the case. This tends towards economy in the conduct of litigation. For instance, much time would be taken up, often at the expense of the Legal Aid Fund, or to the prejudice of the efficient running of the Courts, in argument before the Court about matters such as the amount of aliment to be paid for a wife or child which is avoided by settlements achieved out of Court between Counsel which the clients or their solicitors were unable to achieve". (page 67)

The Government in its Green Paper proposals has taken the opposite course. The Government proposes effective fusion of the barrister and solicitor professions by allowing each to do the work of the other and by permitting barristers and solicitors (and other professionals) to join in the same partnership or company.

RIGHTS OF AUDIENCE

3.14 In Chapter 18 of its Report the Royal Commission considered whether rights of audience in the higher civil and criminal Courts should be extended to solicitors. The Law Society proposed that solicitors should have extended rights of audience in criminal cases in the Crown Court (though not in cases tried by a High Court Judge), and very limited further rights in civil cases in the High Court. The Royal Commission concluded that, with minor exceptions, rights of audience in the higher Courts should not be extended to solicitors. In the judgment of the Royal Commission

- ". . . where the outcome may have very grave consequences for the defendant, it is necessary for his advocate to be able to combine the proper balance between identification and detachment, and to be accustomed to working in an environment in which emotions run high. It is significant that the London Criminal Courts Solicitors' Association regards the element of objectivity which a barrister is able to bring to a case as of value in presenting a case to the judge and jury" (para. 18.37).

- ". . . we consider that, under the present arrangements, the range of informed choice is wider and selection of a suitable advocate more likely" (para. 18.40).

- "... we think that the effect of the present arrangement on prosecution work should not be disturbed" (para. 18.44).

- "There is evidence that it would be contrary to the public interest if substantial advocacy practices in the Crown Court were built up in any one area by a limited number of solicitors' firms, who thereby established a near-monopoly of criminal business" (para. 18.54).

- "There seems to us little sense in making a change which would put additional burdens on the solicitors' branch, which is already overloaded, and at the same time would erode the position of the Bar, in particular its junior members" (para. 18.55).

The present Government's response in its White Paper in November 1983 was that there should be no further general extension of right of audience of solicitors. In its White Paper on Legal Aid in 1987 the Government referred to its acceptance of the Royal Commission's recommendation and re-affirmed its intention not to extend rights of audience in the Crown Court.

Lord Mackay as leader of the Scottish Bar opposed any extension of rights of audience in the higher Courts in Scotland to solicitors. He told the Scottish Royal Commission that "the work of pleading, particularly in the Supreme Courts, demanded the full attention of those who went in for it" (3 July 1978, page 1). He said that "a Supreme Court case merited an independent person to review what a solicitor had found out, and a client in the High Court deserved the judgment of more than one mind" (3 July 1978, page 2). "Solicitors' court experience was not the same kind as an advocate gained in the High Court. Furthermore, the Bar accepted an obligation [the "cab-rank" rule] to take on any case from any client and to advise as independently as possible." (3 July 1978, page 2). This was "an important constitutional guarantee".

The Government in its Green Paper proposals has now taken the opposite course. The Government proposes general rights of audience up to the House of Lords for any lawyer who obtains a licence.

THE BAR COUNCIL/LAW SOCIETY COMMITTEE (THE MARRE COMMITTEE)

3.15 The Marre Committee was appointed by the two branches of the profession in April 1986. Its task was to consider the extent to which the profession's services met the needs and demands of the public, how those services could be made readily available to meet such needs and demands, to identify areas where changes in the education, structure and practices of the profession might be in the public interest, and to recommend to the Bar Council and Law Society how and by whom such areas might be examined further in order to consider such changes as might be required. The Committee was composed of 6 barristers, 6 solicitors and 7 non-lawyers. It reported in July 1988, having taken a much less rigorous approach to the collection and consideration of evidence than the Royal Commission.

3.16 On most points of importance the Marre Committee was in agreement with the conclusions of the Royal Commission, subject to one particular exception (rights of audience of solicitors in the Crown Court) on which the Committee was divided. The 6 solicitors and 6 non-lawyers were in favour of rights of audience in the Crown Court for solicitors recommended by a Board (to be composed of 4 Judges, a stipendiary magistrate, 2 barristers, 2 solicitors and a legally qualified magistrates' clerk) and licensed by the Law Society. On this point the 6 barristers and the other non-lawyer dissented. Their powerful Note of Dissent was based on 3 fundamental and connected points:

(1) The legal profession should continue to be organised in 2 specialised branches;
(2) Advocacy in the higher Courts involves special skills and techniques and makes greater demands on those skills and techniques (as Lord Mackay had explained to the Scottish Royal Commission, saying that in the lower Courts, "in criminal cases, an effective defence could sometimes be made by the use of little more than a quick wit, whereas this would be unlikely to suffice in cases brought before a High Court Judge and jury": 3 July 1978, page 7);
(3) The interests of justice as a whole are best served by maintaining and if possible improving standards of advocacy in particular in the higher Courts, where the most serious cases are decided. The skills in advocacy needed to conduct a jury trial fairly and competently, whether for prosecution or defence, are different from the demands made when appearing in the lower Courts: Lord Mackay (see (2) above) and Lord Roskill (see para. 10.39(1) below) gave evidence to the same effect to the Royal Commissions.

Their Note of Dissent dealt with a number of points which would have to be considered in relation to the licensing of solicitor advocates, including the following:

(a) There is a clear difference between a solicitor acting as a general practitioner in daily and direct contact with the lay client, and a barrister acting as a consultant on referral by a solicitor;
(b) The advantage in the present system is that the choice of a barrister for a client is made by a solicitor on the basis of the barrister's performances in Court. If a solicitor could choose between himself and a barrister that would effectively deprive the client of any real choice;

(c) Problems of quality would arise if licensed solicitors could appear in the higher Courts as an occasional occupation, as opposed to the constant occupation of the barrister whose regular appearances in Court are essential to the development and maintenance of advocacy skills. A licensed solicitor would carry out a mixture of functions as both solicitor and barrister (as in the U.S.A.: see Chapter 21 below), undertaking the preparatory work of interviewing clients, correspondence with other parties, conducting discovery of documents, and preparing witness statements as well as the advocacy in Court. So the licensed solicitor would have less opportunity to keep his advocacy skills in regular use, and would not have the advantage of working among full- time specialist advocates who can assist and advise one another throughout their professional lives.

THE GOVERNMENT'S APPROACH IN THE GREEN PAPERS

3.17 The three examples set out in paras. 3.12, 3.13 and 3.14 above illustrate the Royal Commission's recommendations, the acceptance of those recommendations by the Government, and the Government's change of course in its Green Papers.

3.18 As already pointed out in para. 1.9 above, the Green Papers are not based on evidence. No studies, no researches and no surveys have been carried out. The work of the Royal Commission, its Report, and the Government's considered Response to the Report of the Royal Commission have been ignored. The fact that the Green Papers run counter to the Commission's recommendations and conclusions, and to the Government's considered policy declared in a White Paper after more than 4 years careful consideration, is not mentioned.

3.19 The Government's approach is most clearly stated in a letter from the Permanent Secretary, Lord Chancellor's Department, to the Chairman of the Bar dated 31 January 1989 in answer to a letter asking for copies of the reports on which the main Green Paper was based:

> "The Green Paper on the Work and Organisation of the Legal Profession sets out clearly in the first chapter the principles upon which it is based. Competition and the maintenance of standards are mentioned as twin themes to which the Government is committed. Paragraph 1.4 makes it clear that it is against this background that the existing practices and structure of the profession should be judged. The same paragraph indicates that the Government believes that the onus should be on those who support restrictions as a way of achieving standards to justify them.

The Green Paper therefore attempts to set out from these first principles what the organisation of the legal profession should be. It does not proceed from the kind of reports mentioned in your letter; nor does it rely on such material."

3.20 The "twin themes" of "competition and the maintenance of standards" are included amongst the principles to which the Bar also is committed. But they are only two of such principles. Other essential "first principles" are set out in para. 1.3 above, including

- access to justice for all at fair and reasonable cost
- independence of the barrister and acceptance of the "cab-rank" rule
- choice between barristers in strong competition
- the same high quality of service for poor and rich alike
- fair and reasonable remuneration
- efficient administration of justice in the interests of all
- the high quality of the Judges.

3.21 The normal approach to any problem in public life in England is a logical one. The problem is analysed, starting with a careful analysis of the present position. The merits and defects of the present position are weighed in the light of detailed evidence. Then the possible remedies for any defects are considered and analysed, with evidence as to the merits and defects of each of the possible remedies. An assessment is made of the consequences of adopting each of the remedies. Those remedies which would introduce further defects are rejected. If there are remedies which will not only remedy existing defects but also not bring with them further defects, those remedies are chosen. In the choice of remedies it is kept in mind that it is easier to forecast the consequences of one change or a small number of changes, and very difficult indeed to forecast the consequences of making a large number of changes. That is the logical approach.

3.22 The Government's approach is an illogical one. It largely ignores the present position. It makes no careful analysis of the present position or the merits or defects of the present position. No evidence has been assembled. The possible remedies for any defects are neither considered nor analysed. The consequences of the many changes are not analysed or weighed against each other.

3.23 Instead the Government gives the appearance of having started with the large number of changes it wishes to make and worked backwards to the selected "first principles" which, in the Government's view, best support its case for its chosen changes. That was all that could be done in the 3 months allowed for preparing the Green Papers.

3.24 The Government has then placed on those, like the Bar Council, who wish to continue to build constructively, by evolutionary changes, on the basis of the actual present legal system and legal profession, the burden of proving affirmatively that they can meet the selected "first principles". This has to be done in 3 months, as compared with the study by the Royal Commission for 3 3/4 years and the formulation of policy by the Government for over 4 years after the work of the Royal Commission.

3.25 Such a burden of proof is imposed on those whose practices are brought before the Restrictive Practices Court (RPC). But in the RPC the procedure gives to the industry concerned ample opportunity to gather evidence and formulate their case. Similarly the Monopolies and Mergers Commission (MMC) affords a proper opportunity to those whose practices are being examined to produce evidence and state their case. That is what happened when the Bar's rules on the two-counsel rule and on advertising were considered by the MMC. In a White Paper issued in 1988 the Government proposed that practices including those of the professions should be considered by a new Competition Authority, and legislation is to be introduced for this purpose. But the Government proposes in the Green Papers that fundamental changes should be made in aspects of the legal system and the legal profession, which the Royal Commission and the Government considered at length and approved as being in the public interest, without any reasonable opportunity being given for the gathering of evidence and the formulation of a detailed response. The Bar Council would have wished to be able to submit detailed evidence of the economic effects of the proposed changes, and particularly the effects on the costs to lay clients and to the taxpayer. In the short time given by the Government it has not been possible to assemble this detailed evidence. So the Government's assurances of full consultation have not been fulfilled.

3.26 This is a matter for particular concern because

(1) the changes proposed are so numerous and so far- reaching that the task of forecasting all the consequences of all these changes is an impossible one;
(2) many well-qualified observers forecast that the likely consequences will be less competition and less choice of specialist advocate and adviser, less access to justice for those of limited means, lower standards and lower quality of advocates and judges, and higher costs to the lay clients and to the taxpayer. They include the Director-General of Fair Trading, whose principal function is to promote competition. These consequences are the opposite of what the Government hopes for.

The need for more time to assemble and study the relevant evidence is an obvious one.

PROPOSALS NOT THOUGHT THROUGH

3.27   It is apparent from the Green Papers that, because of the haste with which they have been prepared, important matters have either been ignored, or are incorrectly stated. To give just 3 examples:-

(1) The "cab-rank" rule, the duty of every independent barrister to appear for any client, whoever the client and whatever his or her cause, is a unique and fundamental feature of the Bar. It is ignored in the Green Papers, though it is regarded by Lord Mackay as "an important constitutional guarantee" (para.3.14 above).

(2) The proposals for the licensing of advocates, if already in force, would have ensured that all but 2 of the English Lords of Appeal in Ordinary, most of the Lords Justices of Appeal, and many of the High Court Judges could not have become Queen's Counsel and could not have gone to the High Court Bench: see Chapter 16 below. To deprive the public of the benefit of many of the ablest Judges in the highest Courts can hardly have been intended by the Government, but that would be the result of its proposals.

(3) It is stated in para. 13.10 of the Profession Green Paper that

"The Code of Conduct of the Bar effectively prohibits barristers from publishing their charges."

That is not correct. Barristers are now free to publish their charges: see para. 20.45 below.

THE PRESENT CONTEXT

3.28   The context in which the Green Papers have been put forward is:

(1) The evidence, reasoning and conclusions of the Royal Commission have been ignored.

(2) The carefully considered policy of the Government in response to the Report of the Royal Commission has been ignored.

(3) The Green Papers are based on no evidence, and no assessment of the likely consequences of the many changes proposed has been made.

(4) Inadequate time has been given to respond with a full response backed by detailed evidence.

(5) Practices considered to be in the public interest by the Royal Commission and the Government are proposed to be changed fundamentally without consideration of the evidence or of the consequences of the proposed changes.

(6) The proposals have not been fully thought through, and important matters are ignored or incorrectly stated.

4

Legal Professions

4.1 The Government in its Green Papers deals with the provision of legal services primarily in economic terms as a product of market forces in competition (one of the Government's "first principles"), subject to the maintenance of standards (the other of its "first principles"): see e.g. para. 1.2 of the main Green Paper.

4.2 This is a similar approach to that which might be applied to the competition between suppliers of certain goods subject to maintenance of the quality of the goods supplied.

4.3 Competition is an important element in every economic activity. Indeed the Bar is an excellent example of providers of services in strong competition with each other. The Lord Chancellor and the Bar Council agree that "the Bar is the most competitive business going": para. 10.21 below. Competition at the Bar is maximised by the fundamental rule that every barrister in independent practice must be a sole practitioner, not tied to any other person within or outside the Bar by ties of partnership, incorporation or employment. It is a puzzling feature of the Green Papers that the Government proposes to reduce competition by removing this requirement.

4.4 The legal system and the legal profession cannot be viewed solely as an economic activity. In every case, whether criminal or civil, the interests of the community in the administration of justice, as well as the interests of the accused or of the litigants, have to be considered in terms of justice as well as cost. A barrister representing an accused or a litigant cannot be allowed to pursue merely economic ends, and must perform duties going beyond those ends. The barrister

(1) owes special duties to the client, because of his or her

membership of the profession, including the duty to represent the client fearlessly and irrespective of the client's character or reputation or the client's cause;

(2) also owes an over-riding duty to the Court inherent in the administration of justice, not merely justice for that client but justice for all.

These duties frequently conflict. So a barrister is required to take an objective and independent viewpoint when presenting the client's case, and to ensure that in presenting that case the barrister does not go beyond the bounds set by the requirements of justice.

These duties, and the preservation of the balance between them, transcend the mere economic activity of giving a service in return for a price.

4.6 The danger in viewing the legal profession primarily as an economic activity is the danger of placing money before duty to a client and before service to the public. This is a danger which has arisen in the U.S.A., and has had to be faced squarely by the American Bar Association (ABA). In 1984 Chief Justice Warren Burger observed that the American Bar appeared to be moving away from professionalism towards commercialism, preferring profit to principle, and that the American Bar was so perceived by the American public. In response to his recommendation the ABA set up a Commission on Professionalism which reported in August 1986. The Report of this Commission (112 F.R.D. 243), entitled

"In the spirit of public service: a blueprint for the rekindling of lawyer professionalism"

is both a guide and a warning to the legal profession in the United Kingdom and to those who wish to impose on the profession numerous changes the consequences of which are so hard to forecast.

4.7 The starting point for the ABA Commission was to define what a profession is. It adopted one definition by Dean Roscoe Pound:

"The term refers to a group . . . pursuing a learned art as a common calling in the spirit of public service - no less a public service because it may incidentally be a means of livelihood. Pursuit of the learned art in the spirit of a public service is the primary purpose." (page 261)

The ABA Commission, while recognising that the wording was dated, found that the definition had stood the test of time, and stated:

"The practice of law "in the spirit of a public service" can and ought to be the hallmark of the legal profession." (page 261)

The Commission concluded that

". . . the testimony we have heard and the surveys we have examined indicate that the public wants the legal profession to maintain its long-held professional ideals. Indeed the public should expect no less." (page 262)

4.8   The Bar Council follows the ABA Commission in affirming that the primary purpose of the profession of barrister is service to the public, and means of livelihood must always remain secondary to that service.

4.9   The elements of competition, so far as they apply to the English legal profession, are dealt with in Chapter 11 below. But before economic questions are dealt with, the more important aspects of service to the public have to be considered: see Chapter 9 below.

5

Solicitors' and Barristers' Practices

5.1 The main function of a solicitor is to give general advice on legal matters and to conduct the day-to-day legal business of the lay client. Solicitors usually act for clients on a continuing basis. Solicitors have full rights of audience in the Magistrates Courts and the County Courts (the lower criminal and civil Courts). They have only limited rights of audience in the higher criminal and civil Courts, the Crown Court, the High Court, and the Court of Appeal and the House of Lords.

5.2 Some solicitors, especially those in the larger firms, specialise in particular branches of the law. Some act frequently as advocates in the Magistrates Courts and the County Courts.

5.3 Solicitors have the task of preparing cases for trial in Court, whether they or their partners or employers are to be the advocates, or barristers are engaged for this purpose. Barristers have to be engaged to appear in the higher Courts in which they have largely exclusive rights of audience. But solicitors frequently instruct barristers to appear for their lay clients in the lower Courts in which the solicitors also have rights of audience. The barrister is often less expensive for the lay client, and the barrister has the necessary experience or knowledge in a particular branch of the law. Absence from their office in Court makes conduct of their office practice difficult and inconvenient. Smaller firms have few if any solicitors experienced in advocacy. For these amongst other reasons, solicitors very often prefer cases in the lower Courts to be conducted by barristers. One analogy with the different specialised functions of solicitor and barrister is the specialist functions of the anaesthetist and the surgeon. The anaesthetist prepares the patient so that the surgeon can operate. Both remain in continuous care of the patient during the operation, exercising their different but vital skills.

5.4   The main functions of a barrister are to give specialist advice in a particular branch of the law or in matters of procedure concerning a particular case, to draft documents requiring specialist expertise or to represent a lay client in Court or before a tribunal. All barristers in private practice are required to be sole practitioners, though for convenience they work with colleagues in offices (called "chambers") sharing chambers expenses.

5.5   A barrister acts as a consultant on referral by a solicitor or other professional. Lay clients do not have direct access to barristers. This arises from the different function of the barrister as a specialist giving advice and representing the client in Court. It ensures that the choice of barrister does not have to be made by a lay client who may require the services of a barrister only once in a life-time. The choice of a barrister is made by a solicitor or other professional who is able to make the choice with expert knowledge of the right barrister for the particular client's case or problem.

5.6   The distinction between solicitors and barristers is partly (1) a distinction between general and specialist practice, partly (2) a distinction of function, the solicitor usually acting on a continuing basis for the client, while the barrister is engaged only when so required, whether for advocacy in a particular case or for specialist advice on a particular problem.

5.7   The difference of function results in an entirely different organisation of the offices of solicitors and barristers.

5.8   Solicitors' offices must be organised so as to handle efficiently, on a continuing basis, their clients' files, records and money, employing for this purpose solicitors, legal executives and other staff. The size of solicitors' offices ranges from the many sole practitioners' offices with a relatively small staff, to the largest firms in the City of London with as many as 200 partners employing over 600 other solicitors and an immense back-up staff.

5.9   Barristers' offices (or "chambers") on the other hand are relatively small. The largest chambers has only 44 members. Barristers are not involved with clients on a continuing basis and do not handle clients' money or records. The administration of their offices is mainly concerned with the arrangement of Court diaries and the billing and collection of fees. Barristers as sole practitioners employ no fee earners.

5.10   Because of the difference of function, and the resulting difference in the complexity of their offices and staff, the overheads (including salaries) of barristers and solicitors are proportionately very different. The overall practice economics of barristers and solicitors in private practice are roughly as follows:

	Barristers	*Solicitors*
Gross earnings	100%	100%
Salaries and other Overheads	24	70
Net Earnings	76	30

If these figures are put another way:-

	Barristers	*Solicitors*
Net Earnings	100	100
produced by: Gross Earnings	131.5	333
Less Expense of salaries and other overheads	31.5	233

So to earn an income of 100 for a solicitor costs the lay client 333, whereas to earn the income of 100 for a barrister costs the client 131.5.

This large difference in the overheads of the two professions is reflected in the level of fees paid to barristers, especially in publicly funded work (legal aid or Crown Prosecution Service).

SOLICITORS

5.11   At September 1988, the number of solicitors holding practising certificates was 50,337, divided as follows:-

		Men	*Women*
Partners	23,056	21,009	2,047
Sole Practitioners	3,914	3,389	525
Consultants/Retired	1,835	1,722	113
Assistants/Associates	11,635	6,913	4,722
Local & National Government	3,258	2,467	791
Commerce/Other	2,892	2,202	690
Not Known	3,747	2,573	1,174
	50,337		

5.12   The size of solicitors' practices as at March 1987 can be seen from the following figures relating to practices, principals (partners or sole practitioners), assistant solicitors and other staff:-

Size of Practice by number of principals	Number of practices	Number of principals	Assistant Solicitors	Other Staff
1	2,965	2,965	1,353	11,906
2 - 4	3,672	9,841	3,615	35,723
5 - 10	1,128	7,389	3,120	29,536
11 or more	345	6,537	5,730	29,117
TOTAL	8,110	26,732	13,818	106,282

5.13 It can be seen from these figures that
(1) about 80% of all solicitor practices have 4 partners or less;
(2) the concentration of principals, assistant solicitors and other staff is much greater in the practices with 11 partners or more.

5.14 The geographical spread of practices and principals in three broad areas of England and Wales at March 1987 was:-

– North   (Wales, the Midlands and North above the Severn-Wash line)
– South   (including East Anglia, but excluding London)
– London   (the old GLC area)

Area	Practices	Principals
North	3,469	10,476
South	2,528	7,959
London	2,113	8,297
TOTAL	8,110	26,732

5.15 The disparities in distribution of solicitors (practices, principals and all solicitors) in these three broad areas, when compared with the distribution of the general population, is very marked, as shown in Figure 5.1.

BARRISTERS

5.16 At October 1988 the number of practising barristers in independent practice was:-

		Men	Women
England and Wales	5,944	4,698	1,246
London	4,197	3,260	937
Outside London	1,747	1,438	309
Queen's Counsel	601	576	25

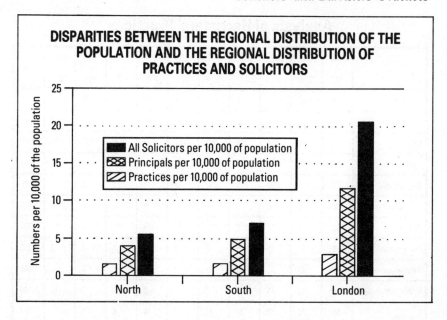

Figure 5.1

5.17 It is difficult to give precise figures for the size of the different specialist Bars. Many barristers specialise in more than one field of law and are members of more than one specialist Bar Association. A rough guide to the specialist work done by barristers is in Figure 5.2.

5.18 The breakdown of gross earnings by area of law for barristers and solicitors is shown in Figure 5.3. In view of the Government's Green Paper proposals, the dominant role of conveyancing as nearly 30% of the total gross earnings of solicitors in private practice is important, particularly because for small solicitors firms in the provinces the percentage may be as high as 55–60%.

TRANSFER BETWEEN THE BAR AND SOLICITORS

5.19 Transfer of solicitors to the Bar is governed by the same regulations 33 to 40 of the Consolidated Regulations of the Inns of Court as transfer from the Bars of Northern Ireland, Scotland, Ireland, Hong Kong and other common law jurisdictions. The Bar Council's policy has been and is to make transfer for solicitors as easy as possible, consistent with the Bar Council's duty to maintain high professional standards. A solicitor of more than 3 years practice since admission and with general experience is normally exempted from all

Analysis of Barristers' Practices

	0% – 10%	10% – 20%	20% – 30%	30% – 40%	40% – 50%	50% – 60%	60% – 70%	70% – 80%	80% – 90%	90% – 100%	Total
Admiralty	71	3	1	18	6	2	15	0	0	0	116
Commercial	544	204	124	72	89	38	45	45	42	62	1265
Criminal	512	275	268	324	344	268	310	408	431	1026	4166
Defamation	144	15	3	5	4	2	3	5	4	9	194
Employment	880	121	30	16	13	8	4	2	3	2	1079
European	73	9	6	5	2	1	0	3	6	10	115
Family	1131	524	367	212	152	79	58	66	47	65	2701
Immigration	188	24	15	5	5	3	1	7	2	2	252
Insolvency	429	63	22	10	11	4	1	2	2	2	546
International	85	19	13	8	8	2	0	0	1	12	148
Official Referees	541	97	50	31	42	16	10	9	1	2	799
Parliamentary	274	53	19	21	12	12	10	14	17	59	491
Patents	192	15	11	3	3	2	3	6	10	31	276
Restrictive Practices and Monopolies	28	4	7	3	1	3	0	1	1	0	48
Revenue	127	21	13	5	10	1	4	4	7	45	237
Chancery	649	136	73	48	43	43	36	67	57	86	1238
Common Law	1349	810	554	435	288	138	122	102	75	84	3957
Other	258	54	40	26	29	12	13	10	13	109	564

Figure 5.2

requirements of the academic and vocational stages, and may be required to do only a shortened pupillage of 3 months before accepting briefs to appear in Court. Each application is considered on its merits by the Joint Regulations Committee of the Inns of Court and the Bar Council (JRC). A solicitor of less than 3 years practice may be required to take some part of the vocational course concurrently with pupillage, and may be required to do a full 12 months pupillage: but exemptions may be granted if the solicitor has had relevant experience, e.g. in advocacy in the Magistrates' Courts or the County Courts.

5.20   The JRC has pursued a policy of removing formal barriers in

Legal Services Market – Percent of Gross Earnings by Area of Law for a) Solicitors and b) Barristers

Solicitors Gross Earnings		**Barristers Gross Earnings**	
3%	General	12%	Other Specialisations
6%	Tax		
8%	Crime	3%	Tax
9%	Matrimonial	9%	Commercial Specialist
9%	Probate	8%	Chancery
		7%	Family
10%	Commercial	13%	Commercial General
26%	Litigation	17%	General Civil (Common Law)
29%	Conveyancing	30%	Crime

Figure 5.3

the way of solicitors or lawyers from other common law countries who wish to pursue a career at the Bar. The changes in the structure of the Bar set out in Chapter 20 below will ease the transfer from the solicitor profession in practical ways. But the person who transfers will still have to build a practice at the Bar on the basis of her or his own performance as judged by the solicitors who give instructions.

5.21 Transfer from the Bar to the Roll of Solicitors is governed by Regulation 50 of the Training Regulations 1987. A barrister seeking transfer is required to take 3 examinations in Conveyancing, Accounts, and Wills, Probate and Administration, and to do 2 years work in a solicitor's office gaining experience in 3 areas of law. Exemption from the examinations may be given if the applicant barrister has practical legal experience and academic or other qualifications relevant to the required subjects. Exemption from the requirement to serve 2 years articles is granted (save in exceptional circumstances) to a barrister if for not less than 3 years during the 5 years before his application he has practised in chambers at the independent Bar otherwise than as a pupil.

6

The Bar

INDEPENDENCE AND THE "CAB-RANK" RULE

6.1 Barristers in private practice are required to be sole practitioners, independent of all other professionals and not tied by partnership, incorporation or employment with other barristers. The requirement of independence of practice has these great advantages:-

(1) *Available to All* Each barrister is available for consultation to every solicitor to give specialist advice or to represent the solicitor's client in a case within the barrister's specialist field.

(2) *"Cab-Rank" Rule* As entirely independent practitioners, barristers in private practice can undertake the vital duty arising from what is called the "cab-rank rule". This rule of practice (contained in paragraph 13 of the Code of Conduct of the Bar of England and Wales) requires a barrister to accept any brief to appear before a Court or tribunal in the field in which he or she professes to practise (having regard to experience and seniority) at a proper professional fee having regard to the length and difficulty of the case and his or her availability. Exceptional circumstances such as conflict of interest may justify refusal of a brief. The "Cab-Rank" rule is unique to the English Bar and to those other Bars which practise as sole practitioners. It is not compatible with partnership, incorporation or employment. An advocate in partnership would have to consider the requirements of his or her practice before accepting a brief, particularly where acceptance might affect the relations between the partnership and, for example, a licensing authority or existing clients.

It is within the knowledge of members of the Bar that in some countries in which advocates practise in partnership, partnerships are reluctant and often refuse to allow their advocates to appear for those who have fallen foul of the Government, for fear of the consequences for their partnerships in their relations with Government and their other clients. This is a matter of considerable importance when considering the Government's licensing proposals in the main Green Paper.

In a speech on 6 March 1989 the Lord Chancellor suggested as an unlikely but possible scenario that it would be

> "quite open to the Bar to drive a coach and horses through the 'cab-rank' rule and decide to insert a provision in its Code [of Conduct] prohibiting its members from prosecuting or defending in certain cases."

This he put forward as an argument for Government control of the Bar's Code of Conduct. The Bar Council's simple response is that the "cab-rank" rule is and has long been a fundamental and self-imposed part of the profession of barrister in England and Wales and in Scotland, a self-denying ordinance which it would be unthinkable to remove while the profession continues to be regulated by itself under the supervision of the Judges. Lord Mackay as leader of the Scottish Bar said to the Scottish Royal Commission (3 July 1978, page 2):

> ". . . this obligation was an important constitutional guarantee from the point of view of a citizen's freedom of access to the Courts, as an advocate had to represent people even though he did not like their views, and whether they had legal aid or not. For this reason, advocates had to be independent and could not be employed nor become partners in a practice."

The Bar Council's reaffirmation of the "cab-rank" rule and its intended revision of that rule as contained in the Code of Conduct are set out in para. 9.22 below.

(3) *Fearless Representation* Because of the "cab-rank" rule lay clients can secure representation by barristers of their choice, irrespective of the unpopularity (whether with other clients, the Government, the public or the media) of the lay client or the lay client's cause, and irrespective of Government or other powerful pressure or influence brought to bear against the lay client. There are numerous well-known examples of this in the history of the Bar, such as Erskine's defence of Tom Paine, the author of The Rights of Man, and Brougham's defence of Queen Caroline. The "cab-rank" rule "secures for the public a right of representation in the Court which is a pillar of British liberty": see para. 3.20 of the Royal Commission Report. A man or woman charged with a criminal offence, however nasty, or suffering from abuse of power by Government or other powerful bodies, can be sure of being represented by an independent barrister.

(4) *Constant and Varied Practice* A further advantage of independent practice is that a barrister who has any success appears constantly in Court in a large variety of cases, and advises on a large variety of problems, brought to him or her from a wide range of solicitors and other professionals. The Bar's development of professional direct access (which came into force on 3 April 1989) will enable professionals from other recognised professions to come direct to barristers, as for example patent agents have long been able to do, without the interposition of solicitors. This will increase the variety of cases and problems brought to the Bar for representation and advice. Constant practice in a variety of cases in Court is the only sound basis for good advocacy, and (see Chapter 7 below) one of the principal bases for the excellence of the English Judiciary. Those who appear in Court rarely (as is all too often the case in a fused legal profession, as in the U.S.A. where the "oncer" who appears in Court only once a year is a potential disaster for his client and for the administration of justice) do not gain the knowledge, the familiarity with evidential and procedural matters, and the expertise of firm but courteous advocacy.

As the main Green Paper states in para. 5.3:-

> "An inexperienced or incompetent advocate who cannot present a case properly is not only unlikely to be able to do justice to his or her client's case, but is also likely to waste the time of the court and may by his failure bring about injustice. The ensuing delay, additional expense and inconvenience can affect not only the case in question but also other cases waiting their turn to be heard; and indeed the state of the law generally."

This regular and varied practice in advocacy above all makes for swift and efficient despatch of cases. The barrister who is expert in the art of Court advocacy, and the Judge promoted from the ranks of such a background, are able to administer justice much more speedily and much more efficiently than those who lack this expertise. The strengths of the English Bar and Judges in this respect have received strong commendation from the former Chief Justice of the United States (see Chapter 21 below) by comparison with the American legal profession and Judges. As is shown in Chapter 7 on the Judiciary, in those countries which lack these advantages the number of Judges required in the administration of justice far exceeds the small number of Judges in England and Wales.

BARRISTERS AS CONSULTANTS

6.2 The independence of barristers in private practice from ties of partnership, incorporation or employment is closely connected with another feature of practice at the Bar. Barristers are consultants. The lay public do not come to barristers directly, but only via solicitors or other professionals. There are many sound reasons for this: in particular

(1) The assembling of evidence, both documentary and in the form of witness statements, is carried out by a solicitor. By regular practice solicitors acquire considerable specialised expertise in the preparation of evidence for trial. Barristers have only an advisory role in this regard.

(2) Barristers do not have to maintain the offices, staff and records necessary for the "behind the scenes" work required in preparation of cases by solicitors, and thereby keep barristers' overheads to a minimum.

(3) Barristers are able to concentrate on advocacy and advice, enabling them to deal with cases and advise more speedily and efficiently. Their independence of the lay client enables them to fulfil without hindrance their duty to act with integrity towards the court, for example, in never knowingly misleading the court, and to monitor the performance in this regard of the client's solicitor in the preparation of the case.

(4) In advisory work barristers are able to develop specialist expertise in particular areas of law, advising on a range of problems coming from a number of different solicitors and other professionals.

6.3 This specialisation of function in the barristers' and solicitors' professions is part of the universal movement from generalist professions to specialist professions, which can be seen most clearly in the field of medicine: the separate roles of the anaesthetist and the surgeon have already been mentioned in para. 5.3 above. It leads to efficient use of the scarce human resources of intelligence and acquired skills, to reduced cost to the public as clients of the professions, and to reduced costs to the taxpayer in the administration of justice. It is another remarkable feature of the Green Papers that the Government proposes to remove this benefit, and to try to turn the clock back to a generalist legal profession without any clear division of function. There is a clear conflict in the main Green Paper between Chapter 3 which seeks to promote specialisation, and the other Chapters which would push the profession back towards generalist practice.

THE BAR TODAY

6.4 The wigs and gowns, and the often antiquated Court buildings and procedures, have sometimes led to an inaccurate picture being given of the Bar in the 1980s.

6.5   One inaccuracy is that the Bar is a self-perpetuating elite, drawn almost entirely from Oxford or Cambridge Universities and from wealthy parents.

6.6   The true position is this:-

(1) The Bar is virtually an all-graduate profession, the minimum qualification for entry to the Inns of Court School of Law being a second-class honours degree, with exceptions being made for mature students.

(2) The entry to the Inns of Court School of Law is from a wide range of universities and polytechnics. The registrations for entry for the 1988/89 year of those intending to practise at the Bar of England and Wales were as follows:

Non-graduates	10
Cambridge College of Arts and Technology	1
Ealing College of Higher Education	13
Essex Institute of Higher Education	11
Hertfordshire College of Higher Education	1
University of Ghana	1
Trinity College, Dublin	3
University College, Dublin	1
University College, Galway	1
University of the West Indies	1
City of Birmingham Polytechnic	6
Bristol Polytechnic	6
Polytechnic of Central London	16
City of London Polytechnic	16
Coventry Polytechnic	2
Hatfield Polytechnic	4
The Polytechnic, Huddersfield	9
Kingston Polytechnic	18
Lancashire Polytechnic	13
Leeds Polytechnic	4
Leicester Polytechnic	16
Liverpool Polytechnic	11
Manchester Polytechnic	20
Middlesex Polytechnic	4
North East London Polytechnic	16
Newcastle-upon-Tyne Polytechnic	6
Polytechnic of North London	9
North Staffordshire Polytechnic	10
Oxford Polytechnic	6
Plymouth Polytechnic	1
Polytechnic of the South Bank	16
Trent Polytechnic	11

Polytechnic of Wales	2
The Polytechnic, Wolverhampton	13
University of Bath	1
University of Birmingham	21
University of Bradford	2
University of Bristol	19
Brunel University	5
University of Buckingham	15
University of Cambridge	56
University College of Cardiff	5
University College of North Wales, Bangor	1
City University	1
University College of Wales, Aberystwyth	19
University College of Swansea	2
University of Dundee	2
University of Durham	10
University of East Anglia	5
University of Edinburgh	2
University of Essex	11
University of Exeter	11
University of Glasgow	3
University of Hull	10
University of Kent at Canterbury	13
University of Keele	8
University of London	94
University of Lancaster	10
University of Leeds	7
University of Leicester	15
University of Liverpool	9
University of Manchester	14
University of Newcastle-upon-Tyne	5
University of Nottingham	5
University of Oxford	82
The Queen's University, Belfast	1
University of Reading	7
University of Sheffield	11
University of Southampton	12
University of St. Andrews	2
University of Surrey	1
University of Sussex	8
University of Warwick	8
University of Wales, Institute of Science & Technology	5
St. David's University College, Lampeter	3
University of York	3

(3) There were included in the list in (2) above 32 students with first

52

class honours degrees: 1 each from Ealing College of Higher Education, Polytechnic of Central London, Hatfield Polytechnic, Leicester Polytechnic, Polytechnic of North London, Polytechnic of the South Bank, University of Birmingham, University of Durham, University of Leicester, University of Sheffield, and University of Southampton, 2 from University College, London, 7 from University of Cambridge and 12 from University of Oxford. Those with 2:1 degrees were even more widely spread among the listed institutions.

(4) The forms for admission to the Inns of Court have in the past provided for entry of the occupation of the father of the student. A comparison of the occupations of the fathers of students admitted to the Inner Temple in 1964, 1974 and 1984 showed an increasingly wide range of occupations reflecting the widened social mix of those entering the profession. The number of sons and daughters of barristers or solicitors was very small. The majority would probably be considered "middle-class" occupations. But that reflects the dominance of the middle-class in the universities and polytechnics.

(5) About 70% of students in the Inns of Court School of Law receive LEA discretionary grants. The grants they receive range from large to very small. Given the reluctance of most LEAs to give any discretionary grants, and the fact that such grants are usually not given to students with greater means, this provides another indication of the wide range of social and economic background of students' families.

(6) Evidence from barristers and benchers of the Inns of Court (senior barristers and Judges) supports the conclusion that there is now a wide mix of students from different social backgrounds which is growing wider year by year.

6.7 Another inaccuracy is the suggestion that the Bar is generally resistant to change.

6.8 The true picture is that:

(1) The Bar is a young profession, both because of its recent rapid growth, and because uniquely the Bar loses many of its leading members to the Judiciary when they reach the age of about 48 to 53. About half of the barristers in independent practice are 12 years or less since their call to the Bar.

(2) Some of the major changes achieved by the Bar during the last five years and now in progress are these:-
   – The new vocational course at the Inns of Court School of Law developed by a team of English and foreign lawyers and academics led by the Hon. Mr. Justice Hoffman. This will from September 1989 provide a course principally devoted to the

teaching of the skills of advocacy, negotiation, and communication with lay clients and others involved in the administration of justice.

- The new pupillage system being put in place by a committee chaired by David Latham QC. This requires the registration of pupil-masters and the training of pupils by their pupil-masters in accordance with check lists prepared by the Bar Council with the help of the specialist Bar Associations.
- The new Code of Conduct and written professional standards.
- A new Bar Council and a new Council of the Inns of Court, constituted for the purpose of more efficient promotion of barristers' services and cooperation between the Inns of Court and the Bar.
- Provision of continuing education with particular emphasis on EEC law, on the teaching of accounting for the purposes of fraud trials in line with Lord Roskill's Fraud Trials Committee Report, and on preparing pupils for the practical aspects of practice at the Bar. Proposals for systematic continuing education of the Bar have been approved in principle by the Bar Council and by the Council of the Inns of Court.
- Compulsory professional indemnity insurance of barristers has been extended by the adoption of a mutual scheme covering up to the first £2 million cover.
- Arrangements have been made for barristers to appear in Magistrates Courts and the Crown Court without the attendance of the instructing solicitor or his representative, in cases in which the interests of the lay client and the interests of justice will not be prejudiced.
- A Code of Advertising and Publicity has been included in the Code of Conduct permitting advertising and publicity. This now allows the advertising of barristers' charges. The Bar Council proposes to extend further the freedom to advertise: see para. 20.47 below.
- Direct professional access to the Bar by professionals from further recognised professions (in addition to solicitors and patent and trademark agents) including ombudsmen, arbitrators, accountants and surveyors (see para. 12.42 below).
- A major revision of the position of employed barristers under the Code of Conduct to bring them into line with employed solicitors.
- The extension of lay representation on the Bar Council's Professional Standards Committee and Professional Conduct Committee (PCC), and on Disciplinary Tribunals. Of particular note is the requirement that complaints against barristers may not be dismissed unless that course of action is approved by a lay representative on the PCC.

- The considerable extension of the part-time judicial work by the Bar.
- The redrafting by the Joint Regulations Committee of the Consolidated Regulations which govern, amongst other matters, transfer from the solicitor profession and entry by lawyers from other common law countries. This has made transfer easy as indicated in paras. 5.19 and 5.20 above.
- The introduction of modern technology and democratic decision-making into chambers administration.

(3) The earnings of independent barristers are not large in relation to those in commercial solicitors' firms, or in domestic and criminal solicitors' firms, or in commerce, finance and industry. Sir Robert Andrew in his Report on his Review of Government Legal Services included (in the Annex to Chapter VIII) an extract from a report on lawyers' remuneration by the Public Sector Unit of Incomes Data Services Ltd. for the Cabinet Office. This shows that earnings are comparable, provided that the necessary adjustments are made for

(1) benefits in addition to salary, such as pension rights, cars, health insurance, and loans at low interest, which are made available to employed solicitors and barristers, and solicitors in private practice

(2) the overheads of barristers in private practice (usually 20–25% of gross earnings) and the payments for private pensions (at a higher rate since the 1989 Budget).

7

The Judges

7.1 One of the most striking facts concerning the Judges of the higher courts in England and Wales is that there are so few of them. The full-time Judges (at the end of 1987) were (see Judicial Statistics: 1987):-

Lord Chancellor	1
Lords of Appeal in Ordinary	8
Lord Chief Justice	1
Master of the Rolls	1
President of the Family Division	1
Vice Chancellor	1
Lord Justices	23
High Court Judges	79
Circuit Judges	393
	508

Their work was assisted by part-time Judges (Recorders and Assistant Recorders) numbering 1026.

Even if the other full time Judges (Registrars, Masters and Stipendiary Magistrates) and Chairmen and members of various Tribunals are added, the total of full-time Judges did not exceed 1,000.

7.2 A second striking fact is how few cases have to be decided by the Judges of the higher Courts whether at first instance or on appeal. Judicial Statistics 1987 published by the Lord Chancellor's Department does not show clearly the exact number of cases dealt with on appeal or at first instance by the full-time Judges of the higher Courts. But it is possible to give a general indication by means of some examples:

– Appeals heard by the House of Lords (including
many appeals heard together)   109

– Appeals heard by the Court of Appeal	
– Criminal Division	3,394
– Civil Division	1,648
– Appeals heard by the High Court	
Divisional Courts	1,189
– Trials at first instance in the High Court	
– Chancery Division	999
– Queen's Bench Division	1,921
– Official Referees	151
– Trials of criminal cases at first instance in the	
Crown Court	28,006
of which there were heard by High Court Judges	
only	2,388

7.3 In the time available to the Bar Council (in practical terms much less than 3 months) it has not been possible to obtain even tolerably accurate up-to-date figures from other countries. Examples were given by Professor F.A. Mann C.B.E. F.B.A. in his article entitled "Fusion of the Legal Professions?" in (1977) 93 LQR 367–377, included at Annex 1. Broadly, the comparison he made in 1977 remains correct today. The comparison with the position in France and Germany shows that

(1) the number of full-time Judges in France and Germany is much greater than in England and Wales, after full allowance is made for the practice by which French and German Judges hearing cases at first instance sit in benches of 3 Judges;

(2) the number of cases tried and appeals heard in France and Germany is far greater than in England and Wales.

7.4 The position in the U.S.A. is even more markedly different from that in England and Wales, the number of full-time Judges and the number of cases tried and appeals heard being also much greater.

7.5 The reasons for the small number of full-time Judges and cases tried and appeals heard in England and Wales are very important. They go to the heart of the English legal system and to specific features of that system which the Government proposals will overthrow. The cost to the taxpayer, through the expense of a larger Judiciary and Court system and through legal aid, and to those who are involved in criminal or civil cases, is central to the consideration of the public interest.

7.6 The reasons are these:

(1) *Expertise* Barristers appearing in the higher Courts acquire by training and by regular appearance in the Courts, in strong competition with each other, expertise in advocacy which enables

them to deal with cases more speedily and efficiently than the inexperienced advocate can: see para 21.28 below.

(2) *Expertise of Judges*   The Judges in the higher Courts, both full-time and part-time, with the benefit of long training in the Courts can with the help of counsel deal with cases speedily and efficiently. Their ability to deliver judgments extempore is often surprising to Judges and lawyers from other countries.

(3) *Familiarity*   Because barristers appear regularly in the higher Courts, and Judges are drawn from those regularly appearing, the barristers are well known to the Judges, who know how far they can rely on barristers for an accurate statement of the law or an accurate summary of the facts.

(4) *Settlement and guilty pleas*   The regular experience of barristers in the higher Courts in criminal cases enables them to judge more accurately the likely results of the cases, and to give firmer advice to defendants than they could if they had less regular experience. The result is fewer cases going to full trial in which guilty pleas should have been made. In civil cases, the accurate forecast of the likely result leads to a greater proportion of settlements on sensible terms, where both plaintiff and defendant are independently advised of their likely chances of success or failure: see Lord Mackay's observations at para 3.13 above.

(5) *Standards of integrity*   The constant appearances of barristers in the higher Courts result in standards of integrity and accuracy being higher than they are in legal professions where appearances in Court are less constant and by less experienced advocates.

The reasons set out in (1) to (5) above are the prime reasons why so much commercial and other litigation and arbitration takes place in this country rather than in the countries of the litigants. The experience of the Commercial Court is one clear example of how a strong Bar backed up by strong firms of solicitors and strong Judges can earn substantial "invisible exports" for this country not only in the cases brought or tried, but also in the advisory work which the strength of the Commercial Court's reputation draws to this country.

But there are other reasons in addition.

(6) *Oral hearings*   Hearings at first instance and on appeal are mainly oral hearings. The introduction of written evidence in chief and written skeleton arguments has served to focus with even greater emphasis on the oral hearing. There is room for improvement, but experience shows that where too much has to be committed to paper, trials and appeals become longer, less efficient and more expensive, as in the U.S.A. (Chapter 21 below).

(7) ***Single and continuous hearing***   The trial of criminal and civil cases by Judges sitting on one occasion and continuously from day to day is another major factor in the efficient and cost-effective disposal of cases. In those countries e.g. in the EEC where cases are heard at intervals over a long period, the advocates have to reprepare themselves for each separate hearing. The advantage of a single and continuous hearing of a case is that this focuses the concentration of all involved, Judge, jury, barristers, solicitors, lay clients and witnesses, to the greatest extent and for the shortest time on the factual and legal issues arising in the case. It is a part of the English system best adapted to Judges and barristers working in harmony together. It is equally a feature which would not be possible if the advocates were, as most solicitors are, involved in an office practice requiring regular daily conduct of the legal affairs of several clients.

(8) ***Research in the law by lawyers, not the Judge***   Under the English system research into the law is carried out by the lawyers, both solicitors and barristers, and is presented to the Judge. It is the duty of the barrister to cite the relevant case-law including cases against his client's interest. This much reduces the burdens on the Judge who therefore needs no back-up office to assist in the researching of the law. But this is a system possible only where the advocates have sufficient experience and appear regularly so that they are trusted by the Judges to present all the relevant law to them.

(9) ***Independence and objectivity***   Where as in England and Wales barristers are both entirely independent and acting on a consultant basis, the balance between the duty to the lay client and the duty to the Court in the administration of justice can be kept more readily, than in a system where the advocate is part of a large partnership or corporation and is dealing with the lay client direct and on a continuing basis. The balance between the duty to the lay client and the duty to the Court, which not infrequently are in conflict, is difficult to keep. Independence, the role of a consultant, and constant practice are each important factors in enabling barristers to achieve this balance satisfactorily. The absence of contingency fees adds to their independence and objectivity: see Chapter 24 below.

7.7   The reasons set out in para. 7.6 for the small number of Judges and of cases tried and appeals heard in England and Wales are well-known to all who take part in the administration of justice in England and Wales. These reasons were fully covered in the evidence of the High Court Judges and that of the Circuit Judges to the Royal Commission, which is not referred to in the Green Papers. Copies of that evidence are contained in Annex 2.

7.8 The reasons set out in para. 7.6 above are of particular significance when considering the quality of both advocates and Judges and the cost of justice. Inadequate advocates or Judges and the inefficient handling of cases result in greater costs for litigants and for the taxpayer. The taxpayer is affected in two ways: through the cost of more Judges, more Courts, more Court staff and more Court facilities, and through additional costs to the Legal Aid Scheme. The cost implications for the Treasury of a legal system under which advocacy in the higher Courts would be made available to any lawyer who had achieved the minimum "flying hours" are considerable. As the Lord Chancellor has confirmed in a written Parliamentary answer, no consideration of the cost implications of the Green Paper proposals has yet been made.

8

Accountants' Firms

8.1 One of the major proposals of the Government is to allow barristers and solicitors to join with each other and with other professionals in what are called "Multi-Disciplinary Practices" (MDPs). Since the major accountants' firms are much the largest professional firms, and like solicitors have branches or linked partnerships in other countries, it is important to include some details of the 8 largest accountants' firms.

8.2 The details set out in Figure 8.1 are taken from "The Accountant" for June 1988 and show the position for each of the 8 largest firms at dates between 31 March and 30 April 1988.

8.3 Each of these firms is part of an international grouping in inter-linked firms with offices in many other countries. Details are set out in Figure 8.2 and are taken from "International Accounting Bulletin" of December 1988.

8.4 The economic power of these major international groups of accountants is large. As appears in Chapter 10 below these groups have made clear their business aim to grow larger still, and if the Green Paper proposals are implemented to expand into the provision of legal services of all kinds including advocacy. It is assumed in the Green Papers that this would increase competition. It is the Bar Council's case that, on the contrary, this would reduce competition if barristers, now competing as sole practitioners, became part of these large organisations. It would also have the other adverse effects set out in Chapter 11 below, including substantially increased costs.

U.K. FIRMS

Firm	Fee Income £ million	% Growth over previous year	Number of offices	Number of partners	Number of other Chargeable Staff	Total Chargeable Staff	Total Staff	Fees per Partner £ thousand	Fees per Total Chargeable Staff £ thousand
Peat Marwick McLintock (KPMG)	262.5	26.7	56	478	6,445	6,923	8,614	548	37.9
Price Waterhouse	178.5	28.7	19	317	3,412	3,729	5,030	563	47.8
Coopers & Lybrand	172.0	20.2	37	337	3,460	3,797	5,087	510	45.2
Deloitte Haskins & Sells	151.1	24.8	19	240	3,132	3,372	4,440	629	44.8
Ernst & Whinney	120.9	20.1	25	214	2,986	3,200	3,744	565	37.7
Touche Ross	116.6	24.6	24	230	2,607	2,837	3,638	507	41.0
Arthur Anderson	113.4	24.2	13	136	1,942	2,078	2,734	834	54.5
Arthur Young	108.0	20.0	22	209	NA	NA	3,221	507	NA

Figure 8.1

INTERNATIONAL GROUPS

Firm	Fee Income US$ million	Member Firms	Offices of Member Firms	Partners of Member Firms	Professional Staff of Member Firms	Total Staff of member Firms
KPMG (Peat Marwick)	3,900	104	650	5,000	42,300	62,500
Arthur Anderson	2,800	49	231	2,016	33,568	45,918
Coopers & Lybrand	2,500	102	580	NA	NA	45,000
Price Waterhouse	2,318	97	409	2,626	26,736	38,535
Ernst & Whinney	2,191	86	472	3,159	24,900	35,600
Arthur Young	2,053	74	423	2,900	22,200	33,000
Deloitte Haskins & Sells	1,921	65	456	2,440	22,217	31,030
Touche Ross International	1,840	89	514	3,030	22,650	33,000

Figure 8.2

63

9

Access to Justice for All

WHAT DOES THIS MEAN?

9.1 The major aim of the Bar is to satisfy the need of every person for ready access to independent legal advice and independent legal representation in Courts and tribunals, of a high standard, and of the same standard for poor and rich alike and whoever is paying.

9.2 Para 1.1 of the main Green Paper, entitled "Access to legal services" shows that the Government shares, in principle, this major aim of the Bar. But it is one thing to share this aim in principle, and quite another to ensure that this aim is achieved in practice.

LACK OF ACCESS TO JUSTICE

9.3 Those who can pay for legal services can obtain access to justice, particularly because of the Bar's "cab-rank" rule.

9.4 Those who cannot afford to pay for legal services must seek access to justice

either by getting help with payment for these services through the Legal Aid system
or by getting free legal advice or representation (including help through trades unions and others).

9.5 In theory those who cannot afford to pay can represent themselves as "litigants in person". In practice this is no real alternative. The complexities of Court and tribunal procedures are by themselves enough to baffle a litigant in person. The further complexities of statute law added to each year by Parliament are beyond the grasp of almost all litigants in person.

LEGAL AID

9.6 In 1979 the Royal Commission in its Report at paras. 5.1 to 5.6 stated as the essential principles relating to the provision of legal services that

(1) there should be equal access to the Courts;
(2) citizens will not have equal access to the Courts nor enjoy the full benefit of rights and safeguards provided by the law without the provision of adequate legal services;
(3) financial assistance out of public funds should be available for every individual who, without it, would suffer an undue financial burden in properly pursuing or defending his or her rights;
(4) all those who receive legal services are entitled to expect the same standard of legal service irrespective of their personal circumstances;
(5) so that those who receive legal services at public expense should have the same standard of services as those who pay for them, a lawyer undertaking such work should not be expected to do so for less than a reasonable rate of remuneration;
(6) every individual, whether supported out of public funds or fee-paying, should always have a free choice among available lawyers and should not be required to retain an assigned lawyer (such as a "public defender" lawyer salaried by the state, as in some States of the U.S.A.).

The Bar Council re-affirms those principles, which are an essential part of the freedom and equality before the law of every citizen.

9.7 The Royal Commission's principles, from which the Government did not dissent, have not been met. The main feature of the decade from 1979 to 1989 and of the Legal Aid Act 1988 (which lays down afresh the law relating to legal aid and its administration) has been movement away from those principles. This is mainly due to Treasury opposition to the growth in Legal Aid funding resulting from the major increases in crime and matrimonial proceedings, and from the increase in the number of civil disputes and applications for judicial review of decisions by Government and other authorities.

9.8 It is not the Bar Council's intention in this Chapter to set out in detail all the changes in legal aid provision which have been adverse to the interests of the poor when charged with criminal offences or involved in civil disputes or suffering from abuse of power. But it is necessary to refer to some of the adverse changes in the context of the Green Paper proposals which are put forward by the Government as purporting to improve access to justice for the poor.

LEGAL AID FOR REPRESENTATION IN CIVIL PROCEEDINGS

9.9 The decline in eligibility for Civil Legal Aid since 1979 is well-documented. One of the best qualified observers of legal aid, Mr. Cyril Glasser, showed in 2 articles in the Law Society's Gazette of 9 March and 20 April 1988 that eligibility had declined to such an extent that only just over 50% of the population and under 60% of households (including households with children) were eligible for legal aid. His estimate was that between 1979 and 1986 (when there was a deliberate down- rating by means of a substantial cut in dependants' allowances) just over 25% of all households and of the population went out of eligibility, and since 1986 the position had certainly deteriorated further. This has to be compared with the position when the Legal Aid Scheme came into force in 1950: at that time the financial limits were carefully set so that well over 80% of the population were eligible on income grounds alone. Though this serious deterioration in eligibility was drawn to the attention of the Government, nothing was done to remedy the position when the Legal Aid Act 1988 was passed through Parliament. On 8 March 1989 the Lord Chancellor announced increased eligibility limits for civil legal aid. Most of the financial limits increased by about 4.7% in line with the increase in social security benefits, at a time when the rate of inflation was substantially above this. But some of the limits, relating to capital, dependants' allowances, and changes in resources before reassessment is necessary were altered more substantially: the changes in these limits are welcome.

9.10 Overall, however, the effect of departing from the Royal Commission's "first principles", which were the basis on which the Legal Aid Scheme was founded, has been to leave in existence a large class of persons and households who are too poor to pay for legal representation, but are regarded by the Government as too rich to receive Legal Aid.

LEGAL ADVICE AND ASSISTANCE (THE GREEN FORM SCHEME)

9.11 Under the 1988 Act legal advice and assistance on conveyancing and wills have largely been removed from the Green Form scheme. As the Marre Committee pointed out, badly drafted wills are a costly source of legal disputes, costly to the taxpayer and costly to the litigants: the saving of money is likely to be offset by the increase in costs of representation. The need for legal aid in some conveyancing matters was also stressed by the Marre Committee.

9.12   With regard to advice on welfare benefits, much of the work of solicitors and legal advice centres results from administrative delays in the Department of Social Security and not from any dispute about the level of benefit. This part of the cost of the Legal Aid Scheme could be reduced by removing the serious inefficiencies in the Department's administration. If that were done, the money saved could be used to good effect in improving eligibility for Legal Aid.

9.13   Instead, the Government proposes that the Legal Aid Board should "contract-out" advice on welfare benefits to advice agencies, thereby removing from potential recipients of welfare benefits the advantage of the advice of a solicitor in private practice. This has to be viewed in the context of the Government's proposals on conveyancing, multi-disciplinary partnerships and rights of audience which are likely to lead to the closure of many local solicitors' offices. There are at present more than 11,000 solicitors' offices, which give overall a more accessible local service than can be given by Citizens Advice Bureaux and other advice agencies. The effect of this change would be to worsen the availability of sound legal advice to men and women throughout the country. The advantages to the taxpayer would be less cost, and also, regrettably, lower take-up of benefits. It has also to be added that the advice agencies do not have funds, staff or facilities to take on work now done by local solicitors.

9.14   Assistance by way of representation (ABWOR) is an extension of the Green Form scheme to provide legal representation in some Magistrates Courts proceedings, prison disciplinary hearings and Mental Health Review Tribunals.

9.15   A major concern about ABWOR and legal aid for representation in civil proceedings is that these schemes do not cover most of the important tribunals which decide on the legal rights of individual men and women. Legal Aid is not available for e.g. Social Security Appeal Tribunals, Medical Appeal Tribunals, Industrial Tribunals and Immigration hearings. This is a serious omission. These tribunals have the power to determine matters which may be of greater importance to the individual than proceedings in Court, for example, the right to remain in England and Wales or the right to be reinstated in employment. During the period since the start of the Legal Aid Scheme in 1950 many such tribunals have been set up outside the scope of the Courts, without any proper consideration of the need for legal assistance and representation. The studies that have been carried out show, not surprisingly, that represented applicants have a materially greater chance of success than those not represented. As indicated in para. 9.13 above this may benefit the

67

taxpayer by resulting in the applicant not receiving a benefit which he or she is intended and entitled to receive.

FAIR AND REASONABLE REMUNERATION

9.16 Section 39(3) of the Legal Aid Act 1974 required the Lord Chancellor when making regulations as to amounts to be paid to barristers or solicitors for the provision of legally-aided services to "have regard to the principle of allowing fair remuneration according to the work actually and reasonably done". The failure to operate this principle led to judicial review proceedings against the then Lord Chancellor in 1986. The Government deliberately did not reproduce this provision in the 1988 Act, but replaced it in section 34(9) of the 1988 Act with a statement of relevant factors to be taken into account.

DEFICIENCIES IN THE LEGAL AID SYSTEM

9.17 The new Legal Aid Board is not yet fully in the saddle. How it will deal with Legal Aid, and what constraints will be placed on it by the Lord Chancellor and the Treasury under the 1988 Act, have yet to be seen. But the brief summary in paragraphs 9.6 to 9.16 above shows that the essential principles laid down by the Royal Commission (see para. 9.6 above) have not been adhered to.

9.18 There has been a process of reducing the range of eligibility for legal aid. It has been estimated (by the National Consumer Council) that the income level where eligibility ceases for a married couple with two children has since 1979 changed from 37% to 6% above average male earnings. The effect has been to create a large class of individuals and households needing legal aid because of their inadequate means, but denied assistance through legal aid. The Green Papers apparently indicate an expectation of the Government that through its revolutionary changes legal services would be made cheaper, and so available to more people without legal aid. This is an expectation without foundation. The Government's proposals, if implemented, would in any event reduce competition and increase cost to the consumer: see Chapter 11 below. One necessary remedy lies in developing the Legal Aid system so that it provides genuine assistance to those who need it.

9.19 There is a further ground for serious concern. The rates of remuneration for legal aid work, both civil and criminal, the delays in payment, and the terms of work, e.g. for Duty Solicitors, are such as to make legal aid work unattractive, especially to solicitors. Many solicitors have had to give up this work. The comments of the senior partner of a 4 partner firm of solicitors in the South of England are typical:-

> "There is a real problem with [the Duty Solicitor Scheme] because of the personal inconvenience and generally because Criminal Legal Aid work is too unattractive to most of the local firms of solicitors. In [two large towns] none of the solicitors are prepared to be on the Scheme.
>
> So far as Criminal Legal Aid is concerned at the Magistrates Court, because of the rates that are paid and the general demands of the work itself, the solicitors are simply not interested in doing it. The hourly rates are so much lower than other legal work that many solicitors are declining to do the work altogether.
>
> I have to say that I was very concerned at the time when the Law Society decided that solicitors were appropriate in the Magistrates Court and effectively penalised them for instructing Counsel by the method of assessment in all cases where there is not a certificate for Counsel. I also feel that it is a shame that many young barristers do not get the chance to gain experience in the Magistrates Court simply because of the present rules.
>
> I find it impossible to understand the pressure to give solicitors rights of audience in the Crown Court as it simply does not bear any relation to reality. There may be a handful of solicitors who want to conduct cases in the Crown Court but I frankly cannot think of one in this area. The real problem is to get people to do the work at all and to ensure that the work is done competently. There is an acute shortage of solicitors so that the salaries we now have to pay weighed against the rewards of criminal defence work simply do not balance.
>
> I personally believe that Legal Aid is in a time of crisis and that Criminal Legal Aid is probably the most unattractive area of work for the majority of practices".

Another example is the submission of a managing partner of a 9 partner firm of solicitors in the South of England, specialising in criminal law:-

> "*Matrimonial Legal Aid*
> There are already serious problems in this field of work. The rates allowable are so low that this firm after considerable soul searching and thought have had to withdraw from Legal Aid Matrimonial work. The Green Papers ignore the fact that the vast majority of matrimonial cases are settled out of Court with orders being made by consent. These settlements are reached by expert professional advisers who have a detailed knowledge of the law. The suggestion that this role can be undertaken by . . . charities and advice agencies staffed by unqualified people is so far from the realities of life as to beggar belief. Proper professional advice is increasingly only available to those with the means to pay. The Government proposals will only serve to perpetuate this inequality and cannot in any way contribute to the professed objectives set out in paragraph (1) of the Green Paper.

Criminal Law

So far as Criminal Legal Aid is concerned, there are already a number of firms of Solicitors who do not undertake Criminal Legal Aid work. There are also a large number of firms of Solicitors who are unable to maintain Specialist Criminal Solicitors because of the unremunerative rates. Practitioners in a great many firms have to combine their Criminal work with other work (often Conveyancing) in order to earn the necessary fee income to support the practice. Those firms therefore are subsidising Criminal Legal Aid Rates with fees derived from other work. I am only able to maintain my Criminal Practice with the assistance of Litigation Clerks and a huge throughput of work. It is only by virtue of volume that I am able to bring in sufficient fee income to justify what I do. I doubt that I could handle more cases that I do at present. Since 1st January this year myself and my Assistant Solicitor have handled 220 cases in the Magistrates Court. In addition to this we have both been Court Duty Solicitor on a total of 10 occasions. One would also have to add to this, various appearances, usually outside office hours, under PACE when warrants of further detention are being applied for.

Tribunals

We are asked to provide advice on Tribunal hearings and at Solicitors Advice Bureaux frequently. With regard to Tribunals, in the absence of there being any basis on which we can be paid, we just cannot help the large numbers of people who clearly really need assistance. We believe that the refusal of Government to extend legal aid into this field stems from a realisation that this would result in substantial increases in the Social Security and other budgets.

May I quote a case in point. My mother-in-law is entitled to a special hardship allowance which follows her for the rest of her natural life. Both my in-laws are Pensioners. Shortly before my mother-in-law reached pensionable age the determining officer ruled that she was no longer entitled to her allowance because she was capable of performing alternative work. Simply because of my own position, we were able to mount an appeal which was successful. In particular I was able to refer her to a Consultant who demonstrated beyond any doubt that she was unable to carry out any of the kinds of work suggested by the determining officer. My in-laws would not have had the means to have instructed a Solicitor privately and no longer had the benefit of Trade Union Membership. There is no Law Centre in this part of . . . . The benefit preserved is worth many thousands of pounds. How many others have slipped through the net?"

9.20 The choice is between these two alternatives:-

either   (1) to continue to deny to those of limited means, but above the Government's Legal Aid limits, access to paid legal services, and to continue to provide a second-class service to those who do receive legal aid;

or   (2) to organise the legal aid service properly and to spend the relatively small sums required both to bring within the legal aid limits those who cannot afford to pay for legal services, and to provide to those who receive legal aid a service reasonably comparable with the service given to those who can pay themselves.

The creation of the Legal Aid Board could give the opportunity to achieve the better alternative (2). But the restraints imposed on legal aid by the Government over the last decade are an indicator that the Government prefers alternative (1).

WHAT CAN THE BAR DO?

9.21 There are two steps which the Bar can take to mark its strong commitment to improving access to justice for all.

THE DUTY OF THE BAR TO DO LEGAL AID WORK

9.22 The Bar Council re-affirms the duty of every barrister to comply with the requirements of the "cab-rank" rule, and to represent any client whether legally aided or not in cases within each barrister's field of practice. The Bar Council regards it as wrong that instructions of any kind should be refused on the ground that the barrister does not do legally aided work. The Bar Council will revise the terms in which the "cab-rank" rule is drafted so as to make it absolutely clear that it applies (1) to instructions of any kind, and (2) to all work whether legally aided or not. The Bar Council will deal with any case of a barrister failing to abide by the "cab-rank" rule through the Bar's disciplinary procedures. If the Government will respond to this re-affirmation of the basic rule which is central to the role of the independent barrister by ensuring that reasonable fees are paid (and paid without the present serious delays) to barristers appearing for legally aided clients (as well as to solicitors), that will go a long way towards ensuring that there is access to justice in the Courts for every citizen.

9.23 This would not deal with the tribunals which are outside the legal aid system. It is the Bar Council's view that proper consideration should now be given to the importance of the decisions of some tribunals to the individuals affected by the decisions and to the urgent need for legal representation in those tribunals. It is fully recognised, however, that there are budgetary restraints on every Government. The increase in legal aid funding necessary to ensure proper legal representation in the Courts would be a first step, to be followed later by extension to tribunals.

FREE REPRESENTATION BY THE BAR

9.24 The second step for the Bar to take is to extend the excellent free "pro bono" work done by the Bar through its Free Representation Unit (FRU), through Citizens Advice Bureaux, Legal Advice and Law Centres, and in many other ways.

9.25 FRU is one of the Bar's best initiatives. With the dedication of a small staff and many young barristers and students it copes with a large burden of representation of lay clients in those tribunals for which legal aid is not available, including (1) The Criminal Injuries Compensation Board, (2) Employers Internal Disciplinary Hearings, (3) The Employment Appeal Tribunal, (4) Immigration Adjudicator Hearings, (5) Industrial Tribunals, (6) Local Valuation Courts, (7) Medical Appeal Tribunals, (8) Rent Assessment Panels, (9) Rent Tribunals, (10) The Social Security Commissioners, (11) Social Security Appeal Tribunals, and (12) Vaccine Damage Tribunals. About 900 cases in London and the area round London are referred to FRU each year by solicitors, Citizens Advice Bureaux, Advice Centres and other agencies. In 1987/88 FRU was successful in 78% of these cases.

9.26 Free "pro bono" work in the public service is a vital ingredient for any profession worthy of that title. The Commission on Professionalism of the American Bar Association (Chapter 4 above) made a strong call for an increase in the pro bono activities of the American Bars, and for every lawyer to accept the obligation to perform pro bono services. That obligation is one which has traditionally formed part of the ethic of the Bar of England and Wales.

9.27 FRU needs to be expanded in London, so as to reduce the number of people who are without representation in tribunals deciding on their legal rights. The Bar's Circuits will also need to develop their own FRU work as it has already been developed in Birmingham by the Bar in collaboration with the City of Birmingham Polytechnic. It is often in the areas furthest from London, for example the North-East of England, that the consequences of unemployment and poverty hit hardest. The services of a FRU in each of those areas is needed, so that the talents of barristers are available to serve those whose need is not met by legal aid. FRU can, as in London, work in amicable collaboration with Citizens Advice Bureaux and other agencies to which the Bar's talents are also directed.

THE FURTHER DEVELOPMENT OF FRU

9.28 The needs of the public for legal advice and representation go much further. The needs exist in at least 4 areas:-

(1) the difficulties in tribunals before which legal aid is not available, faced by individuals, whether applicants or defendants who can not afford legal representation at all and have no Union or similar support, and in Courts by individuals who are outside the eligibility limits for legal aid, have no other support and cannot afford legal representation;

(2) a similar problem in taking cases to the European Commission of Human Rights;

(3) the need felt by many small and indeed medium sized charities, especially those which are not national, to have access to legal advice;

(4) legal advice and assistance to Citizens Advice Bureaux and Law and Legal Advice Centres.

TRIBUNALS BEFORE WHICH LEGAL AID IS NOT AVAILABLE

9.29 The statistics in Figure 9.1 show that for 1987/88 in Social Security Appeal Tribunals where there was an oral hearing, in some 59% of cases the applicant was unrepresented. They also show that in represented cases 51.2% succeeded, whereas in cases where only the applicant appeared, only 31.9% did so.

FRU volunteers appear in about 8% of cases in the London area before Industrial Tribunals. Nevertheless the lack of legal representation denies justice to far too many, and there is an urgent need for expansion of this service.

9.30 There is a number of types of tribunal for which legal aid is not available and where free legal representation is needed:

(1) *Immigration* – FRU takes 2 or 3 cases per year but cannot increase this with its present capacity.

(2) *Criminal Injuries Compensation Board* – FRU appear in about 45 cases per year at present. The need for legal representation will increase.

(3) *Legal Aid Committees* – this work sometimes requires greater experience than other tribunal work. There is a need for representation which could usefully involve more experienced members of the Bar.

(4) *Small Claims Cases in the County Court* – this is an area in which free legal representation would be valuable.

(5) *Appeals to Social Security Commissioners* – since 1986 the DHSS has instructed counsel in a number of appeals. Claimants are generally unrepresented.

REPRESENTATION AT
SOCIAL SECURITY APPEAL TRIBUNALS 1987/88

	TOTAL IN GREAT BRITAIN	LONDON NORTH	LONDON SOUTH
TOTAL HEARD	165,307	19,800	16,269
DECIDED IN APPLICANTS FAVOUR	40,258 (24.3%)	5,278 (26.7%)	3,942 (24.2%)
REP & APPLICANT ATTENDING	27,471	2,985	2,050
DECIDED IN APPLICANTS FAVOUR	14,059 (51.2%)	1,511 (50.6%)	998 (48.7%)
APPLICANT ONLY ATTENDING	50,067	5,636	5,168
DECIDED IN APPLICANTS FAVOUR	15,988 (31.9%)	2,106 (37.4%)	1,773 (34.3%)
NON ATTENDANCE	80,684	10,307	8,358
DECIDED IN APPLICANTS FAVOUR	7,643 (9.5%)	1,284 (12.5%)	951 (11.4%)

Figure 9.1

9.31 For many tens of thousands of people the SSAT is their only point of contact with the legal system. Most types of Social Security Benefits are dealt with. The legal points raised are points of construction and points concerning the interrelationship between benefits; complex points of law involving trusts and matrimonial law also arise. A small but highly significant number of appeals from SSATs are referred by the Commissioners to the European Court of Justice.

ADVICE TO CHARITIES

9.32 So far as smaller charities are concerned, the Bar of Scotland already operates a voluntary scheme under which general advice, often on the telephone, can be obtained by charities from volunteers who, rather than advising on a particular case or problem, are available to point the charity in the right direction.

PRELIMINARY PROPOSALS FOR FRU

9.33   The following are preliminary proposals as to the ways in which FRU could be expanded:

(1) *Involvement of pupils and junior barristers in the work of FRU*
   (a) The FRU training programme could be linked to the Council of Legal Education course to encourage a wider spread of representatives.
   (b) Chambers could assist with the practical stage of FRU training by arranging for FRU representatives to attend Tribunals with members of Chambers.
   (c) FRU work could be encouraged as part of pupillage. Pupil masters could assist by providing some supervision of the pupil's preparation of a case.
   (d) Barristers of all seniorities could provide the necessary pool of expertise to advise in the more complex cases.

(2) *A Chambers FRU Scheme*
   (a) It would be important for FRU to know where to refer cases for assistance or representation by pupils or tenants.
   (b) Chambers which were willing to provide such assistance would subscribe to a "Chambers FRU Scheme".
   (c) FRU would approach such Chambers for assistance with urgent cases where no representative had been found, in the more difficult cases to provide more experienced representation, and generally with advice on difficult cases.

(3) *Involvement of the more Senior Bar with FRU*
   More senior barristers could assist by:
   (a) Providing a panel for advice in specialist areas to FRU representatives.
   (b) Representation in difficult cases, and in the European Commission of Human Rights.
   (c) Assisting in the training process by lecturing and acting as advocates and judges in "mock tribunals".

9.34   The members of FRU believe very strongly that the basis of a barrister's involvement with FRU should be a voluntary one. But the Bar Council's policy is that every barrister however senior should be encouraged to provide some free legal services every year in fields not covered by legal aid. The Bar could greatly assist in the function of an expanded FRU as considered above.

9.35   Members of the Bar could assist in the provision of free legal services in a variety of other ways. The services could be provided within the umbrella of FRU:

(1) Advice by telephone, as a first reference point for referral agencies such as CABX. The Chancery Bar already runs a scheme for licensed conveyancers.
(2) Advice in writing - legal advice beyond the "first aid" stage.
(3) Advising charities in a similar way to the Bar of Scotland: para. 9.32 above.
(4) Assisting the establishment of FRU in centres other than London and Birmingham.
(5) Assisting in the training of CABX personnel.
(6) On an individual basis, more barristers could (as many already do) attend CABX and Law and Legal Advice Centres to give advice to clients.

9.36 The Bar Council calls for a strong commitment from the Bar and from solicitors to meet the needs of the poor and the not-so-poor whose rights may now go unvindicated, just as in appeals from Jamaica to the Privy Council, particularly in cases involving the death penalty, the Bar and solicitors have so readily provided their services free.

9.37 The Bar's services to the public are provided also in another way. About a thousand barristers sit as part-time Judges (Recorders, Deputy High Court and Circuit Judges, Assistant Recorders). In 1987 they sat for 26,665 days (nearly double the 14,152 days sat by High Court Judges including the President of the Family Division and the Vice-Chancellor). They are paid so to sit, and this work helps to make them eligible for promotion as full-time Judges. But the main motive is public service. One consequence of the Government's proposals would be likely to be a reluctance on the part of the new breed of lawyers and their employers or partners or co-directors or shareholders to continue this large element of public service. Experience in other countries, especially the U.S.A., shows that where trial lawyers are grouped in partnerships or corporations, there is less readiness to do this service, as the ABA Commission on Professionalism recognised (page 299). One factor which would militate against this public service would be the pressures of the employer, partner, co-director or shareholder to keep the in-house advocacy department at work.

CITIZENS ADVICE BUREAUX AND OTHER AGENCIES

9.38 The Citizens Advice Bureaux (CABX) play a significant role in giving advice of a generalist nature to members of the public. Individual CABX are largely funded by local authorities, while the central National Association (NACAB) is grant-aided by central Government. It refers many legal problems to solicitors and legal advice and law centres, and FRU receives many referrals for representation in tribunals.

9.39 The Government in the Green Papers and its proposals for Legal Aid appears to assume that CABX and other agencies can directly, or by contracting out by the Legal Aid Board, provide much legal advice now given within or without the Legal Aid system by solicitors and in some instances by barristers. This cannot be a well founded assumption unless the necessary resources (funds, staff and other facilities) are to be made available to CABX. The CABX are hard put to provide even the services now provided at the present level and standards. Funding of CABX by local authorities is under pressure. CABX could not provide services in substitution for those of lawyers without adequate funding, including funding sufficient for the employment of lawyers or to pay for the referral services of solicitors, and where required, barristers. Further, the other proposals in the Green Paper which would be likely to diminish the number of solicitors' offices would make it more difficult for CABX to refer matters to local solicitors, and therefore more important for CABX to have lawyers in-house.

9.40 As regards representation before tribunals CABX try to provide some representation where they can, including some by referral to FRU. But para. 22 of Annex E to the main Green Paper is largely misconceived. Many matters before tribunals require qualified legal assistance. Many involve matters of great importance to the applicants of which examples such as the right to remain in England and Wales have already been given. Some applicants can be helped by non-lawyers from CABX and other agencies with reasonable experience. Most applicants are not able to represent themselves adequately. The representation of applicants before tribunals requires a mix of lay and legally qualified representation in which the Bar through FRU will play a part. But the CABX will not be able to play any effective part without adequate resources, including some assurance of continuity of funding, and the Bar cannot fill all the gaps which will remain.

LAW CENTRES

9.41 In the last 10 years the number of Law Centres has doubled, the source of their funding has become dominantly local authority programmes, and their funding has in many cases come under severe difficulties. A consequence of the financial pressures on Law Centres has been that they have had to give priority to legal advice under the Legal Aid Scheme, rather than to their work in areas not covered by

Legal Aid which should be their priority areas of work. Because of the reduced eligibility for Legal Aid, the scope of work of the Law Centres has been further narrowed. The ability of Law Centres to complement the work of agencies such as CABX is therefore in doubt.

AGENCIES GENERALLY

9.42   The work of these agencies has been adversely affected by the decline in funding, the changes in the systems of funding, and the uncertainties whether funding will be continued and at what level. The agencies have been less able to plug the gaps left by the increasing inadequacies of the Legal Aid Scheme. What is now needed is some overall planning, covering the Legal Aid Scheme and the work of the various agencies, so that for the next 3-5 years there is a reasonably settled policy for the agencies as a complement to an equitable and efficient Legal Aid Scheme.

9.43   Priority should be given to ensuring that everyone has access to a general advice centre such as a CABX (this has been described by the National Consumer Council as the "fourth right of citizenship"). At present advice centres are very unevenly distributed e.g. London has on average one advice worker (paid or unpaid) for every 3,750 people, whereas in the East Midlands there is one advice worker for every 32,250 people, and counties such as Lincolnshire and Derbyshire and metropolitan districts such as Barnsley, Bolton, Gateshead and Solihull have minimal provision.
    Funding of general advice has to be additional to, and not a substitute for, legal aid. Local authorities should be placed under a duty to fund general advice, with the assistance of central government. One government department should be given overall responsibility.

CONCILIATION AND OUT-OF-COURT SETTLEMENT

9.44   The Bar has a good record in the giving of independent, objective advice leading to conciliation and settlement out-of- Court of civil cases, and to sensible guilty pleas in criminal cases, thereby avoiding the costs of unnecessary and time-wasting trials, including trials which would be potentially most distressing to the victims of crime. This was a matter referred to by Lord Mackay (see para. 3.13 above) when he stressed the ability of an independent barrister to achieve settlements out of Court which clients or their solicitors were unable to achieve.

9.45 It is not always appreciated by the public how much the Bar's record of expert out-of-Court resolution of civil and criminal cases has contributed to

(1) the relatively small number of cases heard in England and Wales as compared with other countries;
(2) keeping down the cost to the public of the Court system;
(3) reducing the delays in both the civil and criminal courts, which, though far from satisfactory, are better than most other jurisdictions.

9.46 There are already excellent initiatives in further promoting out-of-Court resolution of civil disputes, especially matrimonial disputes, including the schemes promoted by the Family Law Bar Association and the London Common Law and Commercial Bar Association. Sensible conciliation of disputes between wives and husbands over financial provision and the custody of children can achieve much in avoiding divorce's legacy of bitterness. The experimental methods so far used need to be developed into a definite pattern of active conciliation in matrimonial cases.

9.47 The same is true in other fields of civil dispute in which experienced barristers on each side can promote settlements by accurately advising as to the likely result of cases and conducting amicable negotiations. This is in the interest of litigants who avoid the delay, worry and expense of trials, and in the public interest in reducing delays to other trials and cost to the taxpayer. The new vocational course at the Inns of Court School of Law will include specific training in techniques of negotiation.

9.48 But there is more to be done. In civil cases, both barristers and solicitors should be required to certify in writing at a suitable period before trial that each of them has personally endeavoured to secure a reasonable settlement of the matters in dispute. It is generally unwise for Judges to take an active part in securing settlements. But they can help to promote the likelihood of settlement, by ensuring that issues are clearly defined before trials begin and that through Counsel the minds of the parties are concentrated on the likely outcome of the individual issues and of the case as a whole. A requirement for a pre-trial review can also help in achieving settlements.

9.49 In criminal cases the aim should be to ensure that those who plead guilty do so, on the basis of independent advice, at the earliest appropriate time. That will not be achieved, unless defendants are represented by independent lawyers with the objectivity derived from being at one remove from the persons who have the task of preparing statements of witnesses and collecting the defence evidence: see Lord Mackay's views in para. 3.13 above. That is now the role of the independent barrister, with the advantage of regular appearance in the Crown Court, on the basis of evidence assembled by or under the direction of an experienced solicitor. It is clear that this separation of function is a necessary and desirable one, both for the benefit of the defendant, and for that of the prosecution (as is recognised in paras. 5.10 and 5.22 of the main Green Paper). In jurisdictions where this is not the rule or the normal practice, such as the U.S.A., it is noteworthy that too many cases proceed unnecessarily.

9.50 The Bar Council proposes that for both civil and criminal cases working parties should be set up, composed of Judges, barristers and solicitors to lay down effective means for ensuring that cases which do not need to be fought at trial are brought to an early and satisfactory conclusion before all the costs of preparation for trial have been incurred.

SIMPLIFICATION OF COURT AND TRIBUNAL PROCEDURES

9.51 Court and tribunal procedures are still unnecessarily complex and baffling to the defendant in criminal cases and to the litigants in civil cases. It has always been the Bar's wish that procedures should be as clear and as simple as the needs of justice dictate. It is of particular concern that tribunals which were intended to provide simple justice open to all applicants have often become as complicated in their procedures as the Courts.

9.52 The Bar Council proposes the immediate formation of a committee composed equally of Judges, barristers, solicitors and users with the urgent task of reviewing and proposing means of simplifying the procedures of each Court and tribunal. For the civil courts this committee could take forward the proposals made in the Civil Justice Review, on which the Bar Council has already made its submissions, and which the Government intends to implement. For the tribunals this could be done in collaboration with the Council on Tribunals which has done much valuable work and is now engaged on the production of draft model rules of tribunal procedure.

ADMINISTRATION OF COURTS AND TRIBUNALS

9.53 It is inevitable that in any large and complex system of Courts and tribunals there will be inefficiencies and inadequacies. It is right that a tribute should be paid to some of the steps taken by Government to improve administration including the provision of new Courts and the greater consultation with the users in the design of new Courts. But there is much scope for improvement.

9.54 The Magistrates Court system, which primarily through lay magistrates deals with all the minor and some of the serious criminal cases and many of the straightforward cases involving children and family relationships, is particularly subject to delays and inefficiences in local administration. The Justices Clerks are underpaid and undermanned. Listing is often inefficient, leading to unnecessary delays and serious inconvenience to police, witnesses and defendants. The computerisation of listing has begun, but is proceeding too slowly. There are as yet no proper arrangements for the computer assisted monitoring of cases to the detriment of efficiency and to the inconvenience of all concerned. Communications between the Courts and other authorities are seriously inadequate. To take one small example, if a defendant is given bail by an Inner London Magistrates Court on condition that he lives in a bail hostel, it may be necessary for a probation officer to ring round all the bail hostels to find a place. There is no computer link and no system for ensuring that each Court is aware each day of available places. This is no more than one example of inadequacies which multiplied many times seriously affect our busiest Courts. Administration of Magistrates Courts exhibits all the British symptoms of inadequate thought and insufficient resources over a period of many years. This is now being examined by a Home Office scrutiny team.

9.55 A similar picture can be seen when the County Courts and the Crown Court are examined. There are fewer cases in the Crown Court, and some more thought and resources have been devoted to upgrading its administration. The lack of computer listing and computer monitoring of cases is, however, a serious deficiency, and an improvement much overdue.

9.56 The efforts of the Judges of the High Court and Court of Appeal have led to considerable improvements in procedures and in those aspects of administration for which the Judges are able to take responsibility. But some aspects of administration for which the Judges are not responsible are most inadequate for Courts of higher jurisdiction. For example, the Commercial Court which is the focus of much international litigation lacks Courts able conveniently to accommodate many parties, barristers and solicitors and their many files of documents. There is a lack of proper word processing facilities leading to undue delays in the handing down of judgments. Computer listing and monitoring needs to be speeded up.

9.57 Despite the high standards of Judges and Magistrates and of the justice which they deliver, the inefficiencies of the Court system, within which they are expected to work, adversely affect all participants in the judicial process, causing unnecessary delays, inconvenience and expense. Not infrequently barristers and solicitors find themselves being blamed for this though the real cause lies in the administration of the Court systems.

The Bar is often attacked over the return of briefs. Briefs have to be returned by one barrister and his or her place taken by another barrister when a clash of engagements occurs. Sometimes this happens due to the fault of the barrister or the chambers organisation. But far more often it occurs because of either unforeseeable problems, such as the unexpected lengthening of a case, or inadequacies in the Court administration including the listing of cases. Lay clients and solicitors may blame the barristers, whatever the cause of the return of a brief, and even though the fault, if any, should be laid elsewhere. If there is a justified complaint against a barrister that is pursued through the Bar's disciplinary procedure.

But it must be remembered that the Bar has a major advantage over other professions in coping with a clash of engagements. Because barristers are sole practitioners it is usually easy for the solicitor to find a substitute barrister of equivalent standing to the barrister who has had to return the brief. That is much more difficult for a legal partnership or company which is likely to make available a substitute only of lower standing, if indeed it has a substitute lawyer available at all. The Bar's response is a more flexible one.

9.58 The Government in the main Green Paper proposes a Legal Services Ombudsman with a remit over the complaints procedures of the Bar and the solicitor's profession. This is a proposal which, with some qualifications, the Bar Council welcomes (see also para. 18.12 below). But it would not be appropriate for any Legal Services Ombudsman to have a remit which did not cover the inadequacies of the administration of the Courts by the Government Departments concerned, which may affect litigants as much as the inadequacies of barristers or solicitors. The Ombudsman should naturally not be permitted to intervene in any matter falling within the jurisdiction of the Judges. The Bar Council proposes that the Legal Services Ombudsman should have power to examine allegations about the way that complaints about the administration of the Courts have been handled, to recommend the payment of compensation by the Government Department concerned, to recommend changes and improvement to the administration of the Courts, and to publicise his or her decisions.

CONTINGENCY FEES

9.59 These are considered fully in Chapter 24 with reference to the Contingency Fees Green Paper. But under the heading of "Access to Justice for All" it is important to state that contingency fees, in the context of the Courts of England and Wales, could not increase access more than marginally. The use of speculative actions in Scotland is small. The same would be true in England and Wales. Any suggestion that contingency fees could be a substitute for the devoting of adequate resources to Legal Aid, Citizens Advice Bureaux and other agencies would be quite wrong.

10

Fundamental Flaws in the Green Papers

10.1 The main proposals affecting the availability to the public of the services of barristers are

(1) that barristers should be enabled to join in partnership or corporate practices with solicitors and other professionals (multi-disciplinary practices – MDPs) (Chapter 15 below);

(2) that barristers should be enabled to join in partnership with each other (Chapter 15 below);

(3) that the Bar should cease to be a purely consultant profession, and the public should have direct access to barristers (Chapter 12 below);

(4) that rights of audience in the higher Courts should cease to be reserved to barristers and should be made available to solicitors or other professionals as licensed advocates (Chapter 12 below);

(5) that banks, building societies and other such organisations should be enabled to do conveyancing at cost (Chapter 23 below).

10.2 These proposals are considered separately in other Chapters below, as is the important question of independence from Government. But it is necessary first to examine these proposals together, as a whole, in the light of the assumptions made in the Green Papers in support of the proposals.

10.3 The assumptions made in the Green Papers are that, through the action of market forces, the changes proposed will

(1) increase competition for legal services;

(2) improve access to justice by increasing access to legal representation in the Courts;

(3) improve choice;

(4) result in legal services of sufficiently high quality being available at lower, or at least at not higher, cost.

10.4 The Bar Council squarely challenges each of these assumptions on the basis of the evidence available, including the evidence received by the Royal Commission and the Commission's assessment of the weight of that evidence. Contrary to the Government's assumptions, its proposals would

(1) reduce competition;
(2) reduce access to justice;
(3) reduce choice;
(4) increase cost, *both* to the paying client, *and* to the taxpayer;
(5) lower the quality of service to the public and of the administration of justice (through less good advocacy, through Judges of lower quality, through slower disposal of cases, and through the resulting delays in the administration of justice).

10.5 The absence of any studies, any research or any evidence in support of the Government's assumptions is the more remarkable, when it is borne in mind, for example, that

(1) the questions of widening rights of audience and of allowing lawyers to practise in, effectively, a fused profession have been the subject of debate over centuries;
(2) these questions were put to the Royal Commission which considered the evidence fully and reported at length in 1979, and this Government adopted the Royal Commission's conclusions as its formal policy in November 1983;
(3) the legal professions in other EEC states have more stringent restrictions than those affecting the Bar and the solicitors of England and Wales, designed to ensure high standards of advocacy, conveyancing and other legal work, and full and fair competition between those who provide advocacy and other legal services;
(4) the principal Government agency for promoting the interests of the consumer, the Director General of Fair Trading, was apparently not consulted in the drafting of the Green Papers, and in a speech on 7 March 1989 said this:

> "I think it a pity that the Green Paper does not seem to recognise explicitly the value of the Bar as a separate independent profession each of whose members is available to be drawn upon by solicitors firms, large and small, up and down the country, and through them, by the general public. The Green Paper places great emphasis on the value of competition and on the likelihood that the forces of competition will fill any gaps in the provision of advocacy services that may arise from barristers disappearing into full partnerships with one another or into multi-disciplinary partnerships. But the risk would be considerable that the practising Bar may be seriously diminished in size and quality and range of skills. That would mean

that competition between members of the Bar is reduced and so would that valuable concomitant of competition, namely, choice on the part of both professional and lay clients. This would be a perverse effect of a policy intended to increase competition and widen choice."

(5) It is for others to assess the worth of the Bar. Two assessments by senior Judges from other common law countries may perhaps be mentioned. The assessment by Chief Justice Warren Burger of the U.S.A. is in Chapter 21 below: see paras. 21.28 and following. The assessment by Sir Robin Cooke, now President of the New Zealand Court of Appeal, is also quoted in Chapter 21 below: see especially para. 21.51(1) where he is quoted as saying that he regards the evolution of a separate Bar as "one of the great British achievements".

A LITTLE HISTORY

10.6 The Bar Council does not rely on tradition, but on the simple facts that

(1) the system with separate specialist professions performing different functions has operated for many years, and has in practice stood the test of time;
(2) the system has been examined at regular intervals, and has, on each examination of the evidence, passed the test of efficient administration of justice in the public interest.

10.7 By 1292 at the latest the Judges were regulating those who were entitled to appear in their Courts and supervising their training and selection through the Inns of Court.

10.8 In 1280 rules were laid down for the Courts in the City of London (1) regulating those who might appear as barristers on the basis of standards of advocacy, (2) requiring the separation of the different classes of lawyer fulfilling different functions, and (3) forbidding contingency fees. These rules were expressly laid down in the public interest.

10.9 In the busiest of the King's Courts, the Court of Common Pleas, by the time of Edward III regulations had been imposed by the Judges limiting rights of audience in the public interest to a select cadre of specialist advocates. As long ago as 1357 the "cab-rank" rule was re-affirmed by Thorpe C.J. who assigned to a defendant three named lawyers to take her case on pain of never being heard again in the King's Courts. This was re-affirmed in 1471 by Choke J. By the early 16th century new serjeants (the specialist advocates in the Court of Common Pleas) were exhorted by the Judges:

> "You shall refuse to take no man under the protestation of your good counsel; all partiality and hatred laid aside, be as glad to tell the poor man the truth of the law for God's sake as the rich man for his money."

By that time the degree of barrister was recognised as the minimum and indispensible qualification for practice at the Bar of the King's Courts.

10.10   The division of function and work between the barrister as the specialist advocate in Court, and the solicitor (and earlier the attorney) as the specialist to whom lay clients came and who prepared evidence and briefs, was also established very early, and was firmly in place before the turbulent 17th century.

10.11   In the years of civil war and the Commonwealth during the 17th century, when some fanatics were urging the abolition of lawyers, it was generally recognised that to relax the professional requirements would result in unsuitable practitioners being let loose on the public, whether in Court or out.

10.12   In the 19th century, from the time when in 1846 the new system of County Courts was created in which the Bar and solicitors had rights of audience, there was extensive discussion and examination of the possibility of "fusion" of the two professions into a single profession. In 1888 the then Solicitor General, Sir Edward Clarke Q.C., suggested as his personal view, and not the view of the then Government, that there should be a fused profession. This led to a lengthy debate. The Lord Chancellor and the Attorney-General expressed the Government's view that the divided profession was important to the public in securing efficiency of legal service. Mr. Punch indulged in some humour at the prospect of "barsolistors" fumbling in unfamiliar areas of practice. Attention was drawn to the experience in America, where all-round lawyers had been found not to work well.

10.13   The debate followed lines familiar to readers of The Times during the last three months. Solicitors wrote to The Times stressing the advantage of independent advice from Counsel, and protesting that fusion "would undoubtedly be disastrous to the best interests of the public". In a speech in February 1888 reported in 84 Law Times 248 Mr. Finlay Q.C. (later Lord Chancellor) said this:-

> ". . . he had to respond for a body which at the present time was, to a certain extent, upon its trial. He had been informed from a somewhat unexpected quarter that the division of labour which had so long

prevailed in this country in the great profession of the law was a mistake, and that we had to cast all our old traditions to the winds and begin again and see if we could do better than we had done. A fascinating picture had been drawn of the results of such an experiment. It was said that from the fusion of the two branches of the Profession there would arise a gifted being, equal to receiving the instructions of a client, dealing with every detail of a case, and at last presenting it without too much prolixity, and with all the material points sufficiently developed for the consideration of a Court of Appeal. Whether that fascinating picture was likely to be realised he did not know. It was the habit of reformers in these matters to consult only their own inner consciousness, and not to have any regard to experiments that had been made in similar matters elsewhere. For his own part he was disposed to believe that the division between the profession of an advocate and that of a solicitor was a natural division corresponding to the facts of the case. In those countries where advocacy had been thrown open to both branches of the Profession, it had been found that, by a system of natural selection, the work of advocacy had fallen into different hands from those employed in getting up the case. He believed that the division to which we had been so long accustomed in this country was best. A distinguished American jurist recently said to him: 'Our system works very well with us, but I advise you, as you have a different system which has yielded excellent results, not to be in a hurry to try experiments with a system which may not suit you so well.' Change that was made for the sake of change was always an evil unless undoubted advantages were to be gained; and in this case he did not believe the advantages were such as to compensate for the evils that would attend the change."

In 1889 the Law Times closed the debate with these words:

"An old subject has once more been revived for a moment, and has once more died its usual and inevitable death . . . the separation seems to us not only most expedient, but quite indispensable if the legal profession is to be fully efficient . . . Practice in America fully disproves the theory of our would-be reformers at home."

10.14 Between 1976 and 1979 the whole question of the future shape of the legal professions was considered by the Royal Commission, which reached conclusions on fusion of the professions and on rights of audience in the higher Courts as referred to in paras. 3.13 and 3.14 above, on direct lay access to barristers, and also conclusions on e.g. multi-disciplinary practices and partnerships at the Bar. The Government accepted those conclusions as its policy in November 1983.

THE PRACTICAL CONSEQUENCES OF THE GOVERNMENT'S PROPOSALS

10.15 The Government's proposals would not directly involve the compulsory fusion of the professions, but rather legislation to enable solicitors and others to be advocates in the higher Courts, to enable multi-disciplinary partnerships to be entered into by barristers and solicitors and others, and to enable lay clients to have access to barristers directly. It is necessary to examine the practical consequences of the main changes set out in para. 10.1 above, and to examine those practical consequences over a period of some years. No one suggests that the practical effect of the proposed changes would be instantaneous (except to the extent that recruitment to the two legal professions may immediately be affected). From the only relevant standpoint, that of the public interest, the effects over a period of years are what have to be considered.

10.16 What the consequences of the proposed changes would be depends on an informed judgment, backed by evidence directed to the position in England and Wales, and in other jurisdictions. The consequences are set out in paras. 10.17 to 10.48 below. In this book it is possible to refer only to some of the available material, and there has not been time to carry out any rigorous assembly of evidence.

SOLICITORS AND BARRISTERS IN THE SAME PRACTICES

10.17 The largest firms of solicitors in London and outside have indicated in private to members of the Bar Council and other barristers that their general intentions would be, if the Green Paper proposals became law,

(1) not at the moment to seek to recruit many established barristers or Queen's Counsel wholesale, but to recruit (a) where a barrister has a particular specialist expertise and it would be an advantage to one firm to have that expertise in- house (and so deny it to their competitors), (b) in order to have a small nucleus of experienced barristers to run their advocacy departments (some have already begun to attempt such recruiting), and (c) if any of their major competitors, including accountants firms, did so;

(2) to establish advocacy departments building mainly from young men and women recruited from universities and polytechnics year by year: they foresee that young men and women may be enticed by large initial salaries to start their advocacy practice within a large firm which will give them in-house work rather than sending it to independent barristers;

(3) to build up those advocacy departments until they are able to do much of the work now done by independent junior barristers briefed or instructed by these firms: they foresee that they will give preference to their in-house advocates over outside independent barristers in most instances, unless there are

exceptional reasons why they need to go outside e.g. for specialist expertise or because a client insists on doing so; by keeping advocacy work in-house they will keep the profits in-house, cover overheads, keep the in-house advocacy department busy, and build up its expertise; and the market forces of competition with rival solicitor/barrister practices would tend to lead them towards this course;

(4) they would anticipate continuing for quite a long time to instruct independent Queen's Counsel;

(5) but once their advocacy departments were built up to full strength they would anticipate having Queen's Counsel in-house (in Chapter 9 of the main Green Paper the Government proposes that any advocate with a "full general advocacy certificate" would be eligible to be Queen's Counsel whether independent or in a partnership or incorporated practice: as appears in Chapter 21 below the Commonwealth experience shows that this would be another change adverse to the maintenance of advocates in independent practice).

As this summary of the intentions of the large solicitors shows, the tendency over a period would be to reduce their use of independent barristers, whether juniors or Queen's Counsel, and to build up within their in-house advocacy departments a body of tied advocates as partners, directors or employees (whether barristers or solicitors). Given the economic power of the large solicitors, they would be well placed to persuade the young not to embark on the uncertainties of independence at the Bar, pointing out that advocacy can be provided in-house with security and without those uncertainties. The end result of that process is likely to be large law firms on the American model providing expensive services to business and the rich.

An example of the evidence from these firms is from a litigation partner of about 15 years experience which reads as follows:-

"My experience of civil litigation leads me to regret greatly proposals which, if implemented, could, and I believe will, bring about the demise of the independent Bar.

The present system provides an efficient, cost-effective and consumer-sensitive way of handling litigation. The client chooses his Solicitor, and the Solicitor, subject to instructions, chooses whether to use Counsel, and if so, whom, when and how. Solicitor and client can call on the particular skills of Counsel, i.e. specialist advice, drafting of pleadings and advocacy. On occasions, Counsel is or are intimately involved in the case; on others, a particular Counsel is called upon for a particular purpose, e.g. to give specific advice or to appear on a specific hearing. The Solicitor calls upon Counsel's services and therefore pays for his services, only as and when required. The cost of those services does not include all the overheads of the Solicitor's office.

There is something very valuable in the isolation of Counsel from the pressures and complications of the Solicitor's practice, including direct client contact. It must enhance the quality of Counsel's worth. It underpins Counsel's ethical integrity.

If the independent Bar disappears, the element of choice of specialist and advocate will go. No Solicitor with a large litigation practice will go to another Firm for specialist pleading, advice or advocacy; he will stay in-house. Where will the Solicitor without in-house resources turn. He will have to go to a larger firm. Thus, demise of his litigation practice and a reduction in consumer choice.

The relative cheapness of the Bar's services on an as-and-when required basis will be lost.

One cannot predict with certainty whether or not the Bar will disappear, if the present proposals go forward, but I believe that there is a strong likelihood that the Bar will disappear. Under the proposed new regime, young lawyers will simply not be attracted to the Bar. It will wither from the bottom up.

I therefore consider it most regrettable that an institution which serves the consumer so well should be put at risk for the sake of changes from which a saving of cost and an increase of choice are hoped but will not in reality result."

CONFLICT OF INTEREST

10.18 The solicitor firms would have this clear advantage in competing with the Bar. They would receive the client direct. They would have the power to decide either to keep the case in-house within their advocacy department, *or* to instruct an independent barrister. Their financial interest in keeping a case in-house (covering their overheads, increasing their profits, helping to build up the size, experience and degree of qualification of their in-house advocacy department) would conflict with their duty to advise their client (in her, his or its best interest), who would be the best advocate for the client to use. No means of avoiding this obvious clash of interest and duty has been suggested by the Government. The reason is that there is no means of avoiding it or of policing it. If the Green Paper proposals go through, every solicitor will be faced with this conflict, and will be able to gain a substantial advantage for himself by the way he makes his decision. The Government is for competition, fair competition. This would be, at best, unfair competition.

10.19 In an interview with "Counsel" magazine in the autumn of 1988 the Lord Chancellor pointed out how unfortunate it would be to place this kind of decision in the hands of solicitors. The Lord Chancellor said this:

"Solicitors are not obliged to make their living through advocacy. The barrister is. The level of work in the Crown Court has a huge variety. To extend a general right of audience to the Crown Court would create an enormous transfer and might not best suit the client. The client comes in off the street to seek the help of a solicitor. His whole life in the sense of his reputation and freedom may depend on the skill of the advocate.

It could be a mistake to put the decision, whether to do the case oneself or pass it on to a barrister, into the hands of those with first access to the consumer." (Our emphasis).

10.20 Following this approach, which the Bar Council believes to be a correct one, it would be unwise to place in the hands of the firm or corporation of solicitors (or multi-disciplinary practices (MDPs) of solicitors and barristers, or other professionals, solicitors and barristers) the decision whether to do the case for the lay client in-house, maximising profits for the firm or corporation itself, rather than to instruct an independent barrister or Queen's Counsel.

10.21 In the same interview the Lord Chancellor went on to say this:

"At present the solicitor can judge the range of advocacy skills available to him from the barristers practising at each particular court. *The Bar is the most competitive business going.*" (Our emphasis).

10.22 The financial backing available to the Government's proposed new forms of solicitor/barrister/accountant partnerships and corporations would be very large. They would be able to have non-lawyer shareholders seeking to maximise their return on money invested and their dividends. This would go far beyond the present position in the U.S.A., about which the Chief Justice and the ABA Commission of Professionalism expressed such concern (Chapter 4 above).

10.23 The largest solicitor firms, like their colleagues in medium sized and smaller firms, have expressed the wish that the independent Bar should continue and should thrive. That wish derives from the realisation that the change to in-house advocacy departments could not take place overnight, and equally from a desire not to see the specialist skills of particular barristers, now available to every solicitor and to every lay client of every solicitor, disappear into one firm's in-house advocacy department and become available only to that firm's lay clients. But they have at the same time made clear their intentions as set out in para. 10.17 above, as well as their fear that if one major solicitor firm (or a larger firm of accountants: para. 10.24 below) were to secure for itself alone the services of certain established barristers, the rival firms would be bound to try to follow suit.

ACCOUNTANTS AND OTHER PROFESSIONALS IN PRACTICE WITH SOLICITORS AND BARRISTERS

10.24 As the figures in Chapter 8 above show, the largest accountant firms are much larger than the largest solicitor firms. The international group of firms, KPMG, has 5,000 partners and its member firm in England and Wales, Peak Marwick McLintock has 478 partners. The largest firm of solicitors has about 200 partners.

10.25 A working party of the Institute of Chartered Accountants, chaired by Mr. Jeffrey Bowman, the senior partner of Price Waterhouse, has concluded that accountant firms should be permitted to practise through multi-disciplinary partnerships or limited companies. In "reserved work" such as auditing, the partnership or company will have to be controlled by chartered accountants (the EEC 8th Company Law Directive on regulation of auditors, and the Companies Bill now before Parliament, clause 27(5) and Schedule 8, paras. 4 and 5). Even this restriction could be side-stepped by the device commonly used by accountants of parallel partnerships (or companies). In any other work the control of the partnership or limited company would not have to be in the hands of accountants, or indeed any professionals, and might be in the hands of one or more shareholders whether a single businessman or a large financial organisation or a number of shareholders.

10.26 It is suggested that in such an environment (in which the making of money would be the driving force) the essentials of professional integrity would survive, despite the warnings of the ABA Committee on Professionalism: Chapter 4 above. But the Marre Committee, when considering the possible position of solicitors in MDPs, expressed doubts about the effect of MDPs. The adverse record of serious negligence claims against the major accountant firms shows that these doubts are not unfounded.

10.27 The large accountant firms have indicated their intention, if permitted, to establish MDPs with barristers and solicitors. This was confirmed by the Vice-President of the Institute of Chartered Accountants on 6 March 1989. They wish to secure the services of established barristers for tax advice and for other forms of non-litigious legal work. They also will wish to recruit lawyers from the universities and polytechnics for this purpose. They have already established "litigation support" departments which provide back-up work for the conduct of civil litigation and also defences to criminal charges of fraud. The intention of these large accountant firms would be to develop these departments from merely "litigation support" into departments able to deal with all aspects of Court and tribunal work, including advocacy. Like the major solicitor firms, they would intend to start with a few established barristers, and to build up the advocacy element in these departments over a number of years from university and polytechnic recruitment. This process would be speeded up if one major firm (whether a solicitors or accountants firm) secured the services of a number of established barristers, because its rivals would see this as a threat to their competitive position and would feel bound to follow its lead. Because of their relatively much larger size than the present solicitor firms, the accountant firms see themselves as well placed to gain a growing and substantial share of the "market" for advocacy services.

MEDIUM SIZED SOLICITOR FIRMS

10.28   These range in size from about 11 to 50 partners. At the upper end of this range it might just be possible for the firms to organise an advocacy department to compete with the larger firms, though not on equal terms. At the lower end of this range the firms would find it impossible to organise an advocacy department of sufficient depth to provide an acceptable service to clients. For firms of medium size the continued existence of an independent Bar of sufficient size, and varied specialisms and range of expertise, would be essential if they were to be able to continue to provide an acceptable service.

10.29   The hope of many of these firms is that there would continue to be such an independent Bar. But their fears of what may happen to the independent Bar over a number of years have been strongly and widely expressed in the letters numbering over 1,400 received by the Bar Council mainly from medium and small solicitors firms. They fear a diminution of recruitment to the independent Bar, aggressive recruitment by the largest solicitors and accountants, and a serious reduction in the availability of the services of independent barristers to the public through the large range of solicitors firms and offices throughout the country.

10.30   The Government has sought to discount these fears, on the assumption that the independent Bar will continue in strength whatever the Government may do. That is too facile an answer. These firms of solicitors have a deep concern for the future service to the public. For example a medium sized firm in the City of London in a letter dated 6 February 1989 stated:-

"As a long-established firm with an extensive international commercial and litigation practice, we should like to place on record our opposition to any changes which might result in a reduction in the size of the Admiralty and Commercial Bar, and our concern that the Government proposals would have that effect. In common with many other firms in our sphere of practice, we believe that it is in the interest of our clients that there should be a body of independent advocates from whom we may select those who have the appropriate level of experience and expertise to deal with a particular matter, often in a highly specialised area.

The continuing preeminence of London as a forum for international commercial litigation and arbitration reflects the confidence in the present system felt by many clients world-wide; we would greatly regret any change that might threaten that preeminence, which makes a substantial contribution to the invisible earnings of the United Kingdom.

It is likely that the adoption of the present proposals would result in a fall in the quality and number of independent advocates, in the short-term by barristers becoming in-house advocates with solicitors' firms, and in the long-term by a reduction, because of the uncertain future, in those going to the Bar.

We note that the Government's view, as expressed in paragraph 8.8 of *The Work and Organisation of the Legal Profession*, is that such consequences are unlikely to follow. However, we believe that the empirical evidence referred to, and the experience of English barristers in Europe, constitute a most uncertain basis for such a fundamental change, and provide no safeguard for our clients' interests.

We urge that no steps are taken which would threaten the continued existence of a substantial and independent Admiralty and Commercial Bar."

A senior partner in a London firm of around 50 partners wrote to the Chairman of the Bar in March 1989 expressing his view

"that there is an overwhelming need for the Bar to be maintained as a wholly independent separate and distinct profession on more or less the same lines as at present. Despite comments to the contrary which have appeared in the public Press, emanating from senior partners of the largest firms of solicitors and accountants, and others, recent experience in the City has shown that a significant number of top quality specialists would be "head hunted" by such firms and commercial organisations. If this were to happen to leading members of the Bar, either, in practice sooner or later they would cease to be available to give independent legal advice and advocacy to other firms of solicitors, or in any case, other firms of solicitors would no longer wish to give instructions to such barristers, because of the risk of losing their clients to the firms with whom those barristers were in partnership. To put it crudely, and without disrespect, so long as Desmond Fennell (for example!) is an independent Queens Counsel, I know that I can consult or brief him knowing that for the purposes of that exercise his loyalty is exclusively to me and my lay client. The moment Desmond Fennell becomes a partner in, say, [a large firm of solicitors or accountants] in a multi-disciplinary partnership, I would run the risk of losing the client to the other firm if I instructed Desmond Fennell.

I would, therefore, be forced to choose either between a rump independent Bar which I suspect would find it difficult to survive as an independent profession, or my firm would need to expand to take into partnership barristers who would become part of our own multi-disciplinary firm. To my mind this would greatly lessen the freedom of choice of Counsel available to me and my lay clients.

Even in my own rather specialised practice, I instruct a wide range of Counsel, partly because of availability, but partly because I take the view that particular Counsel known to me are especially suitable for particular types of case. Moreover, such Counsel would not be working full time with me because the work of the two Professional Bodies is sessional and, therefore, intermittent.

Moreover I am only a very small part of this firm, . . . and most of my partners will have need of other specialties such as taxation Counsel, civil injuries Counsel, building arbitration Counsel and so on. Obviously, unless one became a mega firm of mind-boggling size, one could not take into partnership Counsel to cover every range of expertise, all of which may be needed from time to time for strictly limited periods by any average firm of solicitors."

A detailed submission by a solicitors firm in Central London to the Lord Chancellor states (inter alia):

"We firmly believe that the combined effect of permitting barristers to enter into partnerships with solicitors and others and the grant of general rights of audience in the Higher Courts to solicitors fulfilling certain training requirements will be to condemn the Bar at best to a substantial contraction particularly and importantly amongst the most able and specialised members thereof and at worst to wither away completely through lack of recruitment. Either we consider will be to the immense detriment of the public interest.

The Bar by its present rules and structure (whilst needing improvement, one accepts), whether deliberately or unwittingly, fosters the greatest element of free competition for the provision of a specialist professional service imaginable. The quantum of free competition for the provision of the specialist service depends upon there being:

(i) the largest number of providers of that service in competition with each other; and
(ii) no artificial constraints upon that competition.

The Bar by its present rule that each member should be a self-employed individual practitioner creates a market consisting of the largest number of providers of the specialist service together with real and effective competition between each individual member of the profession.

Moreover, competition is at its fiercest because the service by the independent specialist is provided to the immediate consumer best able to judge the quality of that service, namely the solicitor. If he does not rate highly the barrister's performance he does not brief the barrister again. *Per contra*, if the barrister is or becomes one of the solicitor's partners, or if the barrister is or becomes one of the solicitor's employers!

. . .

Solicitors presently have the widest possible choice of full-time advocates on behalf of their clients, the public. Solicitors can and presently do have a free choice of barristers out of the 6,000 individual practising members of the Bar. If solicitors use that choice wisely they can hand-pick a barrister best suited to the particular requirements of any particular case, whether it be in specialist legal expertise, experience, a fine analytical brain, particular advocacy skills required such as mastery of detail, the art of persuasion, or cross-examination skills, and the personality and temperament best suited to the individual client, and last but not least, cost. The solicitor can tailor-make the exercise of that choice to the needs of the particular case on behalf of his client and that is so only because there are a large number of individual barristers, all in effective and real competition with each other. There are admittedly solicitors who do not take full advantage of the choice available, preferring to limit their selection to a couple of favourite chambers. But the service provided by the Bar should not be judged by reference to solicitors who fail to take full advantage of it.

Solicitors and their clients, wherever they are in England and Wales, therefore have today a wide choice and almost the best possible access to the provision of the specialist legal services provided by the Bar. They will indeed have the best possible access, if the remaining restrictions within the Bar and upon entry to the Bar are swept away by the reforms proposed in Chapter 11 of the Green Paper.

At present, choice may be limited in practice because a barrister may be engaged on a long case or enquiry and be unable to accept a retainer on behalf of the particular client for that reason. But few practising barristers are at present permanently unavailable. Solicitors and their clients are also able to take advantage of the 'Cab-Rank' rule of the Bar. That rule should not be undervalued. It is unique. We believe that there is no wholly comparable rule in any other profession.

By contrast, choice will be drastically curtailed if large numbers of members of the Bar and the advocates of the future, and in particular the most talented section thereof, cease to be engaged in free competition with each other, and to be available to all solicitors and their clients. If many members of the Bar and the advocates of the future were to devote their talents only to the clients of a handful of large solicitors' firms and were to say to the vast majority of solicitors and their clients, 'sorry, we can no longer serve your specialist requirements', the provision of competitive legal services in this country will have suffered a serious setback. It would be a sad day if that were ever to happen particularly because it would have been brought about by proposals submitted in the name of competition, only to produce the very antithesis of competition.

. . .

If the right of audience is thrown open to the solicitors' branch of the profession there is a real likelihood that those holding a full advocacy certificate but nonetheless engaged in a more generalised practice will in reality be less practised in the skills of advocacy. There is unlikely to be any means in practice for ensuring after the grant of a full advocacy certificate that all those holding the same spend sufficient time practising advocacy in the higher Courts to enhance or at least maintain the necessary skills. Even if there were to be introduced bureaucratic monitoring of the amount of time spent by each advocate in Court, that we suggest would be grossly detrimental to the public interest. No advocate should have an incentive to litigate rather than compromise.

. . .

Our belief is that the proposals relating to advocacy in the higher Courts and partnership will have the effect that whereas there are currently some 50,000 solicitors who have available to them the specialist services, both in advocacy and other specialisms, of some 6,000 members of the independent Bar, there will upon the implementation of the said proposals be a disintegration of the Bar, as we know it, and the more able advocates and other specialists, especially the advocates and other specialists of the future will enter into partnerships with other solicitors as 'trial lawyers'. There is also the second possibility that some of them may set themselves up as advocates taking their clients direct from the public, although we doubt whether that will apply to the more complex commercial litigation.

The result will be that which is stated at paragraph 8.7 [of the main Green Paper] namely a serious contraction of the corps of independent advocates available to all solicitors and an increasing practice amongst lawyers of all kinds to choose their own in-house specialist or trial lawyer in preference to the independent specialist best suited to the needs of a particular case. The choice of advocates available to all clients will be substantially reduced.

. . .

There has been a notable tendency in some quarters since publication to play down the effect of the Green Paper proposals. It is suggested that they will not bring about the fundamental change to the structure of the profession which many predict. We think that the proposals will unleash market forces which will inexorably lead in the medium to long term to fusion, whether intended or not, especially since the proposals will give no career incentive to a young advocate to choose the Bar when he or she can have exactly the same practice with much greater security as a 'trial lawyer' attached to a large firm of solicitors. Furthermore, that kind of fundamental change must be the intention, else why introduce the proposals at all.

. . .

To remove professional constraints on how practitioners should conduct their business and what legal services they may perform may appear superficially attractive. However, we suggest that on deeper analysis such proposals will not foster greater competition in the provision of legal services. On the contrary, they will encourage the monopolisation of the most talented echelon of the Bar and the most talented advocates of the future by a relatively few large firms of solicitors. That will result in more restricted access on the part of the majority of the public to such members of the Bar and those advocates in the future. The proposals will also result in the higher costs which run hand in hand with monopolies and which will be the product of the natural desire of the best advocates to continue to earn well coupled with the expectation and the ability of the larger firms to charge out their advocacy services at a level which provides an additional contribution to overheads and profit on top.

To avoid these adverse consequences the Bar should remain

independent and proposals encouraging partnerships between barristers and solicitors and others should be considered as working against the public interest. Extension of rights of audience should be limited.

We firmly believe that the proposals work against the public interest in the respects which we have stated and illustrated above and will lead in the medium to long term to the disintegration of the Bar and in particular the specialist Bars. Even if the reader (unlike ourselves) is not convinced that the proposals will surely bring about those adverse consequences (see again paragraph 8.7), can he equally be certain that they will not result from what is proposed. If not, then the public interest is not, we suggest, served by placing the attainment of justice and the beneficial and competitive provision of legal services in this country in such jeopardy.

The proposals set out at paragraphs 11.4 to 11.12 inclusive, 11.19 and 11.25 [of the main Green Paper] on the contrary, we consider to be very much in the public interest and we hope that they are implemented."

We have quoted at some length from this submission because it summarises helpfully what is said by a very large proportion of the solicitors firms who have written to the Bar Council. It is not possible within the confines of this book to include a large number of such quotations.

SMALL SOLICITOR FIRMS

10.31   These firms (and 80% of all solicitor firms have 4 partners or fewer) are the backbone of legal service to the public, to the men and women who need legal help with criminal charges, matrimonial problems, problems with children, conveyancing, wills and other legal matters both one-off and on a continuing basis. They depend above all on the availability of the 6,000 barristers from whom they can choose at will to enable them to provide a full range of specialist advice and a full range of representation in Courts and tribunals.

THE THREAT TO SMALL SOLICITOR FIRMS

10.32   *Independent Bar*   One limb of the threat to their continued existence which these small firms see is in the reduction in the availability and choice of independent barristers of the quality their clients need for advice and advocacy.

10.33   *Conveyancing* These firms are also seriously threatened by the loss of conveyancing work (for them more than 30% of their fee income and in some cases up to 55–60%) which the Government proposes to allow the big institutions, the banks and building societies, to do on an unfair basis, *at cost*. It is well known that the allocation of overheads and other costs is an art, not a science, and that one of the most difficult matters in litigation is to challenge such an allocation. The result of allowing the big institutions to compete unfairly in the field of conveyancing, which is a vital element in the maintenance of local solicitor firms and offices, would be to reduce their availability to the public, particularly in areas distant from the cities.

10.34 An example of the carefully considered views of smaller firms of solicitors is from a partner in a firm with 4 partners in the West of England: he wrote:

"I am the litigation partner in a four partner firm of country solicitors, employing some 26 staff in one town. I believe that if the proposals are implemented, then in 20 years time, there will no longer be any small country or suburban solicitors left, the independent Bar will be much reduced, and the public will have to travel to large city firms (by then dominated by accountants) for any legal services, at fees geared to company and commercial clients. There are two proposals in particular which will bring this about.

1. The widening of rights of audience to solicitors in higher courts will not benefit small firms, with 1, 2 or at most 3 advocates, or indeed the public. Cases in the Magistrates Court and the County Court are usually on fixed dates with cases listed far enough in advance for litigation solicitors to make arrangements to take their own cases: not so in the Crown Court and the High Court. The need to keep the courts processing cases efficiently and not to waste judges' time means that many cases are listed for hearing at short notice, and most cases last longer than the average Magistrate's Court or County Court case. Smaller solicitors' firms will continue to find it more convenient to brief a barrister in such cases. If the case is listed at short notice, and the barrister originally briefed cannot take the case, another barrister can take it more easily than the instructing solicitor, who has other client's business to attend to and other fixed court appointments in the Magistrates' Court or County Court.

However I believe the larger city criminal practices will seek to employ criminal advocates in house, and the large city firms dealing with company and commercial work will seek to employ civil advocates in house. I do not believe that established barristers with thriving practices will be tempted to join forces with big city firms. They value too highly their independence and freedom from the constant attentions of clients by post and telephone.

However, for potential barristers the situation is very different. In the past a potential lawyer, with sufficient confidence in his own ability and desire for the lifestyle to wish to practise as a barrister, was prepared to risk the probability of earning very little money in his early years and the difficulty of finding chambers, for the prospect of advocacy in the higher courts.

. . .

If the solicitors have rights of audience in all the higher courts, there will be fewer aspiring advocates who will be able to resist the blandishments of the big city firms of solicitors and the security and money offered, for the insecurity and initial poverty of starting at the Bar. City firms will therefore attract a body of in-house advocates at high salaries or as partners, who will have little contact with the public but will spend their time at court and in legal research.

. . .

Only the big city firms with a sufficient volume of litigation will be able to recruit a body of solicitor advocates. If those solicitors are to be able to take cases listed at short notice in the High Court, and to spend several days at a time out of the office, they will have very little time or capacity to prepare any cases for trial. Accordingly there will become two kinds of litigation solicitors in such firms, the one dealing with the clients and preparing the cases, and the other the specialist advocate. The public will therefore not have the same solicitor preparing the case as appears in court. Moreover, in cases of any complexity, it is likely that the solicitor or staff member preparing a case will have to be in the court with the specialist advocate for most of the hearing. The cost to the client is likely to be greater than if an independent barrister had been instructed. Meanwhile, if the independent Bar begins to wither away, the small firm will have difficulty in dealing with High Court litigation at all.''

The second proposal he dealt with was the Conveyancing Green Paper: see Chapter 23 below.

There are so many letters and submissions from small firms of solicitors that only a few other representative examples can be quoted from.

— A firm in a large town in the North of England with 2 partners:-

"All the subsequent remarks are subject to our single greatest concern about the Green Papers' proposals that, taken together, their knock-on effect will be the destruction of an independent Bar of the highest quality to which we can turn for specialist advice and advocacy, and which we are convinced is vital to the quality of legal service given to a very large proportion of the population.

. . .

We take it for granted that all firms in [this town] depend upon Counsel to provide the quality of service we wish for our clients. We think that there is a real possibility that the combined effect of these proposals will be to make young and able lawyers reject a call to the Bar and draw many present barristers away from it. We also take it for granted that firms [in this town] will not be able to persuade such people to join them. We therefore think that there is a real possibility that firms [in this town] will be unable to provide a service as good as now provided, and that there may shortly be a marked distinction between the quality of service available to the few and that available to many ordinary people.

. . .

We are deeply concerned that the effect of these proposals will be, if not the extinction, the squeezing out of rural and general high street practitioners.

We conclude that these proposals will narrow choice, increase cost and reduce the quality of service for the vast majority of people living in and around [this town]. We think that they will lead to a legal system which favours the survival of the fittest, not so much among solicitors, which may be acceptable, but effectively among the public, which is not."

– A firm with 2 partners in North London:-

"One of the greatest advantages of our legal system is that everyone has access to an independent and specialist bar. The Marre Committee considered that Barristers should not be allowed to practice in partnership in its Report, after about two years' deliberation. We should not run the risk of a few big firms with big clients being able to secure the services of the cream of the Bar, thus preventing direct access for all to that cream."

– A firm in Anglesey:-

"At the present time Solicitors in this area are providing a full range of legal services. The existence of an independent and competent Bar is important in this respect. Although Conveyancing fees no longer subsidize other legal work in view of the reduction in legal charges for Conveyancing work during recent years, they do form a major portion of the total remuneration. If a substantial proportion of that work is to be lost then there is a grave danger that Solicitors will cease to be available to provide other essential legal services."

– the senior partner of a 4 partner firm in the North-West of England wrote to the Lord Chancellor:-

"On behalf of myself and my partners, I would like you to be clear about our own view of that portion of the Green Paper which concerns partnerships between Solicitors and Barristers. We do not support such a change as it is bound to lead to many members of the Bar being swallowed up into Solicitors private practice and thereby reducing the numbers and ability range of the other Barristers that do remain. Far from producing a greater freedom of choice, this must be seen as a retrograde step.

So far as rights of audience are concerned, although I see nothing intrinsically wrong in Solicitors of sufficient competence being allowed audience in the Higher Court, I think the long term effect will be for young men and women to choose a Solicitors rather than a Barristers profession as it would seem to give them a far wider range of options. As such it will inevitably lead to a decline in members of the Bar. I am sure you do not need me to remind you of the importance to the legal profession and society as a whole of the range of expertise, advice and representation which are presently available to us and which your proposals now seek to jeopardise."

– In another letter to the Lord Chancellor, this time from the senior partner of a 4 partner firm in the North of England, it is stated:-

"As a small provincial firm, we find that from time to time we need to seek expert advice from those pre-eminent in the legal profession who deal with various subjects on a specialist basis such as taxation and we have always been very impressed with the courteous and efficient service that we have obtained from members of the Bar.

We are concerned that the proposals relating to partnerships between Barristers and Solicitors will inevitably bring about head-hunting of the Bar by larger firms of Solicitors; the Bar will be much reduced and the range of choice and availability of specialised services which all firms can presently obtain from the Bar will simply not be available. Smaller firms such as our own will then be unable to compete with the larger firms and the clients choice of advocate and specialist adviser will be virtually nil.

We have always advocated the need for a Bar which is independent and cost effective as we believe it is at present and would ask you, respectfully, to bear in mind the concern of firms such as ours before embarking upon any structural change."

THE INDEPENDENT BAR

10.35 The great majority of independent barristers now in practice would *wish* to remain as independent barristers whatever changes the Government might seek to force through, but whether they *could* remain at the independent Bar is a different matter altogether. Similarly no doubt many young graduates would continue to *wish* to join the independent Bar, but whether they *could* do so successfully would again be a different matter. Whether they could, would depend on the decisions of solicitors, accountants and others in firms and companies, who would (as the Lord Chancellor foresaw: para. 10.19 above) be able to choose whether to keep work in-house or refer it to an independent barrister.

It is clear both from the intentions of the larger solicitors and accountants firms and from the natural pressure of the "market place" that in-house advocacy departments would be developed and expanded. It is also clear that they would recruit in competition with the Bar, not as now in fair competition, but with the added inducement of being able *both* to offer an advocacy career in-house *and* to feed work to the in-house advocate in preference to the independent Bar whenever they chose to do so. As the Lord Chancellor said in his interview with "Counsel" magazine:

"It would be a mistake to put the decision, whether to do the case oneself or pass it on to a barrister, into the hands of those with first access to the consumer. A trained advocate hits the point very quickly. It is not easy to do. Some quite distinguished solicitors take part in committal proceedings and receive wonderful client reaction without actually achieving very much in their client's interests. The client wants the best advocacy going, and if the solicitor fancies himself as an advocate, he may not be the best person to judge his own skills against those of colleagues (i.e. barristers). It is a crucially important decision for his client."

But the new firms or companies, whether only solicitors, or MDPs of solicitors and barristers, or MDPs on a wider scale, would have the economic incentive of greater profit leading them to try to keep as much work as they could in-house.

It is instructive at this point to refer to the views of those who use the legal services of independent barristers and solicitors in private practice. The Chairman of one of the largest companies in the U.K. has summarised its views on the main points in the Green Papers as follows:-

"In our experience no system is superior to that in the U.K., although all systems have their drawbacks. In summary, these are our views:

Service	We like the legal service we are getting in this country. It is competitive and cost effective. The intellectual standard of the Bar is as high as anywhere in the World. Solicitors whom we utilise work as long hours and are as well organised as lawyers in any other jurisdiction.
Best Legal Advice	Because any solicitor has access to the Bar his firm can provide the best legal advice without employing the adviser full time. This promotes competition. We are receiving an outstanding service not only from the City of London but also from many firms of provincial solicitors.
Conflicts and Choice	Because barristers cannot be partners of one another there are fewer conflicts of interest and more competition.
Separate Bar	The separate Bar is therefore very valuable to us.
Protecting the Bar	We do not think the Bar will continue to exist just because we want it to. If barristers become available as partners we fear the best ones will be bought up to secure market share. We are very concerned about the threat that the largest firms of accountants will do precisely this.
Professional Collaboration	We do not need multi-disciplinary partnerships. We can get different professions to work together without MDPs.

. . .

The Split Profession

We think that the split profession operates in our favour and provides us with the service we want.

The fact that any solicitor, including our own, can instruct or seek advice from a member of the Bar means that there is effective competition throughout the country amongst solicitors to provide legal services. What is more, the separation of the professions means that a barrister does not have to carry significant overheads or to spend his time on administrative or managerial work or on collecting evidence.

We support the view that partnership between barristers or between barristers and solicitors would reduce our choice of legal services. We are therefore opposed to any relaxation of the rule against such partnerships.

Do we then believe that other professions, such as solicitors should have wider rights of audience? Because if we do, won't many barristers decide to become solicitors so they can benefit from partnership with solicitors or even other professions? Why should a barrister bar himself from partnership if he receives no benefit in exchange? We do not know the answer to these questions, but we are very concerned that the Bar, which is very valuable to us, will cease to be an attractive profession if its exclusive right to plead in the higher courts is removed.

. . .

If partnerships or MDP's are permitted we are very worried about a legal 'big bang' with the possibility that the top city solicitors' firms and *particularly* the big eight accountants will compete with one another for market share by buying up the Bar. We are afraid that this would lower standards, reduce choice, waste human resources and increase costs."

A solicitor who was for 15 years the head of one of the largest in-house legal departments (he has also been a J.P. for 20 years) wrote as follows:-

"I have studied the Green Papers. Without going into detail, the adoption of their recommendations would in my view have the following consequences:

1. The independent Bar would be weakened – not immediately perhaps, but with the passage of time a significant number of able barristers (particularly certain specialists) would be tempted by the greater rewards and security offered by the large commercial practices. That would operate to the detriment of the smaller firms of solicitors and their clients in particular. In due course the quality of the Judiciary would also be impaired.

2. Banks and building societies would provide mortgage and conveyancing packages. Accountants would move into probate work. In neither case would they need to offer either a cheaper or a better service: since they constitute a first port of call in many instances they would be in a strong position to practise loss leadership and cross-subsidisation. The demand for services from small firms of solicitors would reduce. Those solicitors would be compelled to turn to multi-disciplinary partnerships with accountants and surveyors as a defensive measure. That would lead to a dilution of and decline in professional standards.

105

3. As with deregulation in the financial sector, the private client would suffer a reduction in choice and eventually an increase in cost - the very opposite of what the implementation of the reforms would purport to encourage."

10.36 The pressures described above would lead to the contraction of the independent Bar over the period of years which has to be considered for the purpose of assessing the public interest. The independent Bar would be substantially reduced, in any event, if the Crown Prosecution Service were to take over the prosecution of offences in the Crown Court: that is considered in Chapter 13 below. The effect of that would be over a period to remove from the independent Bar a body of practitioners with experience both in prosecuting and defending those charged with crimes. The loss of that experience would be a serious loss to the public, both directly, and indirectly because that pool of experienced practitioners would no longer be available to provide Judges for the Circuit Court and High Court, both full-time and part-time.

ENDING OF SEPARATION OF LEGAL PROFESSIONS

10.37 The practical effect of the Goverment's proposals, as the evidence shows, would be to end the separation of the legal professions, not immediately but certainly over a period of years. Barristers and solicitors could perform each other's functions and could appear in any of the Courts (once licensed). Barristers and solicitors could employ each other, be partners, join in limited companies, and be shareholders in each other's companies. Barristers and solicitors could equally accept instructions direct from lay clients. Other professionals could employ barristers and solicitors, join in partnerships with them, join in limited companies with them, and be shareholders in their companies. Separation of function would effectively disappear. The legal profession would become effectively fused.

THE ROYAL COMMISSION

10.38 The evidence to the Royal Commission, both oral and written, is so bulky that it is not possible to give any summary within the confines of this book or in the time available (though the Bar Council relies on such evidence as firmly establishing the conclusions of the Royal Commission). But it is essential to summarise the conclusions of the Royal Commission based on the evidence it received, since its conclusions were the opposite to what the

Government now proposes, and the Government in November 1983 adopted those conclusions after long scrutiny.

SEPARATE LEGAL PROFESSIONS

10.39   The Royal Commission concluded unanimously that it is in the public interest for the legal profession to continue to be organised in two separate branches, barristers and solicitors: para. 17.46 and Recommendation R17.1. In reaching this conclusion, the Royal Commission emphasised the following points and evidence.

(1) *Quality of advocacy and Quality of Judicial Decisions*   The quality of advocacy is an essential component of the quality of justice. They quoted Lord Roskill's evidence that

> "No one without judicial experience can perhaps fully appreciate how much a Judge relies upon the advocates before him in arriving at what he believes to be the correct decision. Bad advocacy may lead to the right points being missed, the right questions not being asked, and therefore the right answer not being given by the Judge." (para 17.10)

They also quoted the evidence of the Chief Justice of the U.S.A. He had remarked that cases were dealt with in British courts more quickly than in America, and went on:

> "From time to time I have been asked how I account for this. It is not easy to account for it but an over-simplification perhaps is that in your courts generally you have three experts who have all been trained in the same tradition and in the same pattern. The Judge almost by definition has been one of the leading members of the Bar, and the two advocates appearing before him are trained in the same way the Judge was trained . . . Even if you have [in the U.S.A.] a very experienced Judge and he has two mediocre, badly trained or untrained advocates before him he has difficulty." (para. 17.12).

Nearly all the witnesses, including the Judges, whose evidence favoured the separation of the profession, gave the reason that to end such separation would lead to a marked fall in the quality of advocacy and hence in the quality of judicial decisions (para. 17.29).

The Royal Commission concluded that the amount of advocacy by non-specialist advocates would increase, and that because there would be numerous advocates not appearing regularly in Court, there would be a decline in the overall standard of performance by diluting the specialist knowledge and experience of the Bar (paras. 17.37–17.40).

(2) *Evidence of the Legal Profession*   Members of both branches would find financial advantages from an end to separation. In

spite of these advantages, the weight of evidence from both barristers and solicitors was opposed to ending the separation of the two branches (paras. 17.12 and 17.28).

(3) *More efficient and quicker service* The majority of witnesses gave evidence that the legal service was more efficient and quicker than in countries in which there is a unified profession (para. 17.18).

(4) *Return of briefs* The Royal Commission concluded that if separation of the profession ended, the number of additional advocates is unlikely to lead to an appreciable reduction in the problem of clashes of engagements, and that these would be less easy to cope with, because of the loss of some of the advantage of quick and informal communication (paras. 17.19 and 17.21).

(5) *Cost of legal services* The evidence of the London Criminal Courts Solicitors Association is quoted in para. 3.13 above. Their points were that if separation of the profession was ended there would be (a) enormously increased costs, (b) reduced range of choice, (c) decline in the degree of specialisations, (d) general decline in service at a considerably increased cost. This and evidence to similar effect was accepted by the Royal Commission (paras 17.7 and 17.35).

The Royal Commission were also satisfied that

> "the independent view which is brought to bear by Counsel can have the effect of limiting the issues or bringing about a settlement. Other things being equal, this may represent an important saving in time and cost to the client." (para. 17.26).

(6) *Access to advocates* The evidence to and conclusions of the Royal Commission as to the serious loss of access to the specialist services of the Bar which would result from ending the separation of barristers and solicitors were very powerful. In 1979 82% of solicitors firms had 4 or fewer partners (now the figure is 80%). The Royal Commission stated in paras. 17.30, 17.31 and 17.33:

> ". . . the partners in these firms [with 4 partners or fewer] do not and cannot be expected to have between them all the experience or knowledge necessary to deal with every one of the wide range of problems brought to them by their clients. When court or tribunal work is involved they cannot always absent themselves from their offices for most of the working day, sometimes for many days on end, to represent their clients. It is therefore important that solicitors, especially those in small firms, should have ready access to barristers who can provide services which they cannot themselves provide. Any solicitor may retain a barrister to advise on a particular point of law or to represent his client in court or in a tribunal, sometimes for weeks on end. If necessary, he can obtain for any client the highest skills

which the Bar can offer. It is therefore possible to select a barrister of standing and expertise equivalent to that of the barrister retained by the other party.

If the two branches of the profession were fused, it is likely that the larger firms of solicitors would seek to consolidate their position by inviting the leading barristers to join them as partners. This would enable these firms to provide most services likely to be required by their clients. Medium-sized firms of solicitors might wish to take one or more barristers into partnership to provide some, at least, of the services which they could not provide for their clients without them. To take one barrister only into a partnership would in practice be unlikely to be effective for this purpose. For example, if a firm absorbed a barrister who was skilled in criminal law and advocacy it would need another barrister if it wished to provide a comprehensive service in, for example, chancery work. It is unlikely that many such firms could provide enough work to keep one or more barristers employed solely as advocates unless they were able to obtain instructions on a regular basis from smaller firms of solicitors. In the event, many firms would not be able to recruit barristers because there would be too few to go round. This difficulty would be exacerbated if a large number of barristers decided to set up their own firms which they are not at present permitted to do.

As the law becomes more complex and as the need for specialisation increases, solicitors' firms are likely to continue to increase in size by mergers and amalgamations and by natural growth. Up to a certain point, size has advantages both for the firm and for the clients. It is possible to specialise to a greater extent and thereby to offer the client a higher degree of technical expertise in certain classes of work. For these and other reasons the level of earnings in large firms is higher than in small ones and the provision for pensions is better. *If, however, the pattern of the profession were to move too far towards a small number of large firms,* as we believe would tend to happen in a fused profession, *the effect would be to diminish the number of firms available to the public and thus to limit competition and freedom of choice, especially in smaller towns and rural areas. Such a development would clearly be against the public interest."* (our emphasis).

These conclusions of the Royal Commission were strongly supported by the evidence of local Law Societies (paras. 17.32 and 17.34). The Commission also emphasised the evidence of a barrister with knowledge of practice in England and in California that:

". . . the tendency will be for lawyers to set themselves up as law firms providing a comprehensive service with 'trial lawyers' salaried by the firm. This will lead to bigger firms with bigger premises and the one man firm practising in the poorer areas will have to join the big firms in the richer area. My experience of law firms in California is that none have their offices in the poorer areas; in these parts the only lawyers available are young enthusiasts who set up legal 'co-operatives' and are more concerned with righting political and economic injustices than doing day to day case work. *I believe that the 'local' solicitor makes an important contribution to the present system in the United Kingdom and that his existence would be imperilled by fusion*." (our emphasis).

(7) **Practical Issues** The Commission pointed out that solicitors were not short of work and many were complaining that they were already overstretched (para. 18.55). This is even more the case today. The Commission emphasised that "If the solicitors' branch of the profession is to provide for the needs of the public, it will have a substantial programme before it is to meet deficiencies in many aspects of social welfare work", and to meet other burdens which it had in the Commission's view to discharge. The position today is that solicitors are even harder pressed and even less able to meet all the needs of the public, because of the increases in crime and divorce, and the increasingly complex issues of social welfare, immigration and housing. The Commission concluded with this commonsense conclusion:

"The suggested extension of solicitors' rights of audience would involve considerable changes in the profession over the same period and would distract it from the need of the public for forms of service other than advocacy which, within the present structure, solicitors could and should undertake. By contrast the Bar, particularly the junior Bar, which is already equipped to provide the needs of the public in the Crown Court, has surplus capacity. There seems to us little sense in making a change which would put additional burdens on the solicitors' branch, which is already overloaded, and at the same time would erode the position of the Bar, in particular its junior members." (para.18.55).

(8) The Royal Commission summarised its conclusions on the separation of the two branches of the profession (in paras. 17.45 and 17.46) in the terms already quoted in para. 3.13 above: in particular, that

"With regard to the administration of justice, the weight of evidence is strongly to the effect that a two-branch profession is more likely than a fused one to ensure the high quality of advocacy which is indispensable, so long as our system remains in its present form, to secure the proper quality of justice."

10.40 That was adopted as the considered policy of this Government in November 1983; that was the view of Lord Mackay when he was the leader of the Bar of Scotland. The Government has put forward no reasoning, no research, no evidence, to support any other conclusion.

RIGHTS OF AUDIENCE IN THE HIGHER COURTS

10.41 The proposal was made to the Royal Commission that solicitors be given rights of audience in all courts. That was not supported by the Law Society which proposed only extended rights of audience in the Crown Court and very limited further rights in the High Court (Report, para. 18.23). As the Royal Commission stated in para. 18.24, the general considerations are the same as those arising from the issue whether the separation of the professions should continue: whether it is in the public interest to change the present arrangements, and if so, to what extent. The particular considerations are also the same: so far as concerns the interests of the individual client, the efficiency and quality of the service, its cost, and the client's confidence in it; and from the viewpoint of the public as a whole, the maintenance of the quality of justice and its effective administration.

10.42 The Royal Commission concluded on the evidence that there should be no general extension of solicitors' rights of audience (para. 18.60 and Recommendation R18.5). In reaching this conclusion, based on the interests of the lay client and of the public, the Commission emphasised the following points and evidence:-

(1) *Skills of advocacy in the higher Courts* They stressed in para. 18.37 the need for particular skills in advocacy in the higher Courts, especially when addressing a jury in the Crown Court, "skills which can be maintained only by constant practice". They emphasised also the need for "a detailed knowledge of the laws of evidence, and skill and experience in cross-examination, sometimes prolonged, which is one of the most difficult of the advocate's arts to perfect", as well as the need for the objectivity (see the quotation in para. 3.14 above) which a barrister is able to bring to a case because he acts on referral by the solicitor, not on direct instructions from the lay client. The main Green Paper equally lays emphasis on the development of these skills. In para. 4.11 it is stated that

> "in advocacy work the maintenance of standards both of skill and integrity has much to do with the independence of the advocate, his regular application to his work in the courts,"

and in para. 5.5 it is stressed that

> "The presentation of cogent legal argument is a highly skilled task requiring not only a knowledge of the law but also constant practice in advocacy."

(2) *Different organisation and practice of solicitors* The majority of solicitors' firms are not organised so as to enable one or more

partners to concentrate only on advocacy, and even if they were able to do so, the ready availability of the solicitor to his other clients would make this very difficult. The Commission considered it "unlikely that many solicitors, except in large firms, would be able under present conditions to have the constant practice in Crown Court advocacy which competence and progressive improvement require". The Commission concluded that

> "*if rights of audience were exercised by solicitors generally in the Crown Court, the quality of service would decline.*" (our emphasis: para 18.38)

(3) *Objective selection of barrister* The Commission stressed that the present arrangements ensure a system of objective selection of the barrister by the solicitor, which would not exist if solicitors did Crown Court advocacy. As they stated:

> "At present to judge from the data obtained by our Users' Survey, a client goes to a solicitor, usually by way of personal recommendation, without any informed knowledge of his capacity for handling the class of work required. The number of firms available in a given area and likely to be known to a potential client is limited and the area of choice is not wide. However, when it is necessary to instruct a barrister, it is the responsibility of the solicitor to advise his client which of the barristers practising in the relevant field is fitted to take the case in question. The qualities required are more likely to be found by this method than any other. Accordingly, we consider that, under the present arrangements, the range of informed choice is wider and selection of a suitable advocate more likely." (para. 18.40)

Uninformed choice by a lay client is not a real choice. A real choice of barrister can be made only by an informed solicitor or other professional.

(4) *Independence of the prosecuting barrister* The Commission considered that prosecutions should continue to be conducted by independent barristers seen by the Court, the accused and the public at large to be independent of the police and of the prosecuting authority; by a barrister who, by the nature of his training and daily practice, is more likely to be able to bring the essential qualities of detachment in individual cases (para. 18.44). The Commission stated that

> "*These are considerations which we regard as crucial not only to the actual conduct of a jury trial but also to the proper administration of justice in general, including the institution or continuance of criminal proceedings, the acceptance of proposed pleas of guilty and the proper handling of evidential problems.*" (our emphasis)

The Commission also drew attention to the growth of a practice in the Magistrates Courts in which those who prosecute and those solicitors who defend did so almost all the time with little, if any, interchange between the two groups. The Commission stated that

> "if encouraged, this trend would lead to the loss of the substantial advantages to be gained by practitioners with experience in both types of work, and to the identification of certain lawyers as being invariably on the side of, or invariably in opposition to, the authorities. Experience outside the United Kingdom suggests that this would be a retrograde step to take, and would not contribute to demonstrably just and fair results." (para. 18.45).

These are conclusions of great importance which have been ignored in the proposals for the extension of the Crown Prosecution Service's rights of audience into the Crown Court in the main Green Paper. They are considered in greater detail in Chapter 13 below.

(5) *Near-monopoly by solicitors in some areas*   In para. 18.54 the Commission referred to

> "evidence that it would be contrary to the public interest if substantial advocacy practices in the Crown Court were built up in any one area by a limited number of solicitors' firms, who thereby established a near-monopoly of criminal business. We have evidence that in some provincial areas a limited number of firms have tended to monopolise criminal work in the magistrates' courts. It is said to be one of the advantages of a duty solicitor scheme that, fairly organised, it can help to reverse this tendency. If the firms concerned were in a position to offer a complete service of representation, including advocacy in the Crown Court, their ability to build up and maintain a monopoly position in this class of work would be strengthened. This would be a step towards a system which, as we said in paragraph 18.45, we do not favour, in which all criminal work becomes concentrated in relatively few firms and public offices, each consistently representing only one side, either defence or prosecution."

10.43   The conclusion that rights of audience in the higher Courts should not be extended was adopted as the considered policy of the Government in November 1983 and re-affirmed in 1984, 1985 and 1987. No basis for any other conclusion is now put forward by the Government.

MULTI-DISCIPLINARY PRACTICES (MDPS) AND PARTNERSHIPS AT THE BAR

10.44   The Royal Commission considered the position of the Bar in the light of the many previous detailed examinations of the question whether barristers in private practice should be allowed, in the public interest, to enter into partnerships. The Commission stated the justification for the existence of the Bar in terms which unfortunately have been ignored in the Green Papers:

> "The justification for the existence of the Bar as a separate branch of the legal professions rests firmly on the proposition that the client, or his solicitor acting on his behalf, may select a particular individual by reason of his known capabilities. This freedom of choice goes to the root of the practice and structure of the Bar. It encompasses the right to select a barrister who has a known skill or specialist knowledge; a barrister who will match the skill of counsel acting for the other party in the case; above all the selection of an individual in whom the client can have confidence." (para. 33.64).

The Commission also referred to the potential restriction of the public's choice of barristers, particularly in the small specialised Bars and in provincial centres which have so few sets of barristers' chambers. (para. 33.65). Their conclusion was:

> *"Partnerships would often we think be convenient or advantageous to barristers but the point of overriding importance is the public interest. We therefore consider that partnerships between barristers should not be permitted."* (para. 33.66: our emphasis).

The Commission made it clear in para. 30.1 that this unequivocal judgment applied also to any partnership between barristers and solicitors or other professionals: any such partnerships would equally be contrary to the public interest. This judgment is also today the judgment of the Director-General of Fair Trading: see para. 10.5(4) above.

10.45 With regard to solicitors, the Commission reached a similarly clear conclusion in para. 30.15, in which they stated:

> "Our concern is to raise the level and quality of service to the public by the legal profession. This purpose would not be served by any measures which confused the divisions of professional responsibility in the mind of the client. Divisions of function between different professions and callings are the result of historical development and are not fixed for all time, but we do not think that it would be in the interests of clients or in the general public interest if at present partnerships were permitted between solicitors and members of other professions."

10.46 The recommendations of the Royal Commission based firmly on the interests of the public were:-

> "Barristers should not be permitted to practise in partnership." (R33.14).
> "Partnerships between solicitors and members of other professions should not be permitted." (R30.1)

CONVEYANCING

10.47 The Royal Commission's conclusions can be stated very shortly:-

(1) The public needs to be protected in conveyancing transactions from incompetence, dishonesty and unfair dealing;
(2) A system of licensing those other than solicitors to do conveyancing would be unable to provide the level of positive control required, particularly in respect of standards of competence and ethical conduct.
(3) It would not be in the public interest for building societies and the institutional lenders to provide a conveyancing service. Inevitably conflicts of interest would arise. The public might not in practice obtain from such institutions the independent advice in particular in relation to financial matters which solicitors offer.

Again the Royal Commission's conclusions were based squarely on the detailed evidence they had obtained, and on the assessments of the public interest.

LAY DIRECT ACCESS TO BARRISTERS

10.48 As the Royal Commission stated in para. 17.27 of their Report,

> "The direct object of the rule which prevents access save through a solicitor by the client to the barrister is to ensure that barristers are free from hour-to-hour distractions and that specialist matters with which they deal are presented to them by a lawyer who has already identified the issues and sifted out the relevant facts, rather than by the lay client himself who can only present his problem as a whole. The object is not to put the barrister at a distance from his client, but to ensure, so far as possible, that his specialist skills are efficiently used, that he is ensured, so far as possible, the time necessary to concentrate on them and – this is put forward very much as a secondary objective – that he remains sufficiently detached from his client to be able to give him advice which is wholly objective."

The Royal Commission in para. 19.6 recognised that it is an essential part of the division into the professions of barrister and solicitor, with the Bar being a consultant profession, that clients normally approach a barrister through a solicitor, and said that they did not think

> "that it would be possible to maintain an effective two-branch profession if barristers received clients directly and, in order to compete effectively with solicitors, had to run offices organised in the same way and subject to the same disciplines. The advantages of the present arrangements would be lost. We are not, therefore, satisfied that the public interest would be served by permitting direct access to counsel in all cases."

The Royal Commission recommended that in the interests of the public no change should be made to this rule of practice (R19.1).

THE NEXT STAGE AFTER THE ROYAL COMMISSION

10.49 In this Chapter the main proposals of the Government have been considered in terms of their practical consequences, and in the light of the Royal Commission's assessment of the public interest which this Government adopted in 1983. The next stage is to consider the Government's proposals under the main headings of alleged advantage to the public: *competition, choice, access, quality,* and *cost.*

11

Competition – Choice – Access – Quality – Cost

11.1 It is the Government's thesis (not supported by evidence) that the changes it proposes will increase competition, and thereby improve access, choice and quality and reduce cost. It is the Bar Council's case, based on evidence, that the Government is entirely wrong. Competition, access, choice and quality would be reduced, and costs substantially increased if the Government's main changes were made.

THE PRESENT POSITION

11.2 The Bar Council, like the Government, is for competition, for fair and full competition. The Bar of England and Wales is *now* the most competitive of all professions. 6,000 barristers compete vigorously on equal terms. Each barrister has to be a sole practitioner. Each has to devote the majority of his or her time to practice as a barrister. Each has to rely entirely on her or his intelligence, training, and skills acquired by constant practice in competition with each other. At least this much is agreed by the Government, which states in para. 4.11 of the main Green Paper that "in advocacy work the maintenance of standards both of skill and integrity has much to do with the independence of the advocate, his regular application to his work in the Courts". The Lord Chancellor's view is that "The Bar is the most competitive business going."

11.3 The basic framework of rules governing practice as a barrister has been developed so as to maintain this essential element of maximum personal competition between barristers as specialist advocates and advisers. Some of the rules, such as those relating to the organisation of barristers' offices, are unnecessarily detailed and as appears from Chapter 20 below have been re-considered by the Bar Council.

11.4 The present rule is that barristers may not form partnerships with each other or with solicitors or accountants or other professionals. The reasons for this rule have already been set out in Chapter 10 above and are dealt with more fully in Chapter 15 below. They are directly related to the requirements of independence and the "cab-rank" rule. Because barristers are required to be independent, a barrister who does not have work must in the end leave the Bar. A barrister receives work because a specialist, a solicitor or other professional, wholly independent of the barrister, decides to instruct the barrister. The decision is made, not because the barrister is part of the firm, or to maximise the firm's profits, but because the barrister is chosen as having the actual competence, the actual skills gained by constant practice in a variety of cases, so as to qualify the barrister, not by paper qualifications, but by hard work and proven ability to do the particular work for the particular client of that solicitor.

11.5 This rule against barristers forming partnerships with each other or with solicitors or other professionals is *designed to maximise competition*. That is why it was approved by the Royal Commission as being in the public interest. That is why it is approved by the Director-General of Fair Trading: see para. 10.5(4) above. He is the person with the task of looking after the public interest, of being the defender of the ordinary consumer. His view is that, if this rule is abandoned (as the Government proposes), competition between barristers would be much reduced, and the choice of advocate on the part of both lay and professional clients would also be reduced. If barristers went into partnerships with each other, there would no longer be 6,000 barristers in full competition with each other. If barristers went into partnerships with solicitors or accountants, their services would in practice be available only to the clients of the partnerships. The range of choice would be reduced. As the Director-General of Fair Trading said (para. 10.5(4) above): "This would be a perverse effect of a policy intended to increase competition and widen choice".

11.6 Consider also the rule preventing direct access by lay clients to barristers. This is designed to maximise *informed and therefore full competition*. Lay clients usually have no need for the continuing services of a barrister. Their need is for one-off advice on a legal problem or for one-off legal representation in one case, criminal or civil. They generally do not have the experience, skills or information to make an informed choice of the right barrister for their particular problem or case. The degree of unevenness in information about barristers is larger than in relation to most other professional services, except perhaps medical specialists. It is inherent in the nature of the services which barristers provide on a one-off basis to a lay client but on a continuing basis to solicitors and other professionals.

11.7 In theory reputation and advertising might reduce this unevenness of information. But the nature of the market for the barrister's specialist skills, like the market for the medical skills of a brain surgeon, is one in which reputation and advertising can play little part in providing the necessary information to the lay client. It is not a market in which largely routine services are provided, and can usefully be made the subject of standard information or advertising. In theory certification (the main Green Paper's licensing option) might reduce this unevenness to some extent. But the market is one of many different specialisations. Certification could only be effective in setting minimum standards, such as the Government's suggestion that a requisite number of hours in the Magistrates Courts would entitle an advocate to a "full criminal licence": a low qualification for a potentially low standard. This system of certification would not distinguish between criminal barristers on the basis of expertise in cross-examination, or expertise in addressing the jury, or expertise in analysis of the law, or expertise in long cases or short cases.

11.8 Only a system which removes the unevenness of information can truly achieve the maximum competition. This system is agency, the mechanism of employing a professional on a continuing basis who has the skills and information to make an informed and skilful choice of other professionals for one-off problems. That is the role of the solicitor, one of whose prime functions is to acquire the skills and information needed to choose the right barristers for his clients. An analogy is the medical general practitioner who has to choose the right consultants for a large variety of specialist medical problems. The operation of agency in this way removes the unevenness of information and enables choice to be made on a fully competitive basis. But it goes further. It enables the solicitor as a specialist selector of barristers to monitor barristers' performances, to stop using barristers whose quality and performance is not up to expectations, and also to monitor costs. The lay client has no sound basis on which to choose the right barrister, to choose a barrister on the basis of an informed appreciation of the barrister's quality, or to know whether the barrister's charges are about right or too high or too low. That is the task of the lay client's agent, the solicitor.

11.9 So the rule against direct access by lay clients to barristers does not reduce competition. On the contrary, it ensures full competition. It ensures that the monitoring of standards is achieved by the best means of all, the professional judgment of the solicitor who acquires the skills needed to judge the performance of barristers by seeing their performance in strong competition with each other.

11.10 As regards the limitation of rights of audience in the higher Courts to the Bar, there is no question of an inadequate supply of barristers to perform the specialist work that barristers are required to perform. The number of cases has risen rapidly. So has the Bar increased in size, from under 2,000 in 1960 to 6,000 in 1989. In fact there is a surplus of barristers. Today, as virtually throughout the Bar's history, the number of barristers hoping for briefs exceeds the number of briefs available. As a result there is a proportion of barristers who earn little, who do not make their way in the profession, and who after a while move into other occupations, such as becoming solicitors, or entering the Government Legal Service or commerce, finance or industry, in which they often enjoy successful careers. The Bar recognises that this is a fact of the strong competition under which it operates.

11.11 What are the reasons for this limitation? The rule that barristers alone appear in the higher Courts is *not* a restrictive practice invented by barristers to monopolise the work. It is a rule laid down by the Judges. It has been laid down by the Judges over several centuries, in what they saw, and see, as a vital public interest, in requiring cases serious enough to be heard in the higher Courts to be presented only by men and women (1) who are properly trained under the supervision of the Judges and the Inns of Court, (2) who acquire and retain the necessary skills of advocacy by constant practice in the Courts, (3) who are independent of partnerships and incorporation and therefore subject to the "cab-rank" rule, (4) who are subject to the supervision of the Judges as regards conduct and discipline.

COMPETITION AND CHOICE

11.12 So the present position is one in which competition between barristers as the advocates in the higher Courts is maximised, with an informed choice of barrister being made by another professional.

11.13 In these circumstances the only way in which competition could be adversely affected would be if entry to the Bar were artificially restricted. In fact entry to the Bar has been large, and there has at all times been a surplus of barristers of all seniorities. But the Government appears to be suggesting, in Chapter 11 of the main Green Paper, that the requirement to practise in chambers and the difficulties in obtaining tenancies in chambers operate as an artificial restriction on entry and therefore on competition.

11.14 The Bar Council has been concerned about the development of the problem that some barristers of reasonable ability have been failing to get tenancies. The Bar Council recognises that, whatever the facts about competition, this problem can give rise to an appearance of restriction of competition. It also recognises that, in any event, easier entry to a permanent place in the profession for those who have qualified by their talents, education and training can only add further to the competition and competitive spirit which are so essential to the Bar. Accordingly the Bar Council will be making important changes in the structure of the profession which are set out in Chapter 20 below, including

(1) improved funding of pupils and new entrants;
(2) a supplementary library system, based on the library systems of Northern Ireland, Scotland and the Republic of Ireland, to enable those who are not placed in chambers to start in practice.

11.15 By these means the Bar Council believes that any criticism based on alleged barriers to full competition will be met.

11.16 But what would be the position if the Government's proposals went through? The partnership and multi-disciplinary practice proposals alone would result in a reduction in the number of independent barristers competing vigorously. Some would form partnerships of barristers only. Partners could not compete against each other. Some would be in partnerships, or companies, of barristers plus solicitors and other professionals, and probably with accountants holding the dominant position. Clients of these multi-disciplinary practices (MDPs) would have the services of the advocates of the MDP, who could not compete against each other. Some would enter employment with companies or other large organisations such as banks or building societies. Each of these steps would reduce the level of competition in providing advocacy services and reduce the choice of advocate, by reducing the number of independent barristers on the "cab-rank" and available to any client. As the Director-General of Fair Trading has pointed out (para. 10.5(4) above), this would reduce not only competition, but also "that valuable concomitant of competition, namely, **choice** on the part of both professional and lay clients. This would be a perverse effect of a policy intended to increase competition and widen choice".

11.17 The Green Paper proposals would over a period of time tend to diminish the availability of advocacy services because:

(1) there would be a reduction in the numbers practising at the Bar due to the difficulty of recruiting new entrants to the profession in

competition with solicitors wishing to provide advocacy services; to wastage from the Bar by reason of recruitment from the Bar by solicitors and accountants seeking to build up advocacy departments; and to solicitors providing advocacy services being in a position to dispense with the Bar's services;
(2) advocates employed by solicitors and accountants would be less available to the public than members of the Bar due to the tendency to avoid acting against the clients of the firm;
(3) with the reduction in availability of members of the Bar for advocacy services there would be a gradual reduction in the number of separate firms of solicitors caused by:
   (a) lack of access to advocacy services except by sending clients to larger firms with advocacy departments, and the consequent loss of clients;
   (b) tendency to merge with larger firms having advocacy departments in order to enlarge client bases;
(4) with the development of partnerships between members of the Bar and others, conflicts of interest would reduce availability.

The combination of the reduction in the Bar and the number of firms of solicitors, the increase in size of the average firm of solicitors (and accountants) and the natural disinclination of the larger firms to provide advocacy services against established clients means that the choice of advocate available to a member of the public in any given case would probably be significantly reduced by comparison with that available at present. The Green Paper proposals, if implemented, would therefore in this respect act contrary to the public interest.

11.18 Because the Government has made it clear that there has been no study of the effects of the Government proposals, the Bar Council asked a distinguished economist, Professor B. S. Yamey C.B.E. F.B.A., Emeritus Professor at the London School of Economics, who was a member of the Monopolies and Mergers Commission and has written widely on competition and mergers policies, to consider the effects of those proposals from his independent and expert standpoint. Professor Yamey's report is at Annex 3. He concludes that the proposals in the main Green Paper would have unfavourable effects including a reduction in consumers' choice, a less efficient use of advocates' services, and increased concentration in the supply of legal services. He also questions the main Green Paper's expectation that an independent Bar would continue to flourish if the principal proposals are implemented.

MONOPOLIES

11.19   When considering the effects of the Green Paper proposals on competition, it is essential to keep in mind the risks of creating actual or near monopolies. The Royal Commission drew attention to the undesirability of monopolies in the provision of legal services and their adverse effect on the administration of justice, for example, when referring to "evidence that in some provincial areas a limited number of firms have tended to monopolise criminal work in the magistrates' courts" (para. 18.54).

11.20   The Government's proposals would inevitably tend towards the creation of fewer and larger organisations. The largest firms of solicitors or accountants or mixed solicitors and accountants would be given a major advantage in the recruitment of advocates both from the existing Bar and from new entrants. The cost of establishing an advocacy department with a sufficient range of skills to meet the needs of clients would be beyond the resources of all but the largest firms. This is a point which has been emphasised particularly by medium-sized firms (11 to 50 partners) in the City of London, and by the small firms of solicitors (less than 11 partners) all over the country, in their communications to the Bar Council in response to its Consultation Document.

The Green Papers are seen as weighting the scales in favour of the largest firms. The medium and smaller firms would have little or no alternative but to combine in larger firms, particularly since the ability of large finance organisations to compete unfairly for the provision of conveyancing services (Chapter 23 below) would remove the economic base of many of the smaller firms. Above all, the size of the accountant firms, as shown in Chapter 8 above, would enable them quite rapidly to seize a major part of the market, particularly outside London (as the rapid concentration of estate agencies within large finance organisations has shown). The likelihood of local monopolies outside London would be high. Whatever other damage that would cause to the administration of justice, it would certainly reduce choice and reduce competition.

ACCESS

11.21   The aim of both the Government and the Bar Council is to maximise access to legal services, and so to justice, for everyone in the country. At present there is access to 8,000 solicitors firms throughout the country, able to provide a generalist service to lay clients, and able to call on the services of 6,000 barristers for advocacy and specialist advice. The only barrier is money. The Legal Aid scheme is supposed to remedy lack of means and to bring justice in reach of all. Since 1979 it has failed to achieve its basic aim by an increasing margin: see paras. 9.6 to 9.20 above.

11.22 The Government's proposals would make access to legal services more difficult, for reasons which have already been outlined. Unfair competition from large finance organisations in conveyancing would damage or destroy the economic base of many of the smaller firms of solicitors (Chapter 23 below). The need to set up advocacy departments to compete with the larger solicitor firms and the accountants, and to escape from the consequences of the loss of conveyancing, would compel small and medium-sized firms (in London, up to 50 partners or more) to form much larger organisations. As the pattern of the larger accountant firms shows, these larger organisations (whether of lawyers only or multi-disciplinary practices) would tend to be concentrated in the cities and large towns. Their overheads would be higher than those of the present smaller firms of solicitors. To achieve maximum profitability they would have to concentrate primarily on providing services to business clients, for whom legal services are a deductible expense for tax purposes. Less remunerative areas of practice, which include most work for private clients and particularly legal aid work, would, at best, take second place to work for business clients. Many of the larger firms would give up legal aid work, as both unremunerative and wasteful of resources which could be put to more profitable use on behalf of business clients.

11.23 An early victim would be the "cab-rank" rule, which is not compatible with operation in partnerships or companies or as an employed lawyer. As many solicitors have emphasised, the "cab-rank" rule is of great importance in ensuring proper representation of all clients, not just "any old lawyer", but a barrister of a standing equal to that of the prosecuting barrister or of the barrister for the opposing party in civil litigation. The Race Relations Committee of the Bar Council has also stressed the importance of the "cab-rank" rule in securing proper representation for women and men from the ethnic minority communities: see Chapter 25 below.

11.24 The pressures which the Government proposals would create, would tend to make lawyers more remote, less accessible, and more expensive. Because of the nature of those proposals large lawyer organisations or mixed practices would be favoured. Overall the effect would be the opposite of what the Government says it is aiming for.

QUALITY

11.25 The quality of barristers is maintained and raised by a combination of (1) high standards of entry, (2) high standards of education and training, (3) strong competition involving constant practice in Court advocacy, (4) the requirements of independence and the "cab-rank" rule.

11.26 If the Government's proposals went through, quality would fall, for these reasons:-

(1) Direct access by lay clients to barristers would involve barristers in replicating the office facilities and services currently provided by solicitors, with a consequent increase in costs, and diversion of barristers' time and effort to office work at the expense of Court preparation and practice with the loss of the constant Court practice vital for high standards of advocacy.
(2) Involvement of barristers in partnerships and companies would mean that barristers would be involved more and more in the day to day office work, and in the work of preparation of cases, including taking witness statements and preparing documents for Court, in which solicitors now specialise. There would be a lesser degree of specialisation in Court work, and barristers would get less constant practice in Court. If they tried to maintain a constant practice in Court, they could not devote as much time to preparation for Court advocacy.
(3) There would be less competition for the reasons already set out.
(4) The "cab-rank" rule would largely disappear, being incompatible with partnerships, companies and employment, and being difficult for any remaining independent barristers to maintain if competing with those who did not maintain the "cab-rank" rule.
(5) The most able lawyers would be likely, following the pattern of the law firms in the U.S.A. and Canada, to gravitate to the corporate and commercial fields of work, rather than advocacy which has traditionally had a lower order of preference for the most able. A similar pattern already exists in some of the major solicitors firms in England and Wales.

COST

11.27 Overall, barristers are cheaper than solicitors. That is primarily because solicitors' overheads are on average substantially higher than barristers' overheads. The rough practice economics of barristers and solicitors in private practice are set out in para. 5.10 above. Barristers' overheads are in the range of 15% to 25% of gross earnings, whereas solicitors' overheads are in the range from 66% to 80% or higher of gross earnings. It must be emphasised that these are broad bands and there are some barristers' and solicitors' practices which fall outside these bands. But the Bar's experience and the expert advice it has received show that these figures give an accurate general indication of the differences between barristers' and solicitors' practices. Thus, in general, solicitors' overheads are up to more than 3 times the level of barristers' overheads.

11.28 In pointing this out, no criticism whatever is intended of solicitors. Solicitors' overheads are much higher because of the nature of their practices. They deal with and for lay clients on a continuing basis. They need larger staff, larger offices, and space for the retention and storage of files over a long period. They do the physical preparation of cases for trial, sometimes involving the assembly, analysis and copying of thousands of documents. The nature of barristers' practices, involving the retention of papers only while a case is active or advice is being given, enables overheads to be kept to a minimum.

11.29 The differences in overheads are reflected in the differences in the levels of fees. For example,

(1) Solicitors' average charging rates are usually nearly double those of barristers.
(2) The Crown Prosecution Service has been paying solicitors up to double the amount it pays to barristers for work on a sessions basis.
(3) At the higher levels of fees in commercial work, senior partners in solicitors firms have charging rates in excess of the equivalent rates for Queen's Counsel.
(4) It is commonplace for the fees for senior junior barristers to be less than those paid to solicitors for the work of assistant solicitors at their appropriate charging rates.
(5) It is also commonplace for solicitors to instruct young and not so young barristers, on the solicitors' own behalf, to help with solicitors' work such as the drafting of letters, the assembly and analysis of documents for the legal process of discovery together with the preparation of formal lists of documents, or the formal inspection of documents. They do this in the knowledge that the barristers' fees will be less than they would have to charge the client if their assistant solicitors were to do the same work.

11.30 These are merely examples, and they illustrate the general proposition that solicitors' services are much more expensive than barristers' overall. In the short time allowed by the Government it is not possible to analyse in detail the consequences of the Government's proposals in terms of cost. Indeed much would depend on the extent to which, over a period, advocacy services would come to be available largely from firms or companies of (1) mixed barristers and solicitors, (2) mixed barristers, solicitors and other professionals, (3) solicitors alone, or (4) mixed solicitors and other professionals. As Chapter 10 shows, the likelihood is that the independent Bar would seriously diminish, and advocacy would largely come from such firms or companies. That being so, the consequence would be substantial increases in cost to the lay client or to the taxpayer through the Legal Aid scheme. The Government has made clear that no analysis of the cost of its proposals was made by it before the Green Papers were issued. Instead reliance is merely placed on conventional economic propositions which, as Professor Yamey has shown, cannot be applied simplistically to the market for legal services. The decline in competition which would flow from implementation of the Green Paper proposals would further increase the costs to lay clients or the taxpayer.

12

Rights of Audience – Direct Access to Counsel – Attendance on Counsel

RIGHTS OF AUDIENCE

12.1 The starting point for consideration of rights of audience is what the present rights of audience are and why they take their present form. In this Chapter we are primarily concerned with the higher Courts: in criminal cases, the Crown Court; in both criminal and civil cases, the High Court, the Court of Appeal and the House of Lords.

12.2 The present rights of audience are stated in Annex E to the main Green Paper, and can be briefly summarised as follows:-

(1) Barristers in independent practice have rights of audience in all Courts and Tribunals.
(2) Solicitors in private practice can appear in Tribunals and in the lower Courts (the Magistrates' Courts and the County Court); they have limited rights in the Crown Court on appeals and committals for sentence, and wider rights in certain remote areas; solicitors can appear in the High Court and Court of Appeal when sitting in chambers and in some other limited classes of matter; solicitors can only appear in the House of Lords on petitions for leave to appeal.
(3) Barristers and solicitors in employment have the same rights of audience in Courts, other than the Crown Court, as solicitors in private practice, but only on behalf of their employers. They can appear in any Tribunals.
(4) Lawyers from other EEC member States with rights of audience in their own countries can appear before any Court or Tribunal in England and Wales provided that they are instructed with an English lawyer having the right to appear in that Court or Tribunal.
(5) In most Tribunals there is no limitation on who can appear on behalf of a person involved in the proceedings.

12.3   The restriction of rights of audience in the higher Courts to barristers (with very limited exceptions for solicitors, whether in private practice or employed, and for employed barristers) is of long standing. It is not a "monopoly" created by the Bar for the benefit of barristers. As Chapter 10 shows, it has been imposed for centuries by the Judges in the interests of the public alone, and is closely linked to:-

(1) **the "cab-rank" rule** which the Judges imposed on the Bar so as to ensure that every person involved in proceedings in the higher Courts could be represented by an independent practitioner of her or his choice.

(2) **the independence** of each barrister in private practice who under the rules of the Bar as required by the Judges has to be independent of solicitors, the Government or anyone else, so as to be able to act as a sole practitioner subject to the "cab-rank" rule, a rule which cannot apply to those who are in partnership, a company or employment: see Lord Mackay's views in para. 3.13 above.

(3) **specialisation** (a) in advocacy by barristers and (b) in dealings with lay clients and in preparation of cases by solicitors: this specialisation reflects the practical differences in the work and enables each profession to concentrate its energies on what it does best.

(4) the need for **maximum competition** in advocacy which results from (a) the requirements of total independence and the "cab-rank" rule, and (b) from the fact that the Bar is a consultant profession, dependent on solicitors for instructions, and subject to choice by solicitors according to the competence, the specialist knowledge or skills, and the experience of the individual barrister.

(5) the need for **maximum choice** which results in the main from the requirements of total independence and the "cab-rank" rule.

(6) the need **to maximise the constant practice** in advocacy before the Courts which develops the highest standards of competence.

(7) the need for a specialist corps of practitioners in advocacy which under the firm supervision of the Judges and by the pressures of "peer group discipline" enables **high standards of integrity and ethical practice** to be developed, including observance of the over-riding duty to the Court.

12.4   These essential points have been referred to already in Chapters 3, 6 and 10 above. They explain why the Bar's rights of audience in the higher Courts have been imposed over the centuries by the Judges in the interests of the public. The "monopoly" of the Bar is no more a monopoly than, for example, the restriction of anaesthetics and surgery to those who have by their innate talents, their training, and their hard work and experience made themselves acceptable practitioners in the skilled arts of anaesthetics and surgery. The presentation of cases in the higher Courts is a skilled art. The independence of the Bar as sole practitioners and the "cab-rank" rule bring to this skilled art a feature which is unique.

12.5 In paras. 5.3 to 5.6 of the main Green Paper the Government presents arguments for the existence of a "monopoly" in the skilled arts of advocacy, with which the Bar Council agrees. It is noteworthy, however, that the principal features which have long been the strength of the English legal system, namely (1) independence, and (2) the "cab-rank" rule, are omitted. These are also the principal features of the Scottish legal system, and Lord Mackay when leader of the Bar of Scotland drew particular attention to these features. The omission of these features from Chapter 5 of the main Green Paper is apparently because they are inconsistent with the Government's proposals to take the power over rights of audience in the higher Courts away from the Judges, and to grant rights of audience to anyone who satisfies the formal requirements stated in Chapter 5, whether independent or not, and whether adhering to the "cab-rank" rule or not. The Bar Council welcomes the partial statement of the position in paras. 5.3 to 5.6 of the main Green Paper, but regrets the omission from those paragraphs of the two principal features which distinguish the present system in England and Wales as well as in Scotland, Northern Ireland and the Republic of Ireland.

12.6 The effects of the Governments' proposals on rights of audience have already been considered in Chapter 11 above under the important headings of Competition, Access, Choice, Cost and Quality, and in that Chapter it has been shown how adverse the effects of those proposals, if put into practice, would be under each of such headings.

12.7 The Government has not stated anywhere in the main Green Paper

(1) what it regards as being the defects (if any) in the present system;
(2) what is needed to remedy such defects;
(3) how its proposals would succeed in remedying such defects without creating other and more serious defects.

The Government's failure to do this is noteworthy when the extent of the changes proposed is considered. It is normal, if there are believed to be defects in something as important to the public interest as the administration of justice, to set out the defects with care, to analyse them with care, and to devise with equal care remedies which will remedy the defects without in turn creating new defects. This process has not taken place, as the Lord Chancellor's Permanent Secretary has confirmed: see para. 3.19 above.

12.8 In these circumstances the Bar Council trusts that the Government will, before proceeding to initiate changes, which there is good reason to believe would damage the public interest by reducing competition, access, choice and quality and by increasing cost, first

(1) state clearly and fully what it regards as defective in the present system, and what is the evidence on which it relies for such defects;
(2) state clearly and fully how its current proposals could, in its view, remedy such defects and on what research that is based;
(3) state equally clearly and fully how its current proposals could, in its view, avoid creating the potentially serious damage to the public interest set out in Chapter 11 above.

If the Government were prepared to do this, then those affected, the members of the public as well as the Bar Council, would be able to answer a case based on evidence with their equally careful answers also based on evidence.

12.9 In the absence of any such statement or evidence from the Government, the Bar Council can only draw attention to the adverse consequences of the proposals, if implemented, as already set out in Chapter 11 above, and go on, as it now does, to deal with the details of the rights of audience proposals.

CONTROL BY THE JUDGES, NOT THE GOVERNMENT

12.10 The Judges have for centuries supervised those who appear in the higher Courts. To take away their rights to exercise this control independently of the Government and Parliament would be a major constitutional step. The need for an independent Judiciary and an independent legal profession providing the required independent advocates is considered specifically in Chapter 14 below. No basis whatever has been suggested by the Government for stripping the Judges of this power so essential to their independent control of the higher Courts and to the independence of the profession. The power of the Lord Chancellor in relation to the Crown Court should not be exercised inconsistently with the position as determined by the Judges for the High Court.

12.11 The Judges should continue to supervise (1) who may appear before them; (2) what the education and training of those who appear before them should be; (3) what standards of competence, integrity, and professional ethics should be achieved by those who appear before them; and (4) the exercise of discipline over those who appear before them.

AUDIENCE IN THE HIGHER COURTS

12.12 The Bar brings to its specialist role of advocacy in the higher Courts its independence and the important strength of the "cab-rank" rule. Barristers act only as consultants on referral by solicitors or other professionals. Accordingly barristers receive lower fees in Legal Aid work than solicitors, because their overheads as consultants can be lower. If solicitors or members of any other profession were to be given equal rights of audience in the higher Courts, that should be **on equal terms** so that there is **fair competition on equal terms**.

12.13 What would that involve? It would involve, for example, that:-

(1) Either all advocates should be subject to the "cab-rank" rule, or none should be. If **no** advocates were subject to this rule, then the public would be deprived of a significant benefit which has been recognised for centuries as essential for the protection of the ordinary citizen. If **all** advocates were subject to this rule, then the members of the other professions would have to practise as sole practitioners, like the Bar, and not in partnerships or companies or in employment which are in practical as well as legal terms incompatible with the "cab-rank" rule.

(2) Either all advocates should act as consultants, or none. If **no** advocates acted as consultants, then the public would lose the major advantage of advocates standing independently of their lay clients, and able through training and experience to be substituted for each other at short notice whenever the inevitable clashes due to Court listing occur. If **all** advocates acted as consultants, then the members of other professions would have to practise independently. It would not be possible to maintain a system under which barristers as consultants competed with solicitors who took lay clients direct. As the Lord Chancellor himself pointed out (see para. 10.19 above) it would not be appropriate to leave in the hands of the solicitor the decision whether to keep a case for a lay client for himself, or to pass it on to a barrister. "It could be a mistake to put the decision, whether to do the case oneself or to pass it on to a barrister, into the hands of those with first access to the consumer", was what the Lord

Chancellor said. It would be not only contrary to the public interest, but also unfair to barristers to have to compete on unequal terms.

(3) All advocates would have to be paid the same Legal Aid fees. These would have to be **either** the current barrister's fees, **or** the current solicitor's fees, **or** fees at some other level. It would be completely unfair to barristers to expect them to appear for fees substantially lower than the fees paid to solicitors in direct competition. Solicitors already find it difficult enough to do Legal Aid work. If they were paid at barrister's rates, because of their much higher overheads they would find Legal Aid work impossible. The barristers' rates are in any event very low for barristers, but by keeping their overheads as low as possible they have managed to do the poorly-paid Legal Aid work. Whatever rates were agreed, they would have to be the same for all advocates, so as to ensure fair competition. Similarly the Crown Prosecution Service (CPS) and other Government authorities would have to pay the same rates. It would not be fair for barristers to continue to be paid as little as **half** what solicitors are paid for prosecuting cases on a sessions basis.

12.14 These elementary matters of fair competition have not been addressed in the main Green Paper. But they go to the heart of the Green Paper proposals. Are the public to be deprived of the benefit of independent barristers available to them on the "cab-rank" basis? If not, what steps would have to be taken to place other advocates on a basis of fair competition with barristers? The Bar Council's view is that if rights of audience are to be extended, what is unique with the present system should not be thrown away. Those who wish to practise in the higher Courts should be required to adopt the same basis of practice as the Bar, in particular independence as sole practitioners acting only as consultants and subject to the "cab-rank" rule (including the obligation to undertake Legal Aid work). As stated in the Consultative Document (page 8): "If Members of a legal profession other than the Bar met these requirements and were recognised by the Judges, the Bar should welcome them." The Bar Council recognises that this would mean that the members of such other legal profession would be barristers in all but name. Therefore the Bar Council wishes to make it clear that

(1) it would welcome such persons into the profession of barrister;
(2) the changes to the structure of the profession set out in Chapter 20 below would enable transfer to the Bar to take place, **in practice**, without any difficulty;
(3) the Bar Council would take further steps in collaboration with such other profession and the Lord Chancellor to ensure that those persons able and wishing to transfer would be enabled to do

so, and that no barriers whether of form or practicality would be in their way;

(4) this would depend on a requirement of recognition **by the Judges**, and not by the Government however indirectly: the independence of the Judges and the legal profession from Government control or interference would be an absolute requirement.

As Lord Mackay said to the Scottish Royal Commission when opposing the extension of rights of audience to Scottish solicitors (3 July 1978, page 5):

"it was better for a solicitor to become an advocate and make that his work. He would then be subject to the ethics and discipline of the Faculty and particularly, the 'cab-rank' rule".

CERTIFICATION

12.15 The system of certification proposed does not take account of the much greater degree of specialisation of the Bar of England and Wales, than for example in Scotland. It is commonplace for barristers to appear only in criminal cases, or only in civil cases and never in criminal cases. Because of this specialisation, the proposed system would ensure that most of the most distinguished candidates could not become Queen's Counsel or High Court Judges. That would be an unwise system to adopt, and due allowance would have to be made for specialisation.

12.16 The system of certification proposed would be strong on **form** but weak on **substance**. An advocate who wished to move from a "limited" to a "full" certificate would have to meet only two requirements:

(1) to have held the "limited" certificate for a minimum period;
(2) to have completed a prescribed minimum amount of actual advocacy in the lower Court.

(paras. 5.30 to 5.33 of the main Green Paper). Thus all that would be required would be the necessary "flying hours" in the lower Courts. As a test of real ability it would hardly be possible to construct a less impressive test. The test would take no account of ability, of skills in cross-examination of witnesses or of skills in presenting facts or law: simple "flying hours" would suffice, however poor the pilot.

12.17 Compare that with the present position. Solicitors instruct young barristers after a period of pupillage to appear in the Magistrates' Court on the recommendation of chambers that the young barristers have reached the stage where they are ready to do this. Over a period which will differ according to the abilities of each of the young barristers, they will be tested in the Magistrates' Courts. The stage at which a barrister is able to appear in the Crown Court is not based on an arbitrary period or an arbitrary number of "flying hours", but on the assessment of another professional, a solicitor, that she or he is ready to take the step up into the Crown Court, that she or he is good enough and experienced enough not to let down the solicitor's lay client. So the present position depends not on arbitrary and formal requirements, but on an assessment of actual ability. Some come to the Bar and never make the grade, are not regularly instructed to appear in the higher Courts, and in the end leave the Bar. As Lord Mackay said to the Scottish Royal Commission,

> "just after he was called, a new advocate would generally be given simple work. Solicitors would see how he performed and he might then be instructed in more complicated matters where his conduct of the case would again undoubtedly be assessed by the solicitors present. An advocate did not get responsible work until he had built up a reputation and resources. This meant that those advocates who survived were accredited competent counsel by a number of solicitors who had instructed them over a period of time. . . . a solicitor in the Sheriff Court did not require to get business from anyone else, nor did he require a recommendation; so that the amount of work he did might bear no resemblance to his competence" (3 July 1978, page 7).

Under the Government's proposals, after the arbitrary period and "flying hours" in the Magistrates Court had been met, these barristers would receive the accolade of a full certificate, and be able to represent themselves to the public at large as certified as capable of appearing in any Court up to the House of Lords. That would be contrary to the public interest. But that is what the Government's proposals would involve – the substitution of mere formal requirements for the professional assessments of solicitors. If there are to be changes, they must be more carefully thought through than this.

12.18 The whole question whether a barrister should be able to appear in any Court once her or his training is complete (as Erskine appeared, virtually for the first time, in the House of Lords and won the case) is one which requires the most careful consideration by those best equipped to consider it – the Judges. The Bar Council's view is that the proper approach for the Lord Chancellor (who is a senior Judge), is to refer it to his colleagues and ask them to consider it, as they always do, carefully and in detail, weighing the evidence, any defects in the present system, and the possible remedies.

12.19 Whatever system might be proposed it would have to include a proper assessment of ability, made by the Judges in the light of the barrister's actual performances in Court. That the Judges should be in control of who may appear before them in the higher Courts is an essential requirement of independence in the administration of justice: Chapter 14 below. As indicated in para. 12.14 above the Bar would welcome to the Bar from another legal profession those who were prepared to embrace the same principles as barristers now do, so as to increase further the fair competition in the most competitive of professions.

PLEAS OF GUILTY IN CROWN COURT

12.20 It is proposed that all pleas of guilty in the Crown Court could be conducted by any holder of a limited general or criminal advocacy certificate. This would mean that any solicitors now in practice as well as any solicitors gaining such a certificate subsequently could conduct any plea of guilty of any offence from murder to theft of a milk bottle in the Crown Court. Would this be in the public interest?

12.21 Whether an accused person should or should not plead guilty is often a question involving consideration of complex points of law and evidence; for example, the adviser may have to consider questions of the mens rea of recklessness in relation to charges involving injury to or death of persons or damage to property, or the admissibility of evidence e.g. from a co-accused. Such questions call for advice based on a full understanding of the law and a detailed analysis of the evidence. That is why at present a barrister must be instructed. Pleas of guilty and pleas in mitigation following a plea of guilty do not form a simple straightforward branch of work requiring no particular specialisation. Above all, in many cases they involve the liberty of a man or woman. The consequences can affect the accused and her or his family for the rest of their lives.

12.22 It appears that behind this proposal lies the intention to reduce the availability of Legal Aid by denying Legal Aid certificates for a barrister and granting Legal Aid only for a solicitor in pleas of guilty. If barristers are to be required to compete with solicitors in all Courts, as proposed, the competition would have to be fair and the Legal Aid certificate would have to be for a barrister or a solicitor competing as sole practitioners on a referral basis.

12.23 But that would miss another vital point. The essence of a barrister's training is to advise clients to plead guilty where that is the sensible and proper course. The detachment of the independent barrister gives greater weight to the advice he or she gives. If rights of audience in the Crown Court are to be given to others, one necessary consequence will be fewer pleas of guilty and more criminal cases

136

fought through unnecessarily. That is not because solicitors are inherently less likely to advise clients to plead guilty, but because the new "advocates" will be less experienced, will not have the benefit of constant practice in Court, and will be less well trained to analyse evidence and law and advise a plea of guilty. Less experienced advocates tend to play safe, by not advising clients to plead guilty or to settle civil cases. A criminal case fought through and lost would give the advocate valuable "flying time", and would avoid the risk of being accused by a client of having wrongly advised her or him to plead guilty. The cost to the taxpayer of fewer sensible pleas, of more Court and Judge time wasted, of the need for more Courts and Judges, would be potentially a major extra cost.

12.24   All these are matters which require the most careful analysis and consideration. They cannot safely be determined on the footing of the Government's "first principles" approach, ignoring evidence of the present system and of the potential consequences of the changes proposed. The Bar Council wishes to discuss with the Judges and with the Government the precise boundaries for rights of audience in the different Courts, on the understanding that the basic principles set out in this book would be fully safeguarded in the interests and for the protection of the public.

EDUCATION AND TRAINING

12.25   These are dealt with fully in Chapter 19 below.

ADVISORY COMMITTEE

12.26   The Bar Council's proposals for different committees to advise on (1) professional standards, and (2) legal education and training, are set out in Chapters 18 and 19 below. The fundamental objections to control by the Government, whether or not advised by some committee, are set out in Chapter 14 below.

EMPLOYED BARRISTERS AND SOLICITORS

12.27   The position of employed barristers is appropriately covered by the recent change to the Bar's Code of Conduct which brought employed barristers largely into line with employed solicitors, except that (1) their position is to be made similar to other professionals with direct access to the Bar and (2) the need for the intervention of a solicitor in all cases in Court will need to be reconsidered.

CROWN PROSECUTION SERVICE

12.28 The position of employed prosecutors is considered in Chapter 13 below. For the reasons there set out, the Bar Council's view is that CPS and other Government prosecutors should not appear in the Crown Courts. In particular, such an extension of their right of audience would create just the sort of polarisation between those who only prosecute and those who only defend in the criminal courts, which is one of the most unhealthy features of those jurisdictions which use employed prosecutors, such as the U.S.A., Canada, Singapore and Hong Kong.

LAY ADVOCACY

12.29 In Annex E, para. 22, of the main Green Paper, the Government states in relation to Tribunals that "it is generally considered that most applicants should be able to cope with bringing proceedings without the need for assistance from a qualified legal representative". That statement is incorrect because (1) it is generally considered that most applicants need qualified legal representatives; (2) it is generally the case, as the evidence shows, that most applicants need legal representation if they are to succeed: see Chapter 9 above.

12.30 In para. 5.9 of the main Green Paper, the Government proposes an extension of rights of audience in the Courts to lay representatives.

12.31 What underlies these two references in the main Green Paper to lay representation appears to be the desire to restrict the availability of Legal Aid. If lay representatives are given rights of audience in the Courts, the next step will be to deny Legal Aid to any classes of case designated as suitable for lay representation.

12.32 The Bar Council's approach is a simple one. It shares with the Government the aim to make justice available to every citizen, irrespective of means. It tries to help to achieve this through the application of the "cab-rank" rule to Legal Aid work and by "pro bono" work such as the work done by FRU (Chapter 9 above). It points out that unqualified lay representatives are no substitute for the lawyers whom the Legal Aid Acts are supposed to provide so as to meet the requirements of justice.

12.33 In para. 5.9 of the main Green Paper it is suggested, following the Civil Justice Review, that the Court on giving reasons could restrict or exclude lay representatives who were corrupt or unruly. But this would be little if any safeguard. The Court would not know perhaps until the end of the case (if at all) whether the lay representative was "corrupt", for example whether a contingency arrangement had been made (e.g. for the representative to take 75% of the recovery) which was grossly unfair, or due to undue influence or duress. The Court apparently would not have power to exclude the lay representative for incompetence or lack of probity; even if it did have such powers, the Court might not appreciate how incompetent the lay representive was until part way through the case, if at all. What can be said with fair certainty is that lay representatives would take longer than lawyers, leading to longer hearings, greater Court delays, and more expense to the taxpayer. Whether this expense to the taxpayer would be more or less than the amount saved in Legal Aid, no one could foretell with any accuracy. It would be particularly difficult to apply or enforce any code of conduct in relation to a lay person, or to prevent a lay person of low quality continuing to appear.

12.34 Before lay advocacy is extended to the Courts, careful consideration is needed of the consequences both for those who would be represented by lay persons and for the general body of taxpayers. For the ultimate cost might be much greater than any savings that might in theory be achieved.

ADVOCACY BY GOVERNMENT DEPARTMENTS

12.35 One example of inadequate advocacy which adversely affects not the individual of small means but the public purse is in the field of taxation. It has been the practice of the Inland Revenue to appear before General or Special Commissioners by employees of the Revenue. In **Reed v. Nova Securities** [1985] 1 W.L.R. 193 H.L. (E.) the House of Lords drew attention to the adverse consequences for the Revenue if cases before the Commissioners were incompetently conducted on the Revenue's behalf by departmental officials: Lord Bridge at p. 195E-H, and Lord Templeman at p. 200C, where he said

> "Despite ample warnings in the past, the Inland Revenue appear to be persisting in the practice of appearing by a departmental official in cases where millions of pounds are at stake and the law is complex. In my opinion that practice should be reviewed in the interests of the general body of taxpayers."

That practice continues in cases which involve millions of pounds. The clear statement in para. 5.3 of the Green Paper is ignored.

TRANSITIONAL ARRANGEMENTS

12.36 The transitional arrangements proposed would in any event require further consideration. As drafted, they could have unfortunate consequences, for example, for barristers who having practised at the independent Bar for a number of years are temporarily in employment. Such barristers, if they wished to return to the independent Bar, could find themselves having lost the rights of audience in every Court which they would have, as of right, if they returned to the independent Bar now. Anomalies such as these would in any event have to be resolved, if a fair deal for those already qualified were to be achieved.

DIRECT ACCESS TO COUNSEL

12.37 Under this head it is necessary to distinguish between two entirely different types of access to barristers:

(1) direct access by the lay client to the barrister without the intervention of another professional, i.e. the barrister taking direct instructions from the lay client and not acting as a consultant: this is referred to as "Lay Access";
(2) direct access by solicitors and other professionals, who having been instructed by lay clients, instruct barristers on a consultant basis: this is referred to as "Professional Access".

LAY ACCESS

12.38 If the Bar is to continue as a consultant profession, then Lay Access is not compatible with the Bar's consultant status. It is of the essence of practice at the independent Bar that

(1) barristers devote themselves entirely to the presentation of cases in Court (and to specialist advice) and are therefore able to gain the benefits of constant practice;
(2) barristers do not have the facilities or staff to deal on a continuing basis with lay clients or to take witnesses' proofs or to prepare files of documents for use in Court; in this work solicitors specialise and have the necessary facilities and staff for this purpose;
(3) barristers are able to keep their fees to a level below those of solicitors because of the limited overheads that they need to incur.

Lord Mackay recognised the importance of *not* allowing Lay Access to barristers when he said to the Scottish Royal Commission (3 July 1978, page 3) in answer to a question from Lord Hughes "whether there might be a right of direct access to Counsel",

"it was more difficult to be objective in such circumstances, and closer involvement with clients and witnesses made it easier to form a wrong opinion or to get the wrong impression of the case. He thought that being the presenter of the case as well as the investigator led to problems, e.g. a risk of inadvertently omitting to lead in court a point of evidence."

12.39   If the Bar were permitted to accept Lay Access, there would inevitably be pressure from lay clients to come direct. Once some barristers in a particular area had accepted Lay Access, others would have to accept it in order to compete. Over a period if Lay Access were permitted, this would lead to extensive Lay Access. Lay Access would alter the whole structure of the Bar, and with the proposed changes in rights of audience, partnerships and multi-disciplinary practices would turn the Bar into another solicitors profession. There would effectively be fusion of the professions, and there would cease to be any real purpose in having different professions. Further, the lay client would not be able to make a fully informed choice. An uninformed choice is no real choice, as the Monopolies and Mergers Commission (MMC) pointed out in its recent report on advertising by medical practitioners.

12.40   The consequences for defendants in criminal cases and litigants in civil cases would be expensive, in terms of time, cost and quality:

(1) *Time*   Without independent specialists in advocacy, cases would take longer to try, as they do in the U.S.A. and Canada; advocates would have less constant practice because they would have to deal with preparatory work as well as Court work.

(2) *Cost*   The overheads of the Bar would rise towards the solicitors' level. The consequence would be higher costs for the payer of fees, whether the individual or the general body of taxpayers through Legal Aid. Because cases would take longer, more Courts and more Judges would be required.

(3) *Quality*   Barristers are not perfect. But they can justly claim that the overall standards of advocacy are higher under the present system than in countries such as the U.S.A. where there is no division of function between barristers and solicitors. Lay Access, by preventing barristers concentrating on Court work, and achieving higher standards by constant practice, would lower overall standards.

12.41   In para. 8.7 of the main Green Paper the Government recognises the danger that Lay Access to the Bar could substantially reduce the number of independent barristers and the choice of independent advocates available to all. That is one of the few paragraphs in the Green Papers which address, with any understanding, the adverse effects of the Government's proposals.

But the truth is that the Lay Access proposals cannot be viewed in isolation. As has been made clear in Chapter 10 above, what needs to be looked at is the combination of the proposals on (1) multi-disciplinary partnerships (2) partnerships at the Bar (3) Lay Access (4) rights of audience (5) conveyancing. Together these proposals would result in a reduction of choice, access and competition. The Government go on in para. 8.8 to express the hope and expectation that a free market would flourish despite the proposed changes. That is based apparently on undisclosed anecdotal evidence from other common law jurisdictions, and the supposed success of English barristers in Europe. Those matters are dealt with in Chapter 21 below. They do not support the Government's hope or its expectation.

PROFESSIONAL ACCESS

12.42 The Bar as a consultant profession has received its instructions from solicitors in private practice, and also in certain circumstances from other professionals including patent and trade mark agents, parliamentary agents, government, local authority and public authority lawyers, employed barristers and solicitors, and foreign lawyers. The Bar Council decided in principle in 1986 to extend the classes of professionals who could instruct barristers directly without the intervention of solicitors. That was not viewed with favour by the Law Society. The Bar Council agreed to await the views of the Marre Committee, which concluded that a barrister should be able to act on the instructions of a member of another specialist profession (para. 18.63). This was accepted by the Bar Council on 12 November 1988 and the necessary amendments to the Code of Conduct were passed by the Bar Council on 18 March 1989 and came into force on 3 April 1989. These enable barristers to receive instructions direct from members of recognised professional bodies. The bodies recognised by 3 April 1989 were the Institute of Chartered Accountants in England and Wales, the Chartered Association of Certified Accountants and the Royal Institution of Chartered Surveyors. Other such bodies will be recognised in due course: that will be a continuing process. Professional Access will not include instructing barristers to appear in the higher courts or the County Court or Employment Appeals Tribunal, which are regarded by the Judges as requiring a barrister to be instructed by a qualified solicitor. Professional Access will not be allowed if at any stage a barrister considers that the interests of the lay client or of the administration of justice require that a solicitor should be instructed.

12.43 With growth of the existing professions and the creation of new professions, Professional Access will enable the lay public to seek the advice and other services of barristers through referral by professionals other than solicitors in a widening range of matters. That will reduce costs and avoid the structural anomalies which can result if the intervention of a solicitor is insisted on unnecessarily. An accountant can get advice directly from the Bar on a client's tax problems. A surveyor can instruct the Bar direct to appear at a planning inquiry at which the surveyor will be the main witness for the client; the surveyor and the barrister can together prepare the client's case, each fulfilling his or her specialised functions, without the need for a solicitor.

12.44 This Professional Access will be a sensible use of the Bar's skills as specialist consultants. Lay Access would damage or destroy the particular skills and functions of trained and experienced barristers. Professional Access will enhance and make best use of those skills and functions. This is the essence of specialisation.

ATTENDANCE ON COUNSEL

12.45 It is often said by those outside the profession that the English system requires two lawyers (a barrister and a solicitor) where other systems manage with one. That is wrong, as the Chief Justice of the U.S.A. pointed out: para. 21.34 below. The work of preparation by a solicitor and the work of preparation and presentation by a barrister have to be done in any event, whether they are done by one lawyer or by two lawyers. The advantages of the English system are that each kind of work is done by a professional specialising in that work, that the work in Court and in preparing for Court has to be done by the barrister himself or herself, and that because the Bar is specialised primarily in Court work it is cheaper than a solicitor would be. Further, in any case where the facts are complex the task of preparation for trial would have to be done by more than one lawyer, and two lawyers would in any event be involved. The different specialities of the anaesthetist and the surgeon, both of which are essential, are analogous.

12.46 But it has long been recognised by the Bar that, once a relatively straightforward case has reached the stage of trial, it may not be **necessary** for the barrister presenting the case to be attended by a solicitor or even a representative of the solicitor (although this may still be **desirable**, as considered in para. 12.48 below). (The Bar and the Government have expressed concern at the practice of some solicitors to have in attendance on barristers, particularly in the Crown Court, a resting actor or other person not on the staff of the firm who has no knowledge of the case and whose sole function is to give the impression that there is a solicitor's representative present.)

12.47 Accordingly in its Code of Conduct the Bar permits a barrister to appear unattended in Magistrates Courts and the Crown Court if the barrister is satisfied that both the interest of the lay client and the interests of justice will not be prejudiced by non-attendance of a solicitor's representative. The Bar also has under consideration similar provisions for cases in the County Court.

12.48 The cases in which it may be necessary or desirable for the barrister to be attended by a solicitor or a solicitor's representative **with a full knowledge of the case** include, for example:-

(1) All cases involving complex facts: almost all cases in the High Court are of this nature, and many Crown Court cases are also.
(2) Cases in which during the course of the trial there are likely to be or are matters needing to be done which the barrister cannot do at the same time as presenting the case to the Court. In these cases, if barristers are unattended, the time of the Court and the other party to the proceedings may be wasted by adjournments. In such cases the provision of attendance is both efficient and cost-effective, provided that the person attending the barrister knows the case and is competent to do what is required.
(3) Cases in which it is undesirable for the barrister as advocate to be involved personally in the preparation of evidence. In the main Green Paper at para. 4.15(c) it is recognised that in such cases, in particular serious cases in the Crown Court, the advocate should not be involved in this way. The preparation of evidence in any serious or complex case does not stop when the trial begins. So in such cases attendance is always desirable, and may be necessary.

In such cases there is always a balance to be struck, and no rigid rule can be laid down. But the principle must be that the more serious and important the case, the more necessary and desirable is the detachment of the barrister as the advocate from the witnesses; and this applies in criminal cases in the Crown Court, whether the barrister is prosecuting or defending.

12.49 The Government proposes (main Green Paper, para. 7.4) that in all cases those who are paying for in-court work should be allowed to decide whether there should be attendance in Court, and that there should be no requirement in professional codes of conduct for such attendance in certain cases.

12.50 This proposal has to be put in context:-

(1) It is not just the client's interest which is to be considered. The interests of justice require that the public interest in proper use of scarce Court and Judge resources should be considered.

(2) In many cases it is not the client but the Legal Aid scheme which is paying. So the Government's proposal would give to the Government working through the Legal Aid Board an absolute power to veto attendance in court if it chose.

(3) Adjournments made necessary by the lack of proper attendance may make the hearing inefficient, and may, in total, cost more than any saving through non-attendance. The President of the Employment Appeal Tribunal (EAT) has drawn particular attention to the delays to other appeals, the inefficiencies, and the additional costs resulting from lack of proper attendance of solicitors on barristers appearing in appeals from Industrial Tribunals to the EAT. Similar concerns have been expressed by Judges sitting in the Crown Court, the High Court and the Court of Appeal.

12.51 The Bar Council strongly opposes the proposal that the paying client and the Government paying for Legal Aid cases should have the unfettered power to decide on attendance or no attendance. The Bar Council has placed on the barrister the responsibility to balance the interests of the lay client (and the taxpayer through the Legal Aid Scheme) with the interests of justice. There is no evidence that barristers take this decision unwisely.

12.52 Barristers are responsible not only to the client, but also to the Court. It is the view of the Bar Council that

(1) the barrister should be required, as now, to make the decision, after consultation with the instructing solicitor, in the interests of justice and of the lay client;

(2) the barrister should be responsible for justifying her or his decision to the Court as well as to the lay client;

(3) in cases where the balance between the interests of justice and the lay client is particularly difficult, the barrister will be able to consult senior members of the profession before the trial;

(4) at a pre-trial hearing or during the trial the Judge should have power to direct attendance if that is considered by the Judge to be necessary or desirable in the interests of justice.

13

The Crown Prosecution Service

13.1 The creation of the Crown Prosecution Service (CPS) arose from the Royal Commission on Criminal Procedure which, in 1981, recommended a statutorily based Prosecution Service for England and Wales. The Commission defined the functions of the new service in the following terms:-

(1) the conduct of all criminal cases once the initial decision to proceed has been taken by the police;
(2) the provision of legal advice to the police;
(3) the provision of advocates in the Magistrates' Courts in all cases where proceedings are commenced by the police, and the briefing of Counsel in all cases tried on indictment in the Crown Court.

13.2 When the Crown Court was created in 1971 the Courts Act empowered the Lord Chancellor to give directions on the respective rights of audience of barristers and solicitors in the Crown Court. In giving his first direction under the Act, the Lord Chancellor of the day, Lord Hailsham, said in the House of Lords on 9 February 1972:

"I find no sufficient reason for altering the present balance between the Bar and the solicitors' profession in the conduct of prosecutions, whether by public authorities or private individuals. *I must also emphasise that I regard the presentation of the prosecution case in the higher Courts by Counsel, properly instructed by a solicitor, as an added safeguard of individual freedom since it involves that a second opinion is always brought to bear*". (our emphasis)

13.3 Since 1972, the position has been reviewed by a number of authoritative bodies. Between July 1976 and October 1979, the Royal Commission on Legal Services under the Chairmanship of Lord Benson, considered evidence from the widest possible spectrum of interest. The Royal Commission reported in clear terms that the distribution of rights of audience should remain as they were (and now are). The report made special mention of the Prosecution in paras. 18.43 to 18.45 of the report:

"In one significant aspect the arrangements serve what many regard, we think rightly, as an important public purpose, by ensuring that in the Crown Court the case for the prosecution is put by an advocate who is independent both of the police and the prosecuting authority. . . . Whatever the outcome of the Royal Commission on Criminal Procedure, we think that the effect of the present arrangement on prosecution work should not be disturbed. It provides in every case an advocate from the available range of privately practising barristers, who is seen by the court, the accused and the public at large, to be independent of the police and the prosecuting authorities; one who, by the nature of his training and daily practice, is more likely to be able to bring the essential quality of detachment and balance to bear on the problem in individual cases. These are considerations which we regard as crucial, not only to the actual conduct of a jury trial but also to the proper administration of justice in general, including the institution or continuance of criminal proceedings, the acceptance of proposed pleas of guilty and the proper handling of evidential problems".

13.4 The report went on to consider further consequences of enabling employed prosecutors to appear in the Crown Court. It cited the unfortunate separation which had already appeared in some magistrates' courts between prosecuting solicitors drawn from prosecution departments and defending solicitors drawn from private firms of solicitors. The Royal Commission deprecated the lack of interchange between the two groups because, if encouraged, "the trend would lead to the loss of the substantial advantages to be gained by practitioners with experience in both types of work, and to the identification of certain lawyers as being invariably on the side of, or invariably in opposition to, the authorities. Experience outside the United Kingdom suggests that this would be a retrograde step to take and would not contribute to demonstrably just and fair results." (para. 18.45)

13.5 The report of the Royal Commission on Legal Services was not the final word on the subject. The Crown Prosecution Service, as has been noted earlier, came about as a direct consequence of the Royal Commission on Criminal Procedure, which took evidence between February 1978 and January 1981. In para. 7.19 of its report the Commission considered the question of the presentation of prosecutions in the Crown Court. Most witnesses, the report states, thought that in general the structure of audience rights should remain as at present. The Commissioners themselves were split in the recommendation which they made. In the summary of recommendations, "The Balance of Criminal Justice", at pages 13 and 14 of the Commission's Report it was stated:-

"Some of the Commission consider that the new responsibilities of the Crown Prosecutor's department justify the lifting of the restriction on solicitors and barristers in the department being able to prosecute in the Crown Court. Others, however, do not see the need for any change in the existing rules governing rights of audience."

That the majority were in favour of the existing rules is borne out by the recommendation that the functions of the new service should be to brief Counsel in all cases tried on indictment in the Crown Court.

13.6 The Government response to the report of the Royal Commission on Legal Services was presented to Parliament by the Lord Chancellor in November 1983. At page 19 of the White Paper is set out the Government's Response to Chapter 18 of the Royal Commission's report on rights of audience, in which the Government agreed that there should be no general extension of the rights of audience of solicitors.

13.7 The White Paper of November 1983 accepting the recommendations of the Royal Commission on Legal Services was published after the Government had received the report of the Royal Commission on Criminal Procedure.

13.8 On 19 July 1984 the Attorney-General wrote to the Chairman of the Bar concerning rights of audience for the proposed CPS, a letter in which he stated:

"The legislation will hopefully serve as the framework for our prosecution system for many years to come and one cannot predict what circumstances might arise. In its early days the resources of the new service will be fully stretched by its increased workload in the magistrates' courts, the extent of which is illustrated by estimates that the new service will need to recruit on a progressive basis some 400 new lawyers. Furthermore, *such a step could only be seriously contemplated as and when the new service was properly established and had gained the confidence of the legal professions and the judiciary*. I cannot, of course, bind my successor but nonetheless feel confident on this basis to reassure you that *no additional rights of audience are likely to be sought for members of the new service for a considerable period after 1986*." (our emphasis)

13.9 On 2 August 1984 the Attorney-General wrote again to the Chairman of the Bar, stating that:-

"I see it as important that, particularly in the provinces, there should be a strong affinity between the members of the [CPS] and the local Law Society or Bar as appropriate. Such contact would do much to enhance the professionalism of the new service and ensure a sound and judicious attitude amongst its members towards their work. It would also do much to assuage anxieties of those who foresee the organisation either becoming introverted or developing too close a relationship with the police".

13.10 As a consequence of the Report of the Royal Commission on Criminal Procedure, the Government introduced a draft Bill, The Prosecution of Offences Bill, into the House of Lords in the autumn of 1984. On 29 November 1984, when introducing the second reading, the Minister of State, Lord Elton, said:

> "*I should emphasise that the Government holds strongly to the view that rights of audience in Crown Court trials should continue to be confined to an independent Bar which both prosecutes and defends.*" (our emphasis)

This was again confirmed by Lord Elton on behalf of the Government in a letter to Lord Wigoder of 12 December 1984:

> "There is no intention to extend these rights [of audience] any further, for example to include the conduct of criminal trials before the Crown Court: in this connection the Government have recently reaffirmed their acceptance of the Benson Commission's recommendation that in general rights of audience in the Crown Court should be the preserve of an independent Bar."

13.11 These assurances were repeated by the Lord Chancellor in the House of Lords on 17 January 1985.

13.12 In a debate on the Bill in the House of Commons on 16 April 1985, Rt. Hon. John Morris MP (Aberavon) said this:

> "Despite the Government's assurances, I fear the long-term future – perhaps not so long term – of the criminal Bar. What will happen when the Treasury gets its hands on that? Who can put his hand on his heart and say that in 5 or 10 years' time there will not be a Rayner report or something of that ilk, which advocates more and more in-house work? I fear that that will be the Treasury approach as surely as night follows day, and it would strike at the heart of an independent profession which I believe to be one of the bastions of liberty."

Mr. Morris' prediction was more accurate than he could have expected: the period was less than 4 years.

13.13 In the same debate Rt. Hon. Mark Carlisle MP (now Lord Carlisle of Bucklow) asked for further assurances as to the position in the Crown Court. In his view

> ". . . it would be totally unacceptable if the price for an independent prosecuting service was to be the death of an Independent Bar. . . . If the prosecution of cases, whether they be pleas of guilty, committals for sentence or appeals, were to be taken out of the hands of the Bar in the Crown Court, that would have such a deleterious effect on the chance of young members starting at the Bar as to be a grave attack on the future of an independent Bar."

This concern for the public interest in the continuance of an independent Bar both prosecuting and defending cases in the Crown Court was expressed by a number of other Members in the same debate.

13.14 The Attorney General, Sir Patrick Mayhew Q.C. (then the Solicitor-General) responded in that debate on 16 April 1985 by repeating the assurances given by the Lord Chancellor. He said:

> "As was made clear in the other place on 17 January, it is no part of the Government's intention to use that clause as a means of altering the balance of the two parts of the legal profession. *The Government holds strongly to the view that the public interest requires* the continuance of a strong and independent Bar and *that rights of audience in the Crown Court should accordingly continue to be confined as at present to an independent Bar which prosecutes and defends.* That was accepted, I think, by the Right Hon. and Learned Member for Aberavon . . . I confirm that Clause 4 does not confer upon prosecuting solicitors the rights of audience in the Crown Court now enjoyed by defending solicitors under the provisions of a direction made by the Lord Chancellor under section 83 of the earlier Act." (our emphasis)

13.15 On 25 April 1985 the Attorney-General again confirmed that the Benson Commission's recommendation against extension of rights of audiences in the Crown Court had been accepted by the Government.

13.16 It can be clearly seen, therefore, that the introduction of the Prosecution of Offences Act in 1985 and the creation of the CPS as an independent prosecuting authority was to provide for a significant new measure of independence and balance at the stage of preparing a prosecution case and the exercise of the prosecution function at Magistrates' Courts. It was intended (and clear assurances were given by the Government to that effect) that there should be no alteration in the safeguard that prosecutions in the Crown Court should be presented by independent barristers.

13.17 The matter was considered again in the White Paper which was issued by the present Government on 26 March 1987, "Legal Aid in England and Wales: A New Framework". In Chapter 6, entitled, "Procedures", the Government set out at para. 57, that *"the Government does not intend to extend the rights of audience in the Crown Court. This would be contrary to the view, accepted by the Government, of the Royal Commission on Legal Services."* (our emphasis)

13.18 In the Marre Committee's Report of July 1988, that Committee unanimously recommended that "rights of audience in the Crown Court should not at present be extended to lawyers employed by the Crown Prosecution Service." (para. 18.106) It noted that "there seem to be insufficient qualified staff for all the demands currently made for their services in the magistrates' courts."

13.19 The Bar of England and Wales welcomed the creation of the CPS. In addition, at the special request of the Attorney-General, the Bar changed its rules of conduct and practice to enable barristers to accept work in the Magistrates' Courts on a sessional basis rather than a case by case basis, in order to give assistance to the newly formed CPS which was at the outset, and is still today, suffering from a severe shortage of manpower. The Bar has continued to support the CPS and welcomes the CPS's recent efforts to obtain more financial assistance from the Government so as to secure better terms for its employees in an attempt to improve recruitment.

13.20 In the recent report by Sir Robert Andrew, a former senior civil servant, into the Government Legal Services which was published in the week before the publication of these Green papers, the extension of rights of audience in the Crown Court to Crown Prosecutors was suggested as giving "a much needed fillip to the morale of those now serving and [making] the work more attractive to the high-quality recruits who are badly needed." (para. 7.13)

13.21 The statements of fundamental principle set out in the reports of both Royal Commissions were accepted by the Government in November 1983, in the debates on the Prosecution of Offences Bill in November 1984 and January and April 1985, and in particular in the re-affirmed declaration of the Government in the Legal Aid White paper as recently as March 1987. In contrast to those statements of principle, the suggestion that an increased right of audience for Crown Prosecutors in the Crown Court should be considered as a means of boosting morale and making a Civil Service post more attractive is an unacceptable approach to a matter which the Government has always regarded as a vital element in the administration of justice.

13.22 That approach is also wholly contrary to this Government's normal approach, which is to privatise whatever can be sensibly privatised, and not to nationalise what can be done better by independent persons practising in private practice. The creation of a nationalised monopoly is inconsistent with the Government's stated aim of ensuring competition. The Government proposes to substitute to an undisclosed extent for the services of the independent Bar (which the Lord Chancellor regards as the most competitive of all professions) a nationalised monopoly service without competition, and protected from the forces of the market place which the Government regards as an overriding "first principle".

This is the more surprising since it is proposed at a time when the CPS has yet to establish itself firmly in the Magistrates' Courts. It still suffers from recruitment problems. It has lost many of the experienced practitioners whom it inherited from the County prosecuting departments. There remain major problems of organisation and management to be tackled.

13.23   Sir Robert Andrew presented two arguments in support of his thesis. The *first* was to praise the Procurator Fiscal's Department in Scotland as an example of Prosecuting Officers who attain a high degree both of ability and ethical standards within a prosecution role. The *second* was to cite the Treasury Counsel at the Central Criminal Court in London as examples of full time prosecutors who maintain high standards.

13.24   As illustrations of the argument for employed prosecutors for the Crown Court, neither example bears detailed examination.

SCOTLAND AND THE OFFICE OF PROCURATOR FISCAL

13.25   The prosecution of crime by employed lawyers in the Procurator Fiscal Service is of long standing in Scotland, being at least 2 centuries old. Nevertheless the Service suffers from a serious recruitment problem; there is a shortage of staff in general, but particularly of legal staff. As the National Audit Office (NAO) recorded in its recent report on the Service (7 February 1989), the view of Procurator Fiscals is that, at present, to keep up with the demands made of the Service depends on an increasing amount of unpaid overtime and goodwill of the staff. But this cannot continue indefinitely and with the rising crime rate the Service will face difficulties in maintaining standards (para. 5.11).

13.26   The Procurators Fiscal do not see the "success rate" of convictions as being an appropriate measure of adequate preparation or fair presentation of the prosecution case. But it is apparent that this is a matter to which the Service has regard and which the NAO considered in some detail and recommended as a test of "efficiency" (paras. 5.2 and 5.3). The danger of such an approach to criminal prosecutions is an obvious one. Employed prosecutors can readily be pressured to increase their "success rate", and such pressure is inimical to the fair and independent presentation of prosecution cases. Such pressure is a not uncommon feature of the U.S. Attorney and District Attorney systems in the U.S.A. In Hong Kong and

Singapore, though "success rates" are not formally maintained, it is well known that informal league tables of the "success rates" of individual employed prosecutors are kept. Even in the fledgling CPS in England and Wales pressures are sometimes put on barristers appearing for the CPS not to exercise their independent judgment in the conduct of cases, the implication being that if they fail to do so they may not be instructed in future by the local CPS office, and their grading by CPS may be affected.

13.27   It was precisely to avoid this kind of problem with an employed prosecution service that this Government, through the Home Secretary, the Lord Chancellor, the Attorney-General and the Solicitor-General, in 1983 (when accepting in the White Paper the recommendation of the Royal Commission on Legal Services), in 1984 and 1985 (in relation to the establishment of the CPS), and in 1987 (in the White Paper on Legal Aid), gave firm assurances and stated its firm policy not to alter the position on rights of audience in the Crown Court.

13.28   Differences between the Scottish and English legal systems are material. The different sizes of service and the much more dispersed service in England and Wales make it harder to emulate what is good in the Procurator Fiscal Service, so as to gain public confidence, and the confidence of Judges and juries. As a fledgling service the CPS is a long way from gaining that confidence fully.

13.29   In Scotland the Sheriff Court jurisdiction is restricted to offences which carry a maximum sentence of 3 years imprisonment. In England and Wales, since the Criminal Justice Act 1967 abolished the distinction between felonies and misdemeanours, there is a very small number of offences which carry a maximum sentence of 2 years. A useful example is that any offence of theft, even of a bottle of milk, carries a maximum punishment of 10 years in prison. There may be arguments for a re-examination of the classification of offences, and of the jurisdictions which can try those offences. But these considerations directed to the administration of justice are not touched on in the Green Papers.

13.30   Even in the two centuries-old Scottish Service problems of consistency of policy have not yet been tackled or solved. For example in 1987 the proportion of cases in which the Service decided to take no proceedings ranged from 2.5% of cases in Forfar to 25.5% of cases in Edinburgh, 25.3% of cases in Aberdeen, and 25.0% of cases in Glasgow. The NAO found no discernible pattern to the incidence of "no proceedings" cases. In areas with a similar number of cases there was still a remarkable inconsistency: for about 14,000 cases in each of Aberdeen and Dundee the proportion of "no proceedings" cases was 25.3% in Aberdeen and 6% in Dundee. As the NAO observed (para. 4.8):

> "There is a risk to the administration of justice if cases are not pursued for reasons other than the merits of the case, and if there are wide variations between fiscal offices in the chances of an individual reported offence not being pursued."

That such inconsistencies can be present in the long-established Scottish Service is a warning as to the prospects for the CPS in England and Wales which has yet to be established on any sound footing.

One reason for the remarkably high proportion of "no proceedings" cases is no doubt the problem well-known in the U.S.A. and Canada. Those who work as full-time prosecutors in U.S. Attorneys and District Attorneys offices in the U.S.A. or in the Crown Attorneys Departments in Canada need to maintain high "success rates" of convictions in the prosecutions they conduct. Such a success rate can be maintained in part by not proceeding with prosecutions in which, though there is a case to answer, it is thought by the prosecutor to be safer not to proceed so that the danger of affecting his success rate is not risked. Full-time prosecutors are just as likely to fail to prosecute in cases that ought to be brought, as to prosecute with excessive zeal cases that ought (as all prosecution cases ought) to be conducted fairly.

13.31 In England and Wales and also in Scotland the problem is at heart one of resources. One of the reasons why the Government now wishes to go back on its assurances and reverse its policy, by extending the CPS prosecutors' rights of audience, is its desire to make prosecutions cheaper. But a properly funded Service employing adequate staff at adequate salaries would probably not be much cheaper, if at all, than the use of non-salaried, independent barristers, if the full costs of the CPS in terms of administration, offices, salaries, pensions, support staff, libraries, and so forth were taken into account. It should also be noted that the solicitors in private practice used by the CPS in Magistrates' Courts receive a sessions fee which may be as high as *double* that paid to independent barristers.

13.32 Even if the Government were to succeed in making the CPS cheaper, cheapness would be at the expense of quality. Quality in prosecutions is vital

(1) in the public interest, in ensuring that those who are guilty are brought to justice, and duly punished, and

The Crown Prosecution Service

(2) in the interest of both the public and the defendants, in ensuring that prosecutions are fairly conducted and that prosecutors are not under pressure to secure results.

TREASURY COUNSEL

13.33 The second argument in the Andrew Report relies on the existence of a small group of Treasury Counsel at the Central Criminal Court. This is said to demonstrate that the full time practice of the prosecutor's role does not constitute any danger to the maintenance of a rigorous independence.

13.34 An examination of the facts shows that this argument is not well founded. Since the appointment of Sir Harry Poland as the first Treasury Counsel in July 1865, only 54 members of the Bar had joined the ranks of Senior and Junior Treasury Counsel, between that date and the appointment of the present first Senior Prosecuting Counsel at the Central Criminal Court who became Junior Treasury Counsel in July 1977. Each of those appointed as Treasury Counsel has been called to the Bar and has practised in Criminal Chambers for a period approaching 10 years before the date of their appointment. During that period of time they have both prosecuted and defended regularly. They have had the benefit of the Chambers structure in which they share experiences with other members of the Bar, specialising in criminal cases and appearing both for the prosecution and for the defence. Their appointment as Treasury Counsel does not mean they are debarred from accepting work on behalf of the defence, though in practical terms, the demands which are made on them by the Director of Public Prosecutions mean that they can only accept a limited amount of defence work. Each of them, however, accepts a limited amount of defence work during the period of their appointment, and after a certain time they return to general criminal practice after taking Silk.

THE MAIN DANGER, AND HOW IT IS NOW AVOIDED

13.35 The principal danger is that the constant exercise of the prosecution function erodes that essential balance of approach which prosecuting counsel must maintain. The important need to avoid specialisation in prosecution work has been recognised and emphasised by both the Director of Public Prosecutions (Mr. Allan Green Q.C.) and his Deputy Director (Mr. David Gandy).

13.36 This is so intrinsic to the role of prosecuting counsel that in July 1986 a committee under the Chairmanship of the Hon. Mr. Justice Farquharson, who was appointed by the Lord Chief Justice, reported in these terms:-

> "There is no doubt that the obligations of prosecution counsel are different from those of counsel instructed for the defence in a Criminal case or of counsel instructed in Civil matters. His duties are wider, both to the Court and to the public at large. Furthermore, having regard to his duty to present the case for the prosecution fairly to the Jury he has a greater independence of those instructing him than that enjoyed by other counsel. It is well known to every practitioner that counsel for the prosecution must conduct his case moderately, albeit firmly. He must not strive unfairly to obtain a conviction; he must not press his case beyond the limits which the evidence permits; he must not invite the jury to convict on evidence which in his own judgment no longer sustains the charge laid in the indictment. If the evidence of a witness is undermined or severely blemished in the course of the cross-examination, prosecution counsel must not present him to the jury as worthy of a credibility he no longer enjoys . . . it is for these reasons that great responsibility is placed upon prosecution counsel."

13.37 It only has to be stated that at present the CPS has available to it more than 3,500 practising barristers of the Bar in independent practice who hold themselves out as available and specialised in criminal work, to understand that this rigorous maintenance of the role of prosecuting counsel is the reality today. Not only is such a range of counsel open to the CPS, but the CPS has undertaken and continually keeps under review the grading of independent counsel into four classes of prosecutor, both to simplify the task of selecting the appropriate counsel, and to keep under review a monitoring system for the promotion of the more able and the maintenance of standards. This classification of counsel is essentially the responsibility of the CPS as the professional client of the members of the Bar. But in its task it is aided by liaison committees on which serve senior and experienced members of the Bar appointed by or including the Leaders of the Circuits whose opinions are sought as to the particular merits of individual counsel.

13.38 There can be no prospect that an expansion of the state CPS to embrace a Crown Court advocacy division will ever be able to achieve such a range of established and proven skill and ability. Crown Court work, by its very nature, is never trivial. It will always involve the liberty of the subject. If it is to be suggested that there is less important work currently being conducted in the Crown Court, then the solution is for Parliament to identify that work, and to change the nature of its classification so that it no longer merits the privilege of trial by jury, assuming that public opinion were to accept such a reclassification.

13.39 An additional merit of the present system by which independent counsel is instructed in the Crown Court is that the great variety of available barristers enables the CPS to brief suitable barristers for trials. The professional client, the CPS, has the ultimate sanction. It may choose whom it wishes to instruct and may decline to continue to instruct counsel who fail to match the appropriate standards of ability and confidence. A system of employed prosecutors could only mean a lowering of standards.

THE GREEN PAPERS

13.40 All the most authoritative commentators, before the Government's proposed changes were announced in these Green Papers, have made it plain that the statutory division of the function of prosecuting authority from that of the police authority, whilst a necessary and welcome development, is only one stage in the maintenance of the responsible conduct of criminal prosecutions. The main Green Paper recognises this and sets out in para. 5.11 the following proposition:

> "In particular, in the case of prosecution work the Government endorses the principle recommended in the report of the Royal Commission on Criminal Procedure . . . (the Philips Report) that there should be a clear separation of responsibility for the conduct of the prosecution from the conduct of the investigative process."

13.41 The same paragraph (para. 5.11) goes on to state the following tentative proposition:-

> "The Government therefore considers that it is likely to be feasible as a matter of principle for lawyers employed by the Crown Prosecution Service to have rights of audience in all the criminal courts, provided that they can satisfy the appropriate advocacy requirements and undertake to abide by the relevant codes of conduct; and provided that it is adequately recognised by practical safeguards that their duty to the court must take precedence over any responsibility they have to their employer."

13.42 The Government is not proposing to limit such extensions of rights of audience to lawyers employed in the Crown Prosecution Service, but clearly considers that this may extend to other government departments. Para. 5.12 of the main Green Paper states that

> "So far as rights of audience for lawyers employed on prosecution work by other Government departments are concerned, and also for lawyers

employed by other bodies which undertake prosecutions, consideration will need to be given to how they might meet the Philips principle of separation of responsibility especially in the case of the more serious cases which are tried in the Crown Court, before any changes in their rights of audience are made. . . . departments would at least need to be able to demonstrate a clear structural separation in the arrangement of the department of those staff involved in investigations from those responsible for conducting prosecutions; and, in some cases, the solution might be to transfer responsibility for the lawyers who have carriage of prosecution work from the department concerned to the Attorney General."

13.43 These two passages from paras. 5.11 and 5.12 of the main Green Paper underline the undesirability of permitting employed prosecutors from the CPS and other Government departments into the Crown Court. The principle of independence from the prosecuting authority will not be achieved by these proposals. There must be a real separation of responsibility, both in terms of the practical qualities which the prosecutor brings to his duties, and also in the perception with which the prosecutor is viewed by the public.

13.44 The close and essentially confidential relationship between the police as investigators and the CPS as the prosecuting authority inevitably carries with it serious practical difficulties in the maintenance of an independent and uninfluenced approach. The most obvious difficulty is the reality that the lawyers employed in the CPS are exclusively engaged upon the preparation and the presentation of prosecution cases. It will remain a necessary element in the maintenance of public confidence in the CPS that criminal cases in the Crown Court should be presented by those in private practice. In most cases it is only after the case has been committed to the Crown Court that the barrister is briefed. The advantage of this is that the barrister comes to the preparation of the case with a completely fresh mind. He is able to examine the strengths and weaknesses of the case. He may have to come to practical decisions about the case on any one of a range of features of every day prosecutions about which he may find himself to be at odds with senior police officers who have devoted much time and effort to the gathering of evidence in the investigation of the crime. It may well be that, despite all the effort that has been put into the arrest of a particular defendant, there are reasons why a prosecuting barrister has to insist that particular evidence may not be adduced in the trial.

13.45 It is neither a simple nor an attractive task to have to stand out against the introduction of such evidence, nor is it easy or straightforward to maintain a proper balance and fairness in presenting the facts to the court.

13.46 Crown Court prosecutions attract considerable local publicity. There is the danger that the association of particular employed lawyers with the local Crown Court will inevitably lead to the identification of that branch prosecutor as the local "Crown Court Prosecutor", creating the polarisation which is to be seen in the U.S.A. with District Attorneys seeking re-election and U.S. Attorneys seeking future employment: Chapter 21 below.

13.47 It is not suggested that the barrister in independent practice possesses some innate superior moral stance which is denied the employed solicitor or barrister. But the reality is that the circumstances under which the independent barrister receives and prepares his work, the manner in which he is paid for his work, his accountability for his work and the geographical circumstances in which barristers practise from Chambers, all combine together to ensure for the independent barrister freedom from external influence and pressure, and so far as any environment possibly can, the necessary independence and detachment of mind. Even those counsel who regularly attend a particular Crown Court do so in the capacity of defending in one case and prosecuting in another. The experience of appearing both for the prosecution and for the defence in criminal cases enables the barrister to do both jobs better. A barrister who is in an independent position and who is forced to look at cases from both perspectives is more likely to achieve fairness. If a prosecutor were put in a position in which he was not wholly independent (as is the case in the U.S.A. with U.S. and District Attorneys), he might fail to recognise occasions when he was not being entirely fair. It is not so much a lack of judgment, as the substitution of identification with the prosecution in place of wholly independent professional judgment.

13.48 It must equally be understood that there would also be a serious danger in counsel appearing always for the defence, as would be the case if much of the prosecution work in the Crown Court were to be done by the CPS through in-house lawyers. Those who in these circumstances would be instructed to appear only for the defence would run the risk of substituting identification with the defendant in place of independent professional judgment.

13.49 This polarisation between those always for the prosecution and those always for the defence was regarded as a serious danger by the Royal Commission on Legal Services (para. 18.45: see the quotation in para. 13.4 above).

13.50 In July 1985, addressing a conference in Hong Kong attended by a number of English Judges, the then leader of the Hong Kong

Bar, Henry Litton QC made reference to this lack of objectivity which may emerge within a system of state prosecutors. Under the sub-heading "Prosecution Mentality and the Crime Rate", Mr. Litton said:

"It has been said that there is an absence of the 'prosecution mentality' which is apparent under the American system. A state employed prosecutor may feel that his efficiency is to be measured by the rate of convictions he achieves. This pressure is absent where members of the Bar in private practice both prosecute and defend: within such a system an entrenched attitude to 'prosecution results' is unlikely to develop. Barristers who are under no peer pressure to achieve convictions (and such pressure will be particularly strong within the collegiate environment of a prosecutor's office) will be less amenable. Both because of the growth in crime rate and the increasing need to enlarge and strengthen the prosecution offices, a 'prosecution mentality' is likely to grow; no jurisdiction is immune; be it England, Hong Kong or other parts of the Commonwealth".

13.51 It was precisely for this reason that the Attorney-General has required the CPS to maintain the convention, subject only to limited exceptions, that independent barristers who practise on the local Circuit are briefed on the prosecution cases in that area:

"The Attorney-General considers it in the public interest that this convention should be maintained. That is because the maintenance of high standards of professional conduct, not least as regards the duty counsel owes to the Court, depends greatly upon 'peer group discipline'. This has traditionally exercised valuable influence upon the Bar, and the Attorney-General considers it important that it should continue to do so. It is also very helpful to the administration of justice if barristers become professionally known to the local judiciary before whom they appear." (CPS paper on selection of independent counsel instructed by the CPS, August 1987).

13.52 Using employed prosecutors would not achieve this "peer group discipline" now achieved by the Circuits, and standards would fall. But the Government is apparently not prepared to take the advice of two Royal Commissions, the Marre Committee, the Judiciary, the Attorney-General, past Lord Chancellors and many others, or to follow its own policy restated as recently as March 1987 (para. 13.17 above).

13.53 Not every barrister has invariably achieved the standard of fairness required of prosecuting counsel, though transgressions are rare. But the conduct of a prosecution by the independent barrister instructed for the purpose of that one case only is the surest safeguard against the development of the prosecution mentality. The criminal justice system in England and Wales has not always been free of such an influence. It was well known within certain county prosecuting authorities before the enactment of the Prosecution of Offences Act 1985 that individual county prosecuting solicitors took too keen an interest in the vigour and single-mindedness with which defendants were prosecuted. A number of distinguished Judges and senior members of the Bar share the valuable experience of having been removed from a county prosecuting solicitor's list of counsel for declining to conduct cases or to advance arguments in a manner which seemed to them to transgress the accepted role of counsel for the prosecution.

13.54 The consolidation of more than 88% of all criminal prosecutions in this country within the control of a single national prosecuting service has created a unique professional client whose influence and power far outstrips any other single consumer of advocacy talents. The CPS is still in its infancy. Its development has been beset by the consequences of inadequate resources and over-hasty introduction on a nationwide scale. This has caused a consequential loss of morale. Many experienced lawyers have left the service in order to find other positions in private practice or with other employers. Whatever else may be said, this stage of its development is not an appropriate moment to introduce any further rights of audience beyond the existing over-stretched capacity of the CPS.

13.55 Questions have been raised as to the extent to which the CPS is fulfilling its intended purpose, and particularly in relation to administrative problems, morale and under-staffing. It is understood that these matters have been the subject of an extensive internal enquiry, the results of which have not yet been published officially.

The Race Relations Committee of the Bar Council (of which the chairman is a High Court Judge) has expressed concern about the limited extent to which barristers from the ethnic minorities have been instructed by the CPS. This remains a matter of concern which is under regular review.

THE WAY AHEAD: THE BAR COUNCIL'S PROPOSALS

13.56 These are the Bar Council's proposals for the future conduct of prosecutions in England and Wales. They are constructive proposals designed to avoid the obvious pitfalls into which the Government's proposals would fall.

(1) The establishment of an effective pupillage system for CPS recruits has already been agreed between the Bar Council and the

CPS. Recruits to the CPS will first have 6 months pupillage in general common law chambers, gaining as broad an experience as possible: the intention is for the CPS to fund them. They will have a second 6 months pupillage with pupil masters in the CPS approved by the Bar Council for this purpose.

(2) The CPS and the Bar Council have agreed to cooperate fully in the training of barristers in the CPS: in particular, to ensure that they all have an understanding of the problems of those appearing for the defence.

(3) The CPS should ensure that, when filling its complement of *employed* lawyers, the necessary standard is maintained. Gaps in the CPS system should continue to be filled by the instruction of independent barristers on a sessions basis. Since independent barristers instructed on this basis may cost the taxpayer *one-half* of the cost of solicitors, the CPS should save money by instructing independent barristers where they are available and of the required standard. The Bar Council will ensure that independent barristers instructed by the CPS on a sessions basis provide the service to which the public are entitled: the Code of Conduct of the Bar will ensure that the same service must be given to every client, whether paying or legally-aided, or the CPS or other prosecution authority.

(4) Arrangements should be agreed between the Bar Council and the CPS so as to ease the mobility of barristers between CPS employment and independent practice, including temporary secondments from the independent Bar to the CPS and vice versa.

CROWN COURTS

(5) If Crown Prosecutors wished to advance to appearing in the Crown Court, they would apply to a committee composed of the Presiding Judge, the Leader of the Circuit, the President of the local Law Society and the senior CPS Prosecutor. If approved as being of the required standard, they would move to the independent Bar, either taking seats in Chambers with the assistance of the Circuit Leader, or joining the library system.

(6) By this process Crown Prosecutors would acquire a satisfactory career structure (but without the clear disadvantages of the Andrew and Green Paper proposal) and would become eligible for appointment as Queen's Counsel and for ultimate promotion to the Bench.

14

Independence of the Judges and the Legal Profession

14.1 "A strong and independent judiciary is one of the central supports upon which our liberties are based and upon which the rule of law depends": main Green Paper, para. 10.2. The need for an independent judiciary was fought for during the 17th century and won by the Act of Settlement of 1701. Since 1701 it has been settled that as a matter of law the Judges of the higher courts hold office while they are of good conduct and cannot be removed except on an address of both Houses of Parliament, and that as a matter of good governance the Judges are not to be influenced by the wishes of or pressure from the Government of the day, or any other powerful body.

14.2 Such an independent judiciary could not readily be recruited from a legal profession subservient to Government or to other vested interests. A judiciary drawn from lawyers in the Government Legal Service or the Crown Prosecution Service would not have had the constant training in independence of mind necessary for an independent judiciary, and would not be seen by the public as independent. A comparison of the Judges of England and Wales with the politically-influenced Judges of some European countries, and with the elected Judges in many States of the U.S.A., shows the importance of an independent judiciary, and of an independent profession providing an ample number of candidates eligible for appointment to the Bench.

14.3 The proposals in the main Green Paper involve substantial inroads on the independence of the Judges and on the independence of the legal profession, in these respects:-

(1) The Lord Chancellor would have power to decide (a) whether a particular specialist area of expertise of the legal profession

should be recognised as such; (b) what standards of education and training would be appropriate for such specialist area of expertise; (c) what particular body or bodies should be recognised as competent to authorise individual practitioners (whether lawyers or other practitioners) as specialists in that specialist area of expertise; (d) what body or bodies should cease to be so recognised; (e) what codes of conduct should be followed by practitioners authorised by such recognised body or bodies as specialists in that specialist area of expertise (paras. 3.12 and 3.13). It is not clear whether this power would be exercised by the Lord Chancellor directly or by statutory instrument.

(2) The Lord Chancellor would receive the advice of an Advisory Committee composed solely of persons appointed by the Lord Chancellor, with a majority of non-lawyers, and serviced by civil servants from the Lord Chancellor's Department, but the Lord Chancellor would be able to adopt or reject the advice of his Committee as he chose (paras. 3.12 to 3.14).

(3) The Lord Chancellor's power as referred to in (1) above, to decide what codes of conduct should apply to work done by the legal profession, would include power to impose codes specifically setting professional standards in relation to (a) the provision of legal advice and assistance generally; and (b) the particular issues concerning advocacy and connected with the handling of briefs and the general conduct of cases in Court (paras. 4.11 to 4.15).

(4) The Lord Chancellor would have similar power to accept or reject codes of conduct laid down by professional bodies in the legal profession as meeting or failing to meet the requirements for such codes laid down by the Lord Chancellor by statutory instrument (paras. 4.11 to 4.13).

(5) The Lord Chancellor would have power to decide whether each professional body had adequate arrangements for enforcing the codes of conduct, and if at any time he decided that its arrangements were not adequate, either to require it to change its arrangements, or to remove its recognition (paras. 3.12, 3.13, 4.13).

(6) The Lord Chancellor would receive the advice of the Advisory Committee on the matters set out in (3), (4) and (5) above but would be able to adopt or reject the advice of the Committee as he chose (paras. 3.12, 3.13, 4.11 to 4.13).

(7) The Lord Chancellor would have power to decide by statutory instrument in relation to rights of audience in the Courts, (a) which professional bodies satisfied him that their members were fit and proper persons to appear as advocates before any particular Court in order to obtain rights of audience for their members before that Court; (b) which professional bodies did

not so satisfy him; (c) which professional bodies, having previously so satisfied him, had ceased to satisfy him; (d) what lay representatives or what classes of lay representatives should have (or should cease to have) rights of audience before any particular Court; (e) what lawyers employed in the Crown Prosecution Service or in other Government Departments or by any other employer should have (or should cease to have) rights of audience in any particular Court; (f) which professional bodies should be authorised (or have their authorisation withdrawn) to grant advocacy certificates to their members entitling their members to have rights of advocacy in any particular Court; (g) what should be the requirements for obtaining each of the different kinds of advocacy certificate proposed; (h) what courses or other periods of training would have to be taken before any person could obtain an advocacy certificate, and what the length and content of each course or period of training should be; (i) what transitional arrangements for different classes of lawyer there should be (Chapter 5).

(8) The Lord Chancellor would receive the advice of the Advisory Committee and the Judiciary on the matters set out in (7) above, but would be able to adopt or reject such advice as he chose (para. 5.13).

14.4 Put more shortly, the Government through the Lord Chancellor would control

(1) the existence of the professional bodies in the legal profession and how such bodies (if allowed to operate) could operate;
(2) the codes of conduct laid down by such professional bodies;
(3) the education and training of lawyers;
(4) the requirements to be met by any person, whether a lawyer or other professional or a non-professional, and whether employed by Government or any other person or self-employed, before being licensed to have rights of audience in any Court at any level;
(5) the disciplinary procedures for enforcing the codes of conduct of such professional bodies.

The Government would not directly license individual persons to have rights of audience. But the Government would have the power of "life or death" over all the professional bodies; and the Government, by threatening to remove recognition from a professional body or by imposing particular requirements for education or training or for eligibility for licences, could influence the grant of particular licences to particular lawyers or non-lawyers or to particular classes of lawyers or non-lawyers.

14.5 The present position is as follows:

(1) For well over 7 centuries the Judges have had the right to determine who may have rights of audience in the higher Courts. In 1608 James I tried to introduce the then French system of complete regulation by the State of the conditions under which advocates might practise in and out of the Courts, including the fees they charged. But he failed, in face of general opposition from all who wished to maintain the independence of the Courts and the Judges. Between 1608 and 1989 no further such attempt had been made until the present Green Paper proposals. The ambit of the Judges' power to control rights of audience in the High Court was raised and decided by the Court of Appeal in **Abse v. Smith** [1986] Q.B. 536. Following that case the Judges made an alteration to the rights of audience in the High Court to meet the particular point raised in that case.

(2) The education and training of barristers is subject to the Judges' supervision exercised through the Inns of Court, the Council of Legal Education and the Inns of Court School of Law.

(3) The professional standards of the Bar are subject to the supervision of the Judges exercised (a) by direct consultation with the Judges' Council, (b) through the Judges as Visitors supervising the disciplinary system of the Bar, (c) through the Judges sitting in the higher courts and supervising the conduct of cases before them by the Bar.

(4) The disciplinary procedures of the Bar are supervised by the Judges as Visitors, both through the delegation to the Inns of Court and the Council of the Inns of Court of their disciplinary powers which are exercised by Disciplinary Tribunals presided over by Judges, and directly as Visitors deciding appeals from Disciplinary Tribunals.

14.6 The Government's proposals represent a major inroad into these matters which have always been supervised by the Judges.

14.7 That these matters have always been supervised by the Judges has been an essential element in the independence of the Judiciary and of the legal profession from which the Judiciary has been drawn. This independence has been a distinctive feature of the English legal system, particularly since the Act of Settlement in 1701 established the principle that Judges of the higher Courts could not be removed at the will of Government. This independence has always been and now is a feature which has attracted respect from other countries, and which has drawn to this country a substantial amount of commercial litigation and arbitration.

14.8 It has been suggested by the Government that its proposals would represent a minor inroad because in practice the Government would wish to work in collaboration with the Judges, and because any Government, if it ever wished to do so, could subvert the independence of the Judiciary more readily by the appointment of Judges who were not independent of the Government. (It is in part because of this suggestion, that the Bar Council proposes in Chapter 16 below, paras. 16.14 to 16.19, that consideration should now be given to the appointment of the Judges by a Judicial Appointments Board).

14.9 However honourable the intentions of the present Government, the powers proposed to be taken by the Government, for itself and for future Governments, and summarised in para. 14.4 above would encroach to a considerable extent on the existing powers of the Judges, on their independent sphere of action in the Courts and their supervision of the Bar. It is noteworthy that:-

(1) No suggestion has been made in the Green Papers that the Judges have failed to exercise their powers wisely and in the public interest.

(2) No suggestion has been made that there is a mischief needing to be remedied and which requires for its remedy so major a change.

(3) Even if (as the Government suggests) this is only a "thin end of the wedge", it is in principle inappropriate to attack the independent powers of the Judges by a means which would put in the hands of a less wise Government power to subvert the independence of the legal profession and the judiciary. There are warning lessons from other countries in the Commonwealth which have ceased to have Judges and legal professions independent of the diktat of Government.

(4) The proposals go counter to the trend in the European Community and elsewhere for lawyers to be independent of Government. Control over entry to the legal profession is governed by the profession itself in all the member States except Denmark (and as a formality only, in Greece). The lawyers in States other than the United Kingdom and Ireland have rights of audience in the Courts, subject to (a) special rules defining the territories of the Bars to which lawyers belong, as in France and West Germany; and (b) the power of the Courts to limit the lawyers entitled to appear before them, as, in Denmark, the Landsret and Højesteret approve advokater to plead in those Courts. Even in France (to which James I looked for the pattern of Government-controlled Judges, Courts and lawyers) the profession and rights of audience are governed by the Bars of the different regions and the Bar of the Conseil d'Etat and the Cour de Cassation.

(5) There is a danger that the legal profession in England and Wales would no longer be regarded as an "independent legal profession" in some of the member States of the EEC. For example, the CCBE Code of Conduct for Lawyers in the European Community unanimously adopted by the 12 national delegations representing the Bars and Law Societies of the Community in Strasbourg on 28 October 1988 requires (section 1) "the existence of a free and independent profession, bound together by respect for rules made by the profession itself [which] is an essential means of safeguarding human rights in face of the power of the state and other interests in society", and (section 2) a lawyer's "absolute independence, free from all other influence, especially such as may arise from his personal interests or external pressure." It requires this "absolute independence . . . from . . . external pressure" in both litigation and non-contentious matters. It states that: "Such independence is as necessary to trust in the process of justice as the impartiality of the Judge." Similar provisions are to be found in the Declaration of Perugia of 16 September 1977 in Section V.

(6) The Government-appointed National Consumer Council has expressed its concern that these powers should be proposed to be given to a Government minister rather than to persons independent of Government.

(7) Above all, the proposals are entirely contrary to the basic principle which the Government itself proclaims, as quoted in para. 14.1 above.

14.10 The new powers are proposed to be put in the hands of the Lord Chancellor. The Lord Chancellor has a political role as a member of the Cabinet and the head of a large civil service Department. He presides over the House of Lords. Above all, he is a senior Judge. As a senior Judge he has to stand independently of his political role. These proposals would place in the office of Lord Chancellor an undue concentration of power. This power, in less wise hands, could be exercised so as to damage the legal profession and the Judiciary in the interests of political dogma.

14.11 Under the proposals some of the powers would simply be exercised by the Lord Chancellor, while others would be exercised by him through the statutory instrument procedure. That procedure would provide little or no safeguard. Out of the thousands of statutory instruments made each year it is not possible for Parliament to give any effective attention to more than a very small number. Statutory instruments must be accepted or rejected as a whole. Because of the large number of instruments and the lack of parliamentary time, few statutory instruments are ever rejected. The proposal to adopt a statutory instrument would in almost all cases involve Parliament merely in rubber-stamping what the Government through the Lord Chancellor proposed. This was put very clearly by Sir Max Williams, a past President of the Law Society, when he said on 6 March 1989:-

> "Delegated legislation would not provide the necessary protection. It cannot be amended and the opportunities for discussion in Parliament are rare. It is not, I suggest, an adequate protection for the independence of our lawyers and Judges to rely upon the annulment of a statutory instrument emanating from a Minister of the Crown. There is too much authority vested in Government."

14.12 In sum, these proposals would threaten the independence of the legal profession from which the Judges are drawn, and encroach on the independent powers of the Judges, and much extend the range of powers of the Government, without any justification being offered by the Government in the Green Papers for seeking to do this.

15

Partnerships, Incorporation and Multi-Disciplinary Practices

15.1 The Bar Council's simple point is that it would be contrary to the public interest for independent barristers to be permitted to enter into partnerships or incorporated practices with each other or with solicitors or with any other professionals.

To permit such partnerships or incorporated practices would (1) reduce choice, (2) reduce access, (3) reduce competition, (4) reduce standards, (5) increase cost.

15.2 The Bar Council is not alone in holding the firm view that such partnerships or incorporated practices involving barristers would be contrary to the public interest. Reference will not be made to every committee or other body which has investigated this question. But it is appropriate to refer to the bodies the views of which are summarized in paras. 15.3 to 15.7 below.

THE TEMPLEMAN COMMITTEE

15.3 This Committee chaired by Lord Templeman reported in 1969. It concluded unanimously that the rule against partnerships involving barristers should be maintained. It drew particular attention to the advantages to the public of the rule forbidding such partnerships, including

(1) freedom for solicitors to choose any barrister for any work either advocacy or advisory work (para. 40);
(2) the individual responsibility of each barrister for the advice she or he gives in litigious and non-litigious matters, which "results in a high level of competence amongst practitioners and results in good training for those who eventually make decisions in some judicial capacity" (para. 41);
(3) equality between barristers of whatever seniority: "The public pay for competition and experience and not for seniority" (para. 42);

(4) high standards: each barrister finds her or his own level of work according to her or his talents and industry: "Partnerships may attract and preserve the mediocre to the exclusion of the able and to the detriment of the public" (para. 43).

15.4 The Templeman Committee also drew attention to the serious limitations which partnership involving barristers would necessarily impose, in particular:

(1) Members of the same partnership could not be allowed to represent different interests;
(2) A member of a partnership could not be allowed to appear as an advocate before another member acting in a judicial capacity as a part-time judge.

15.5 The Templeman Committee concluded that if a substantial number of barristers were to form partnerships, "this would harm the profession and the public" (para. 45).

> "So far as the profession is concerned, we believe that the existence of partnerships would make it difficult for a beginner to choose independence, difficult for him to prove his capabilities and difficult for him to outstrip his rivals. So far as the public are concerned, we believe that partnerships would restrict the freedom of choice of Counsel, create undesirable monopolies, and preserve the less competent". (Para. 46).

ROYAL COMMISSION ON LEGAL SERVICES

15.6 The Royal Commission was unequivocally opposed to partnerships involving barristers. The relevant paragraphs in its Report and its conclusions have been quoted and summarised in paras. 10.44 to 10.46 above. We draw particular attention to para. 33.64 of the Report of the Royal Commission in which the importance of free choice of barristers in the absence of partnerships was spelled out.

DIRECTOR-GENERAL OF FAIR TRADING

15.7 The recent statement by the Director-General is quoted in para. 10.5(4) above. His judgment is that to allow independent barristers to join in partnerships would be adverse to the interests of the public as consumers.

LESS CHOICE

15.8 If barristers were in partnership (or an incorporated practice) together or with solicitors and other professionals, there would necessarily be a reduction in the choice of barrister. The lay client who engaged a solicitor/barrister partnership would have to take the in-house barrister allotted by the partnership: there would be little or no choice. Such a partnership would be reluctant to use barristers outside the partnership, for the obvious financial reasons that it would lose the contribution to overheads and the profit derived from use of an in-house barrister. Such a partnership would be even more reluctant to use a barrister from another partnership for fear of losing the lay client to that other partnership. It would be equally reluctant to use independent barristers, if lay direct access were allowed, for fear of losing the lay clients to the independent barristers. This can be seen very clearly in the American experience. It is unheard of for any substantial American law firm to use trial lawyers from outside the firm save in very rare and exceptional cases, even if the in-house trial lawyers are lacking in experience in the field of law or practice relevant to a particular case. This is also to a large extent true of the Canadian experience.

15.9 If there were only partnerships between barristers, that would also lead to a reduction in choice, as the Templeman Committee pointed out: see paras. 15.3 and 15.4 above. Partners could not represent different interests. That is an elementary point arising not only from the law of partnership, but also from the practicalities of everyday life. In law each partner is an agent of the partnership and the other partners for the purpose of the business of the partnership, and each partner is responsible for the acts and omissions of the other partners in carrying on in the usual way the business of the partnership (Partnership Act 1890, Section 5). In practice a client looks to and places her or his whole trust in the undivided loyalties of the professional acting for her or him. If the professional has a financial interest which conflicts or may conflict with his loyalties to the client, that client may not be properly served, and certainly will not regard herself or himself as being properly served. No change in the law could alter this elementary feature of commercial life. The answer to the Government's question in para. 11.14 of the main Green Paper is that the problems of conflict are insurmountable, and that lawyers in the same partnership could not be enabled to act for opposing sides in a case. To allow them to do so, as a matter of law, would have a corrupting effect on the practical responsibilities they owe to their lay clients, and it would diminish the standing of the administration of justice in England and Wales.

REDUCED ACCESS

15.10 Reduction in access would result in the same way as reduction in choice. At present 6,000 barristers bound by the "cab-rank" rule are available for access by the public on referral by solicitors and other professionals. Partnerships involving barristers would reduce access, and if barristers entered multi-disciplinary practices access would be effectively limited to the barristers in the relevant practice. The "cab-rank" rule could not apply where barristers were in partnership together or in multi-disciplinary practices. As Lord Mackay said to the Scottish Royal Commission (3 July 1978, page 2), because of the "cab-rank" rule, "advocates had to be independent and could not be employed nor become partners in a practice." Conflicting duties owed to other clients, and conflicting interests of the practice, would be dominant, and would exclude any "cab-rank" rule, just as such a rule cannot apply to solicitors' partnerships now.

LESS COMPETITION

15.11 Now there are 6,000 barristers competing in what the Lord Chancellor has described as "the most competitive business going" (para. 10.21 above). If partnerships between barristers, and the more if multi-disciplinary practices involving barristers, were permitted, it is inevitable that there would be a trend towards the establishment of such partnerships and practices. The removal from the independent profession of any material number of barristers would inevitably reduce competition. 20 independent barristers will compete more strongly with each other than 4 partnerships each with 5 barristers or 2 partnerships each with 10 barristers. The reduction in competition would be greater if barristers joined multi-disciplinary practices, because the barristers would then merely be an adjunct of the practice, automatically being instructed because in-house.

DECLINE IN STANDARDS

15.12 The Templeman Committee drew attention to the decline in standards resulting from the introduction of partnerships at the Bar: see para. 15.3 above. Individuals without ties of partnership or of any other kind, and competing strongly with each other, will, **overall**, succeed in maintaining higher standards of advocacy, than they will if they are grouped together in partnerships, particularly multi-disciplinary ones. Individual responsibility for decisions from the outset of practice, and reliance only on the talents, hard work and acquired skills of the individual exercised constantly in conditions of strong competition, make for higher standards of advocacy.

INCREASED COST

15.13 Partnerships would not reduce the number of lawyers involved in cases before the Courts or in advisory work. If the barristers as advocates were to achieve the same volume of work as now, the preparation of cases would still have to be carried out by other lawyers experienced and specialised in the preparation of cases. If barristers had to prepare cases as well as present them in Court, barristers would appear less often in Court and would be less experienced in advocacy, cases would be prepared less efficiently, and would be presented less efficiently. Less efficiency would mean more time taken, and more time taken would mean greater cost. Further, the likelihood is that partnerships would have higher overheads, probably equivalent to those of solicitors at present. Since solicitors' overheads are now roughly 3 times the level of barristers' overheads, this would be another substantial cause of increased cost.

15.14 The submissions by Lord Mackay (when leading the Bar of Scotland) to the Scottish Royal Commission made similar points to those set out in this Chapter in relation to the suggestion of partnerships involving Scottish advocates:-

"the public interest is best served by preserving the present rule whereby each advocate is required to practise entirely on his own. By this means, the freedom of choice and flexibility essential to the proper working of the system of litigation in this country is preserved". (Page 73).

"The combination of advocates in partnership with solicitors or others would not serve to increase the availability of the services of Counsel. On the contrary . . . it would tend to restrict their availability". (Page 73).

"The combination of advocates into partnership with solicitors and others would also tend to weaken the separate identity of the Bar, its collegiate structure and the forces of competition". (Page 73).

"The combination of advocates into partnership with solicitors would tend to concentrate into still fewer hands the specialist services which advocates are best able to provide". (Page 74).

"The combination of advocates into partnerships, with the inevitable community of interest in the practices conducted by each other that would result, would restrict this freedom of choice". (Page 75).

"If advocates were to operate in partnership, the instructions would go to the partnership and not to the individual. The litigant would have less control over who was to act for him in the various stages of the case. He might well find that his case was being passed down the firm to advocates of lesser experience or qualification than he would have chosen for himself". (Page 76).

"As regards the time taken on legal work, there are sound reasons for believing that the existence of a separate Bar tends to reduce the time spent on a particular case. Greater experience tends towards greater efficiency, and where possible to economy in the presentation of the case". (Pages 78–79).

15.15 The Bar Council agrees, and offers Lord Mackay's statements as one answer to the question in para. 11.12 of the main Green Paper: "why the Bar does not simply permit partnerships." Partnerships involving barristers would militate against one of the present cornerstones of our system of justice: the requirement that a barrister ought, so far as possible, to be free from external influences, and, subject only to his duty to the Court and to the observance of proper standards, ought to be free to give to his clients his undivided loyalty. Partnership would also constitute a significant restriction in the lay client's freedom of choice, particularly in some areas of the country and in specialised fields of practice.

15.16 In para. 11.16 of the main Green Paper the Government suggests that partnership could offer barristers some advantages not now available to them. The Bar Council's view is that the interests of the public must be dominant, not the interests of barristers. But it is necessary to deal with these suggested advantages to barristers:-

(1) *Greater office efficiency* Efficiency in chambers management depends on the will of those in charge of the management to invest in proper accommodation and up-to-date office support systems. This is equally the case in a barristers chambers sharing facilities and expenses as it is in a partnership. The best chambers now are well managed without the extravagances which characterise some of the more expensive solicitors' offices.

(2) *Improving the financial position of the new entrant* Financial security of new entrants is not dependent on partnerships. There is no obstacle to any set of chambers, eager to attract the best talent, offering scholarships and minimum earnings to pupils and tenants. Many of the best chambers already do this, in response to the competition which will increasingly compel chambers to offer financial incentives to new entrants. The Bar Council has committed itself to policies for improving substantially the funding of pupils and new entrants (Chapters 19 and 20 below).

(3) *Encouraging proper supervision of work undertaken by the new entrant* Supervision of work in Court is difficult whether for chambers or for a partnership. Ultimately the test of adequate performance by a barrister is whether solicitors shun the barrister, or compete to instruct the barrister. Within chambers

the young tenant is encouraged to seek advice from more experienced colleagues on a constant basis. Freedom to consult colleagues on any problem arising in the course of practice is one of the major features of every well-run chambers. Partnership would introduce a more hierarchical system and might well reduce the free flow of advice and problem-solving which is characteristic of all good chambers.

(4) *Increased financial stability for chambers*   There are relatively few tenants in the established chambers who cannot support themselves by the end of their first or second year in practice. In some chambers it takes longer to become established. The best chambers guarantee adequate earnings in the early years of tenancy. In chambers where resources are limited, there is a need for help in the first or second year of practice. The Bar Council's policies as set out in Chapters 19 and 20 will ensure that this need is met where chambers cannot do so.

Generally, financial stability of chambers depends on the success of the barristers in the chambers, and on their will to manage chambers efficiently and to invest in the future, in pupils, new tenants and staff, and in good accommodation and equipment. That can be and is achieved already.

15.17   Partnership would make little difference to financial stability. Many partners are reluctant to enter into formal partnership agreements for a fixed term of years, for fear of being "locked in", or simply because the partners cannot agree on the drafting of the agreements. Many small or medium-sized firms of professionals (solicitors, accountants, estate agents and others) operate without a formal partnership agreement but as partners at will. Partnerships at will can be dissolved at any time. They provide no stability beyond what is provided by the day to day relationships between the partners. They are a recipe for disputes over the right to goodwill, the sharing of other assets, and the discharge of tax and other liabilities. Even under a partnership for a fixed term problems often arise as to whether one partner or a group of partners is pulling her, his or their weight, leading not infrequently to disharmony and in the end dissolution. Well-run and successful chambers do not need partnerships. Less well-run and less successful chambers would be unlikely to be better-off in partnership. If barristers were in partnership they would be likely to be less ready to take on more barristers in chambers.

15.18   Any advantages of partnerships to barristers would not outweigh the known advantage to the public interest of barristers strongly competing against one another as sole practitioners and without partnership.

INCORPORATION

15.19   The points made above in relation to partnership apply the more strongly to incorporation. In para. 11.18 of the main Green Paper the Government argues that because some chambers have service companies, barristers should be permitted to practise in corporate form. This is a non sequitur. Service companies for holding chambers assets or employing chambers staff do not affect the fundamental practice structure at the Bar, which requires independent practice by each barrister. The arguments for and against corporate practice are, in essence, the same as those for and against partnerships. The stronger weight of argument is for independent practice, and against partnerships or corporate practice, at the Bar.

OVERSEAS PRACTICE

15.20   In paras. 11.26 and 11.27 of the main Green Paper the Government seeks to rely on the overseas practice rules of the Bar in support of the notion that partnerships of barristers would not be contrary to the public interest. The comparison is unsound. The functions and utility of English barristers depend on, and must be considered in the context of, the legal system in which they practise. In countries which do not have divided professions, and which have no specialist corps of advocates, the role of the barrister of England and Wales has to be different: local rules have to prevail. The Bar has had no alternative but to accept local rules if barristers are to compete in other countries. But that is no reason for abandoning the essential features of an independent Bar **in England and Wales**, which have won respect abroad, and earn a not inconsiderable amount of "invisible exports" through litigation, arbitration and advisory work in England and Wales.

PURSE-SHARING

15.21   In para. 11.13 of the main Green Paper the Government refers to so-called "purse-sharing" arrangements. These were permitted by the Bar Council in recognition of the long-standing arrangements of a particular chambers which wished to continue them. The arrangements did not amount to partnership, and consisted

Quality of Justice

merely of a sharing of receipts in a similar way to the usual sharing of expenses. The experiment proved not to be beneficial. The lack of success in this experiment affords no support for any argument in favour of partnerships at the Bar. The Bar Council will now consider whether purse-sharing should continue to be permitted, except in the form of the provision of finance for pupils and young tenants for which the Bar Council makes detailed proposals in Chapters 19 and 20 below.

MULTI-DISCIPLINARY PRACTICES (MDPs)

15.22 Fusion by another name Partnerships between barristers and solicitors, coupled with the giving of equal rights of audience to solicitors and the other changes proposed by the Government, would amount to effective "fusion" of the two professions. Every committee or body which has considered the position of the Bar in detail has rejected outright any steps towards the "fusion" of the two legal professions: see the views of the Royal Commission, the Marre Committee and the Director-General of Fair Trading summarised and quoted in paras. 3.13, 3.16, 10.5(4) and 10.39 to 10.40 above. Lord Mackay's views, trenchantly expressed as leader of the Bar of Scotland, were equally strongly against fusion of the two legal professions: see paras. 3.13 and 15.14 above. In oral evidence to the Scottish Royal Commission Lord Mackay said: "It was very difficult to see any advantage in fusion to the public, although it would be advantageous to practitioners to be in a larger unit where they could more easily evade responsibility for a mistake . . ." (3 July 1978, page 3). He said "that cost was an important factor in the fusion argument; that to spread the pleading effort through even the central belt [of Scotland] would be to dissipate a good deal of the economy that could be achieved in the Faculty where, for example, the library was unique. Advocates distributed among various firms would find access to the library difficult and costs would escalate". (3 July 1978, pages 3–4). The written evidence to the Scottish Royal Commission by Lord Mackay on behalf of the Faculty of Advocates was that "fusion would have serious disadvantages from the public point of view and few, if any, advantages" (page 64).

15.23 The Government in para. 12.14 of the main Green Paper proposes that barristers should be permitted to enter into MDPs, whether with solicitors or with any other professionals. No arguments and no evidence are put forward as supporting such a change as being in the public interest.

178

15.24 Every argument against allowing barristers to enter into partnerships with each other applies with much greater force against allowing barristers to enter into MDPs with estate agents, surveyors, accountants, solicitors or other professionals. There would be **less choice, less competition, increased cost,** and **lower standards.**

The Bar Council has already set out in paras. 15.8 to 15.13 above the reasons why partnerships at the Bar would have these effects. MDPs involving barristers would have the same effects, and would damage the public interest in the same ways, but the damage would be greater and more immediate.

15.25 MPDs involving barristers and solicitors, accountants, estate agents, surveyors and/or other professionals would have the following further adverse consequences for the public interest:-

(1) *Conflicts of interest* These can be simply expressed. If a client went to an MDP for accounting advice, there would be a strong financial incentive for the accountant to persuade the client to use the accountant's lawyer partner to do legal work for the client, whether or not the lawyer partner was equipped by training and experience to do the work. If the lawyer found that his accountant partner had given negligent advice to the client of the MDP, the lawyer would have a strong financial incentive not the tell the client how he had been let down and not to tell the client that he had a cause of action for damages against the MDP. There is no possible safeguard against the corrosive consequences of conflicts of interest of these kinds within an MDP.

(2) *Difficulties of supervision* Supervision by professional bodies of their members in MDPs would present serious practical difficulties. Much of the work of partners and employees in MDPs would cross disciplinary boundaries. The barrister would answer to his professional body by saying that he had acted as he had because of the requirements of his accountant partner: the accountant would answer to his professional body by saying that he had acted as he had because of the requirements of his barrister partner. Whichever body had the lower standard, those standards would over time tend to prevail, leading the standards of both professions towards the lowest common denominator.

(3) *Distinctions between the professions would be blurred* It would be likely that the barrister would be drawn into doing accountant's work for which the barrister was unqualified, and the accountant be drawn into doing barrister's work for which the accountant was unqualified. This would result in a further lowering of standards in both professions.

(4) *Effect on administration of justice* There is the strongest public

interest of all in the administration of justice by well qualified and experienced practitioners free from problems such as conflicts of interest, and standards affected by the mixture of professions and their differing standards.

(5) *Disappearance of Local Solicitors* The local solicitors' firms, which are the backbone of the provision of legal services throughout England and Wales, and through which the services of 6,000 specialist barristers are available throughout the country, are threatened by the Government's proposals, amongst others, for conveyancing. If solicitors were to be faced with unfair competition from large finance organisations for conveyancing, and if MDPs between solicitors and accountants were permitted, many local solicitors firms would disappear, their place being taken by branches of the large accountant firms in the larger towns and cities. As appears from Chapter 8 above, the size and economic power of the accountant firms is such, that the eight largest of them could easily swallow several of the large solicitor firms. For the accountant firms to take over many of the local solicitor firms and to concentrate their work in the large centres would be even easier. Other solicitor firms would be likely to merge into estate agencies and surveyors firms. What has recently happened with estate agencies (with a large proportion being taken over by the biggest finance organisations) shows the pattern that would probably emerge. There would be large chains of finance organisations with tied solicitors and MDPs offering legal services, with a more limited choice, and at the higher cost necessary to cover the higher overheads. The service provided with difficulty by local solicitors in criminal legal aid work, county court work whether legally aided or not, matrimonial and children work, social security and other advisory work, would either not be available at all, or available further away in a larger centre, and would be more expensive. The choice of barristers now available to local solicitors would be reduced, as the large conglomerate MDPs gathered in more barristers.

15.26 These are potentially adverse consequences to the public interest not mentioned in Chapter 12 of the main Green Paper.

15.27 As stated in the Bar Council's Consultative Document, this would be a charter for the "big battalions", for those seeking to gain a monopoly position in the provision of services in a particular area. The losers would be the ordinary members of the public, needing good, quick, local and above all cheap advice.

15.28 In summary, looking at the position in England and Wales

(1) to allow barristers to enter into partnership whether between

180

themselves or with other professionals would be damaging to the public interest as the Royal Commission, the Director-General of Fair Trading and Lord Mackay have stated.

(2) The proposals to allow MDPs involving solicitors (or barristers) have not been thought through to their likely consequences for (a) the public as users of legal services, or (b) the public interest in the administration of justice.

(3) To bring in changes which would damage the present availability of legal services throughout England and Wales, and promote the provision of legal services more expensively and more remotely through large MDPs and other large organisations is directly contrary to Government policies for the protection of the consumer (see paras. 23.13 and following, below) and for the increase of competition.

THE EEC AND FOREIGN DIMENSIONS

15.29 MDPs involving lawyers are not permitted in any other countries of the Community, except to a limited extent in

(1) *Netherlands* An advocate may practice in collaboration with 3 other professions, those of notary, patent attorney and of the Order of tax advisers, which provide essentially legal services: collaboration with these 3 professions is permitted (inter alia) because no obligation is imposed that could jeopardise the free and independent exercise of the profession of advocate, and it is doubtful whether a non-legal profession could meet this requirement;

(2) *West Germany* It is probable that a rechtsanwalt will be allowed to form a partnership or share an office with patent attorneys, tax consultants or auditors: at present the position is unresolved.

15.30 U.S. lawyers are major competitors of English solicitors and barristers in the international field. U.S. lawyers are protected in the U.S.A. by the reservation of legal practice to lawyers, and are not permitted to practise in MDPs with any other profession. But U.S. lawyers are freer in practice in Europe than in the U.S.A. and freer than European lawyers are in the U.S.A.

15.31 The EEC and foreign dimensions are dealt with more fully in Chapter 21 below. Here it is necessary only to state that

(1) in view of the restrictions on MDPs involving lawyers in other countries of the Community, it would be unwise to proceed with

181

the MDP proposals for England and Wales in advance of agreement on a Community approach to such MDPs, and to multi-national practices;

(2) formulation of an agreed Community approach will require an agreed approach also to the activities of U.S. lawyers in Europe.

16

Appointment of the Judiciary

16.1 "A strong and independent judiciary is one of the central supports upon which our liberties are based and upon which the rule of law depends": para. 10.2 of the main Green Paper.

EX-BARRISTER JUDGES

16.2 The high quality of the Judges of the higher Courts in England and Wales is not accidental. The *strength* and *independence* of the Judges derives from the circumstances in which they have been trained.

16.3 Their training has consisted of an entire professional life in the Courts, in strong competition with other barristers, in regular practice of the examination and cross-examination of witnesses, in weighing and summarising evidence, in exposition of the law, and in testing Socratic dialogue with the Judges. The Judges' qualities of *strength* and *independence* derive from the training of this regular practice in the Courts, and from the responsibilities imposed on a leading barrister in the handling of difficult and heavy cases. *Independence* arises particularly from (1) the fact that barristers are independent of ties with solicitors, and of influence and pressure from Government, and (2) from the requirement to adhere to the "cab-rank" rule. The *strength* arises from the confidence which regular experience over 25 years or more gives to the experienced barrister.

16.4 In Chapter 7 above the reasons why there can be and is so small a number of full-time Judges in England and Wales have been spelled out, especially in para. 7.6. The factors which enable the Bar and the Judges to deal with a large case-load more efficiently and speedily than is achieved in many other countries arise from the particular circumstances of training and experience of the Bar and the Judges.

There is a risk that major changes in such training and experience may lead to less efficient and slower justice, with adverse consequences in terms of increased cost for the taxpayer and for those involved as defendants in criminal cases and litigants in civil cases.

16.5 If the body of "advocates" in the higher Courts is much enlarged, it is inevitable that advocates will spend less time in Court, and will be less experienced and less well trained for the Bench. Chief Justice Warren Burger in distinguishing between American and English Judges said:

> "Another difference is that judges of trial courts of general jurisdiction are selected entirely from the ranks of the ablest barristers. Thus there is little or no on-the-job learning for trial judges as is all too often the case in the United States Courts, both State and Federal. Only the highest qualifications as a trial advocate enter into the selection of English Judges. As a result an English trial is in the hands of three highly experienced specialists who have a commmon professional background".

Change "highly experienced" to "moderately experienced", and there will be a consequential change for the worse in the efficiency of the trial process.

16.6 At a time when the excellence of the higher Judiciary is generally acknowledged, it would be unwise to make any major change in those who may be promoted to the High Court Bench. The present system of promoting from the most experienced barristers, who have proved themselves as part-time Judges, has considerable virtues, as the Lord Chancellor and other members of the Government have acknowledged.

16.7 But the Bar Council also recognises that excellence as a Judge may on occasions be found in those who have not succeeded in becoming leading Queen's Counsel. A good 19th Century example was Lord Blackburn. He had a fairly small practice at the Bar and was best known for his law reporting and text-book writing. He did not become a Queen's Counsel. On his promotion as a Judge of the Court of Common Pleas in June 1859 by Lord Campbell L.C., the Times complained that this was making a farce out of the appointment of Judges. After service for 10 years as a Lord of Appeal in Ordinary, he had "acquitted himself with an ability so consummate as to cause his retirement in December 1886 to be felt as an almost irreparable loss" (DNB, Suppl. p. 204). On his death the Times ate its words of 1859.

16.8 But men like Lord Blackburn are rare. Most of those eligible for promotion as High Court Judges will and should continue to be leading Queen's Counsel with the most appropriate experience. That is essential if the quality of the High Court Bench is not to be diluted. But there will also continue to be some Circuit Judges drawn from the Bar who have shown themselves, like Lord Blackburn, to be able and efficient Judges suitable for promotion. Lord Chancellors have not always been correct in their selection or rejection of candidates for the High Court Bench. Some, who should have gone straight to the High Court, become instead Circuit Judges and then reveal their ability as Judges. They are and should continue to be promoted to the High Court Bench.

EX-SOLICITOR JUDGES

16.9 At present the supply of suitable candidates from the Solicitor profession who are able and willing to sit as part-time Judges has proved relatively small. This results from the different nature of solicitors' practices. They act for clients usually on a continuing basis. It is difficult for solicitors in the smaller firms to make arrangements for the regular absence of one or more partners for 4 weeks a year while sitting as a part-time Judge, in addition to the normal holidays. Partners are not always ready to contemplate a major fee-earner being absent from the office for 4 weeks and potentially losing quite a lot of their fee-earning capacity. But there are able solicitors who can do this and become Circuit Judges.

16.10 The Bar Council agrees that there should be no barrier to an ex-solicitor Circuit Judge being promoted to the High Court Bench if he or she has the qualities required. The ex-solicitor Circuit Judge has not had the experience and training of competitive appearances in higher Courts over a period of perhaps 20 years which the ex-barrister Circuit Judges and High Court Judges have had. But he or she may reveal as a Circuit Judge the qualities required for the High Court Bench, and it would be wrong to continue to bar all ex-solicitor Circuit Judges from promotion.

QUALIFICATIONS FOR PROMOTION TO THE BENCH

16.11 The qualifications stated in paras. 10.3, 10.8(i) and (ii) and 10.13(a)–(d) of the main Green Paper for promotion as a full-time Judge have not been thought through at all. They would bar from appointment as a Lord of Appeal in Ordinary, as Lord Chief Justice, Master of the Rolls, President of the Family Division, or Vice-Chancellor, as a Lord Justice of Appeal, or as a High Court Judge, any "advocate" who had not held a "full general advocacy certificate" for a period of 10 or 15 years. This would be inappropriate for the specialised Bar in England and Wales. If these qualifications had already been in force, they would have barred from promotion all but 2 of the English Lords of Appeal in Ordinary and many of the Lords Justices of Appeal and High Court Judges. The reason for this is that many English barristers do only criminal work or do only civil work and no criminal work. The authors of the Green Paper offer an alternative route via appointment as a Circuit Judge. But the qualification for Circuit Judges is proposed to be either (1) a "full general advocacy certificate", or (2) a "full criminal advocacy certificate" plus a "limited civil advocacy certificate", or (3) a "full civil advocacy certificate" plus a "limited criminal advocacy certificate". This would equally have excluded many of the most distinguished Lords of Appeal in Ordinary, Lords Justices of Appeal and High Court Judges. In any event most of them would not have been prepared to become Circuit Judges with only the possibility of promotion to the High Court Bench.

16.12   To put forward a scheme which would exclude from the higher Courts those who have most to contribute as Judges seems unwise.

16.13   A further change is proposed, which is to remove the present requirement that solicitors should serve a period of at least 3 years as part-time Judges (Recorders) before being appointed as Circuit Judges. That requirement is desirable. Solicitors have not had the training of regular experience in the higher Courts, unlike barristers. It is essential that before they become full-time Circuit Judges, (1) they receive the training and experience which work as part-time Judges gives them, and (2) their merits and defects become sufficiently known, so that those who have the responsibility for recommending and appointing Circuit Judges are able to know whether the solicitors are suitable for appointment as full-time Judges. To reduce the time during which solicitors must sit as part-time Judges before appointment as full-time Judges from 3 years to nil seems an unwise proposal.

WHO SHOULD APPOINT THE JUDGES?

16.14   The Judges are at present appointed by the Crown on the recommendation of the Prime Minister or the Lord Chancellor who is a senior Judge. (It is sometimes not appreciated by the public that the Lord Chancellor is by virtue of the Supreme Court Act 1981 President of the Supreme Court and a senior Judge in England and Wales, with all the responsibilities that being such a Judge entails.)

16.15 The question has been raised whether the Judges of the higher Courts should continue to be appointed effectively by the Prime Minister or the Lord Chancellor (formally, by the Queen on their recommendation) or whether they should in future be appointed by the Judges of the higher Courts as a whole, or by a Judicial Appointments Board with some lay representation.

16.16 The general standard of the Judges of the higher Courts is an argument in favour of the status quo.

16.17 On the other hand, it is apparent that some appointments are recommended by the Lord Chancellor on the basis of inadequate knowledge. In the past, when the Lord Chancellor sat regularly as a Judge and not only in the House of Lords, he was better equipped to gain personal knowledge of the potential candidates for promotion to the Bench. Today his duties as a politician in and out of Cabinet, and as a minister in charge of a large ministry (the Lord Chancellor's Department), leave him little time to gain personal knowledge of such candidates. Many of those promoted to the High Court Bench choose themselves, in the sense that within the profession and in the Courts (both as barristers and as part-time Judges) they have displayed an excellence which immediately commends them for promotion. Others are not so well-known, and their merits and defects need to be found out by careful enquiry in the profession and amongst the Judges. It is in this aspect that the process of selection is not always as well equipped as it might be.

16.18 There is therefore quite a strong argument for placing the selection of new Judges of the higher Courts in the hands of the Judges who know personally the merits and defects of those who appear before them, in a way which the Lord Chancellor as a senior Judge, politician and minister cannot emulate. This would also make clear the independence of the process of selection from the wishes of the political party in Government at the time of each appointment. It would not be difficult to organise a system of selection in which the decisions are taken by the Judges perhaps with some lay representation.

16.19 The arguments for the status quo and for this change are evenly balanced. It is therefore proposed that a committee drawn from retired Lord Chancellors, Lords of Appeal in Ordinary, Lords Justices and other Privy Councillors should be appointed to examine this question in detail and to recommend what changes, if any, should be made in the selection of Judges of the higher Courts.

17

Queen's Counsel

17.1 In Chapter 9 of the main Green Paper, the Government proposes retention of the system of appointment of Queen's Counsel, but goes on to propose that in future those treated as eligible for appointment as Queen's Counsel should be (a) all lawyers (whether barristers or solicitors or others) who hold full general advocacy certificates, and (b) on an occasional and honorary basis, lawyers who are not practising advocates.

17.2 As already stated, it is the Bar Council's view that those who appear in the higher Courts should be independent and sole practitioners, adhering to the "cab-rank" rule, and through the application of that rule available for legal aid work.

17.3 The two-tier system of juniors and Queen's Counsel is a useful part of the system as it now stands because

(a) it makes known to solicitors and others those independent practitioners who are recognised as of an acceptably high standard in specialist advocacy (or in some instances of specialist expertise in a field of law not requiring Court advocacy);

(b) it provides a pool of independent practitioners from whom the High Court Judges can be drawn;

(c) it provides the best training ground, coupled with work as part-time Judges, for those who wish to be eligible for promotion to the High Court Bench.

17.4 It is vital that the rank of Queen's Counsel should be retained as a title designating those who are recognised as independent practitioners in Court work or specialist advice. Independence is stressed because that is the hallmark of recognised merit whether in Court work or specialised advice out of Court.

17.5   The title is given as an honorary one to distinguished barristers who are, for example, teachers of law. The practice of giving the title as an honorary one should continue. But where the title is given to a practising barrister who aspires to judicial office, it would be inappropriate to apply the title to those who do not practice independently, do not adhere to the "cab-rank" rule, and do not therefore hold themselves out as available to all. To do so would devalue the title, and that would not be in the public interest.

17.6   Those who aspire to become Judges are best trained for that as independent practitioners (Royal Commission on Legal Services, para. 33.80). It is in independent practice that the strongest competition lies, and the circumstances of constant competition in Court against others show to those who are involved in the appointment of Judges the merits and defects of those eligible for appointment.

17.7   The title "Queen's Counsel" should continue to be applied only to those who through independent practice have reached the highest standard in court advocacy or specialised advisory work. The word "Counsel" correctly conveys this scope of the work of those who are appointed.

17.8   If the Green Paper proposals for advocacy certificates were to be introduced, it would be unwise to limit the title to those with "full general advocacy certificates", and not to give it to those independent practitioners specialised in civil or criminal work, and so having only a "full civil certificate" or a "full criminal certificate". Such a limitation might be suitable in the very different circumstances in Scotland, where there is less specialisation. But if introduced in England and Wales it would tend to destroy the very specialisation which the Government states that it wishes to foster. If such a system had already been in force in England and Wales, most of the distinguished Judges in the House of Lords, the Court of Appeal and the High Court could not have become Queen's Counsel, because they were specialists. That would not be a wise result.

17.9   At present the title of Queen's Counsel is effectively granted by the Lord Chancellor (formally by the Queen on the Lord Chancellor's recommendation) after consultation with his officials, the Judges and the profession. There have been indications of a lack of knowledge in the Lord Chancellor's Department resulting in the refusal of the title to those of distinction, and in the grant of the title to those not deserving it. The refusal of the title to those of obvious competence has caused some to leave the profession because of their inability to progress any further. There are two possible solutions:

(1) an improved process of selection by the Lord Chancellor by means of which a wider knowledge of the applicants is gained;
(2) selection by the Judges after wide consultation in the profession.

17.10 The main argument for continued selection by the Lord Chancellor is that he effectively appoints the High Court Judges and that it is appropriate for Queen's Counsel to be appointed by him also as the persons eligible for later appointment by him as Judges. The main arguments against are

(1) that it is inappropriate for a Government Minister to control appointments to a higher rank within the profession;
(2) that there would be greater public confidence in a system administered by independent Judges;
(3) that it is very difficult for the Lord Chancellor to acquire sufficient knowledge of all those seeking to be Queen's Counsel, whereas this knowledge can more readily be gathered by the Judges on the basis of Court performance and merit recognised by other practitioners.

17.11 On balance the arguments for selection as Queen's Counsel by the Judges seem to be stronger, particularly the argument that the public would have greater confidence in a system independently administered. The Bar Council proposes that this question should be examined in detail by the same committee as it proposed in para. 16.19 above in relation to Judges of the higher Courts.

17.12 The position in some Commonwealth jurisdictions especially in New Zealand, and in some of the Australian States where an independent Bar exists though the profession is a unified one, show that importance is attached to the grant of the rank of Queen's Counsel to independent practitioners and the selection of Judges primarily from such Queen's Counsel. That approach helps to ensure the maintenance of an independent Bar including independent Queen's Counsel, and the maintenance of a supply of suitable candidates for appointments as Judges: see Chapter 21 below. It is proposed in the Green Paper that Queen's Counsel should be drawn from any "advocate" with the necessary licence, whether in independent practice or in a large firm or company whether multi-disciplinary or not. That would be another factor militating against the maintenance of an independent Bar, as the Commonwealth experience shows.

18

Professional Standards

THE BAR

18.1 The Bar fully accepts the duty stated in para. 4.1 of the main Green Paper. It seeks to achieve the performance of this duty in the following ways:

(1) There is a written Code of Conduct (4th edition, 1 February 1989). It contains most of the professional standards required.
(2) Compliance with the **spirit**, not merely the **letter** of the Code of Conduct, is ensured by formal means, but much more by informal means which are considered in more detail in para. 18.2 below.
(3) Written professional standards for criminal and civil work were drafted in 1988 in conjunction with preparation of the new edition of the Code, and are now out for consultation, before being formally issued.
(4) Complaints about the conduct of any barrister are investigated by the Professional Conduct Committee of the Bar Council (PCC) and its staff. The PCC has the benefit of lay representatives of distinction appointed with the help of the Lord Chancellor. Dismissal of any complaint requires the agreement of the lay representative: if he does not agree, the complaint goes to a Disciplinary Tribunal.
(5) If the PCC considers that the barrister has a case to answer, it brings charges before a Disciplinary Tribunal appointed under the aegis of the Council of the Inns of Court.
(6) If the Disciplinary Tribunal finds the charges proved, it has a wide range of powers of sentence available, including disbarment, suspension from practice, fines, and now new powers in relation to legal aid matters as required by the Legal Aid Act 1988. A Disciplinary Tribunal is composed of 5 persons, a Judge, a lay representative and 3 barristers.
(7) There is a right of appeal to the Judges as Visitors, which is

governed by the Hearings before the Visitors Rules, made by the Judges of the High Court.

(8) If there is no appeal or the appeal fails, then the barrister's Inn of Court gives effect to the sentence.

The Bar Council has initiated a number of steps over the last 18 months with a view to making the disciplinary system more efficient, and removing causes of delay at each stage.

With regard to written professional standards, the Royal Commission recommended that these should be issued. At that time neither the Bar of England and Wales, nor the Bar of Scotland, had a written Code of Conduct. Lord Mackay in 1980 stoutly defended the Bar of Scotland on the ground, which was correct, that the rules of conduct were clearly understood and available elsewhere than in a Code. In 1980 the Bar of England and Wales issued its first Code of Conduct. The Code of Conduct covered in considerable detail all the matters which the Royal Commission recommended should be covered. The third edition of the Bar's Code was in force when the Civil Justice Review reported. Its criticism of the absence of written professional standards appears to have been made without appreciating what was contained in the Bar's Code of Conduct. The Bar Council prepared the fourth edition of the Code together with written professional standards as indicated in (3) above.

18.2 The most important means by which standards are maintained and improved at the Bar are the **informal** means, which include the following:

(1) The example and discipline of fellow-barristers in Chambers, which is the strength of the chambers system.

(2) The example and discipline of the Circuits which exercise "peer group discipline" on those who practise on the Circuits, as the Attorney-General recognised in August 1987: see para. 13.51 above. The influence of the Circuits is at its strongest away from London, not least because of the close co-operation between the Circuit Leaders, the Presiding High Court Judges and the Circuit Judges.

(3) The influence of the Judges, both in Court and out, in restraining poor conduct and encouraging better professional conduct.

(4) One ultimate deterrent to unprofessional conduct by a barrister is the refusal by solicitors to instruct or brief her or him. Because the Bar is a consultancy profession, and solicitors have a wide range of choice between independent practitioners, solicitors directly and indirectly have an important role in encouraging good conduct and discouraging bad conduct at the Bar.

18.3 If informal means do not suffice, then the formal procedures outlined in para. 18.1 above are put into effect. In the House of Lords on 7 April 1989 Lord Murray of Epping Forest said this:

"I speak essentially as a layman and as a lay member of the Professional Conduct Committee of the Bar Council. In serving on that committee, I have been struck in particular by the dedication of the barristers who are professional members; by their toughness on their fellow barristers who are in breach of the code of conduct; by their concern to uphold the standards of the profession; and by their willingness to examine and to improve the procedures which are provided by the Bar Council.

Recently there has been a major overhaul of the procedures and of the standards. That was carried out long before the Green Paper was published. There is no reference in the Green Paper to that overhaul. Nor, incidentally, do I find in the Green Paper any criticism of the Bar Council's procedures in Chapter 4 although I find criticism of the procedures of the Law Society. But the ability of the Professional Conduct Committee to exercise discipline and the diligence of that committee rest, I believe, on two main pillars. The first is the ability of that committee, and of its barrister and lay members, to pin responsibility on to an individual barrister. The second is the accountability of that committee to its barrister peers through the medium of the Bar Council itself. I believe that both those pillars would be very seriously weakened by the proposals in the Green Paper." (Hansard, cols. 1335–6)

18.4 The main Green Paper contains no criticism of the Bar's standards or discipline. But neither is perfect. Complaints can take too long to be dealt with. Standards of advocacy, especially in the lower Courts, are not always high enough. There have been some justified complaints about the conduct of sessions lists for the Crown Prosecution Service (CPS). The Bar has taken steps to ensure better standards of preparation of CPS work, subject always to the need for efficient back-up work by the CPS which is sometimes sadly lacking. The Bar has also taken longer term measures to ensure higher standards of advocacy by newly called barristers, including the new ICSL vocational course, and the proposed advocacy course as part of the continuing education programme (see Chapter 19 below), with the Lord Chancellor's support.

CODES OF CONDUCT

18.5 The Bar's Code of Conduct is subject to the supervision of the Judges in 3 ways:-

(1) through direct consultation by the Bar Council with the Judges' Council and the Council of the Inns of Court;

(2) through the Judges' appellate role in the disciplinary system as Visitors; and

(3) through the Judges' work in the administration of justice in the Courts.

Provisions would be unlikely to be adopted in or omitted from the Bar's Code of Conduct against the considered views of the Judges, and the recent consultation referred to in (1) above has been effective.

18.6 The Government proposes to take power to impose principles of Codes of Conduct on the Bar by statutory instrument after taking the advice of an Advisory Committee. It does so on this basis:

> "The Government is not prepared to leave it to the legal profession to settle the principles which these codes should adopt because they will be of such great importance both to the administration of justice and to the public".

18.7 The independence of the Judges and the legal profession has already been dealt with in Chapter 14 above. By this statement the Government appears to be saying that the Bar cannot be trusted to lay down the basic principles of its Code of Conduct governing conduct in Court, advisory work and generally the Bar's role in the administration of justice. The Government appears also to be saying that the Judges (of whom the Lord Chancellor is a senior Judge) cannot be trusted to supervise the Bar in the basic principles of its Code of Conduct. No grounds have been suggested and no evidence offered for the proposition that the Bar and the Judges cannot be trusted. Recently the Lord Chancellor also suggested that Government control is necessary because the Bar might "drive a coach and horses through the cab-rank rule" (para. 6.1(2) above). No grounds have been put forward and no evidence offered as a basis for this suggestion. The "cab-rank" rule has been at the heart of the Bar's service to the public for centuries. As Lord Mackay explained to the Scottish Royal Commission, it is "an important constitutional guarantee from the point of view of citizens' freedom of access to the Courts" (3 July 1978, page 2).

18.8 It is unfortunate that these suggestions should ever have been made.

18.9 The **letter** of a Code of Conduct is of little value unless the **spirit** underlying the Code is enforced in a liberal sense by those whose task it is to administer the Codes. That is the aim of the Bar as well as the Judges. The Bar should be allowed to continue to maintain its Code of Conduct (free from Government control), regularly altering it in the Bar's endeavour to meet the changing needs of the public and of the administration of justice. The Judges should be allowed to continue to supervise the Bar. More formal mechanisms could be established for this process of supervision, if that is thought necessary.

ADVISORY COMMITTEE

18.10 With regard to the proposed Advisory Committee:-

(1) This should advise the Judges, not the Government, for the reasons spelled out in Chapter 14 and in this Chapter.
(2) It should in any event be a body separate from the Legal Education Committee dealt with in Chapter 19 below.

Advice on professional conduct and standards is not a matter for a committee concerned with education, and the academic representatives on such committee would not be equipped to give informed advice. That is understood to be the considered view also of the Heads of Law Schools.

18.11 The Bar Council proposes that

(1) The Judges should continue to supervise the Bar's Code of Conduct and the actual professional standards of barristers.
(2) The Judges should also supervise the Codes of Conduct of solicitors (and any other profession involved in the administration of justice e.g. patent and trademark agents) and the actual professional standards of solicitors, as proposed in para. 26.8 below.
(3) The Judges should be advised by an advisory committee (perhaps called "the Legal Professional Standards Committee") composed as follows:
   (a) A Lord Justice as Chairman
   (b) A High Court Judge
   (c) A Circuit Judge
   (d) A Stipendiary Magistrate
   (e) A lay Magistrate
   (f) 2 barristers
   (g) 2 solicitors
   (h) 5 non-lawyers, to include at least 3 persons experienced in the maintenance of professional standards in other professions;
(4) there should be more lay representatives on the Bar Council's Professional Standards and Professional Conduct Committees;
(5) there should be an annual report by the Bar Council to the Judges (including the Lord Chancellor).

LEGAL SERVICES OMBUDSMAN

18.12 There are three main ways in which a member of the public may suffer in the administration of justice:

(1) through inadequate management of the Courts and Tribunals systems, and the mishandling of complaints about such mis-management (see Chapter 9 above at paras. 9.53 to 9.58);
(2) through inadequate services provided by solicitors, and the mishandling of complaints about solicitors' services;
(3) through inadequate services provided by barristers, and the mishandling of complaints about barristers' services.

The Bar Council supports the appointment of a Legal Services Ombudsman, provided that he or she can consider matters falling within each of these categories. With regard to the first category, paras. 9.57 and 9.58 above are repeated. Not infrequently complaints about the handling of cases involve all three categories, and barristers and solicitors find themselves being blamed e.g. for delays which are in reality caused by bad administration of the Courts. Subject to this point which will necessitate enlargement of the powers, and to two further points set out below, the Bar Council considers that the powers listed in para. 4.31 of the main Green Paper would be appropriate. The two further points are these:-

(1) It would be appropriate for the Legal Services Ombudsman to investigate the handling of a complaint against a barrister by the PCC. It would not be appropriate for the Ombudsman to have power to consider the handling of disciplinary cases by a Disciplinary Tribunal presided over by a Judge, or on appeal by the Judges as Visitors, for reasons which are obvious: the Judges must be the ultimate decision makers.
(2) The proposal for the payment of compensation by the Bar Council raises a potentially serious practical problem. The Bar is a small profession. The resources of the Bar Council are necessarily small. It would be important not to impose an undue burden, which might damage the Bar Council's ability to perform its functions effectively.

LIABILITY FOR COSTS

18.13 A similar point in relation to liability for costs arises out of para. 4.13 (the last sentence) of the main Green Paper. If the Courts were to be given power to order a barrister to pay personally costs incurred by any party to an action, that could destroy the ability of barristers to continue to practise as sole and independent practitioners bound by the "cab-rank" rule. The costs of an action may range from perhaps £100 in the County Court to millions of pounds in the Commercial Court. Such a proposal would need a full study, in particular of the availability and cost of insurance, and of the potential effects on sole practitioners, before it could be implemented. There has been as yet no such study.

19

Legal Education, Training, and Specialisation

LEGAL EDUCATION AND TRAINING

19.1 The four stages of education and training of a practising lawyer, whether barrister or solicitor, are:-

(1) the academic stage, at a university or polytechnic;
(2) the vocational stage: for the Bar, at the Inns of Court School of Law (ICSL) run by the Inns of Court through the Council of Legal Education; for solicitors, at the College of Law;
(3) the stage of practical training: for the Bar, pupillage with a pupil-master; for solicitors, articles as an articled clerk;
(4) continuing education, continuing throughout a career as a barrister or a solicitor.

ACADEMIC STAGE

19.2 All students wishing to become barristers must have obtained a first or second class honours degree at a university or polytechnic, and have passed either during their degree course or in a post-graduate course the six "core" law subjects agreed from time to time by the Bar and the Law Society.

19.3 The need to teach every law student the "core" subjects restricts the range of courses in law which universities and polytechnics can offer. It is important that the number of "core" subjects is kept to the minimum and that universities and polytechnics are thereby enabled to offer as wide a range of courses as possible. It is better for students to be taught, for example, the basic principles of law, the elements of legal philosophy, and through comparative law how other countries deal with the same legal problems, than to be taught quasi-vocational matters such as evidence which can be acquired quickly in the vocational stage. The suggestions for enlarging the number of "core" subjects contained in Annex C, para. 3, of the main Green Paper would go in the wrong direction. There are however two matters which require separate consideration.

19.4   The first is the law of the European Economic Community, with which must be joined the law of the European Convention on Human Rights (EEC and ECHR laws). No lawyer joining the Bar or the solicitor profession today should be without a basic understanding of EEC and ECHR laws which impinge on our national laws in so many ways. This has to be acquired in either the Academic or the Vocational stage.

19.5   The second matter is the current lack of skills in languages. The lawyer of tomorrow, whether a barrister or a solicitor, will have a much greater need to speak and write at least one foreign language well. At a time of increased need, the range of skills in languages acquired at school is declining. Positive steps need to be taken by schools, universities and polytechnics to reverse this decline. For those already at the Bar and now entering, the Bar Council proposes to arrange language courses as part of its continuing education programme (paras. 19.22 to 19.24 below).

19.6   The Advisory Committee and the roles proposed for it are considered in paras. 19.28 to 19.32 below. Whatever body might be created and whatever its roles, it should not be permitted to dictate to the universities, polytechnics or the professions what subjects are to be taught in the Academic stage. The Bar Council fully recognises the need to collaborate with the universities and polytechnics, so as to ensure that changes in the Vocational course and in the requirements for entry to the Bar are agreed with them. Arrangements to ensure this collaboration have been established by the Bar Council and the Council of Legal Education with the Chairmen of the Committees of Heads of Law Schools at the Universities and the Polytechnics, as well as the Society of Public Teachers of Law and the Association of Law Teachers.

FUNDING OF UNIVERSITY AND POLYTECHNIC LAW SCHOOLS

19.7   It is a matter of deep concern to the Bar that, in a time of increasing demand for well-educated law graduates, the Government should have cut and be intending to cut further, in real terms, the funds available to Universities for their Law Schools. The position of

Polytechnic Law Schools under the new regime for the Polytechnics (independent of local authorities) is as yet uncertain. The decline in funding of the universities has already resulted in declining law teacher – student ratios, making the tutorial system difficult to maintain in many universities. Further worsening in teacher-student ratios is likely to lead to lower standards achieved by law students, with adverse consequences for the standards in the legal professions. To consider the Academic stage without reference to the funding of that stage (which is wholly ignored in the main Green Paper) is to take Hamlet without the Prince. It is all too easy to damage the quality of university teaching, and much harder to restore the quality later. The Bar Council proposes that a working party drawn from the Judges, the Heads of University and Polytechnic Law Schools, the Bar, Solicitors, the Department of Education and Science and the Lord Chancellor's Department should be appointed to consider how funding of Law Schools can be improved, and how their standards can be maintained and improved.

VOCATIONAL STAGE

19.8 The course at the ICSL for intending barristers is being changed from September 1989 so that it is fully directed to training in the skills of advocacy, drafting, negotiation and communication (with lay clients and others with whom barristers deal in the course of the legal process), in professional ethics and conduct and the uses of information technology. The changes have been devised over a period of 18 months by the Hon. Sir Leonard Hoffman and a team drawn from the ICSL and experienced teachers from universities here and abroad. The Lord Chancellor and his Department have fully supported the introduction of this new vocational course, which will for the foreseeable future be the only developed course in this country for the teaching of vocational skills and advocacy. Whatever changes may come (whether the Green Paper proposals or those advocated in this book) students who wish to specialise in advocacy will need to go first to the ICSL to acquire the training and skills necessary before embarking on pupillage.

19.9 The proposals in the main Green Paper for the Vocational stage do not go far enough. The range of requirements set out in Annex C, para. 5, so far as they are relevant to the Bar, is based on the new ICSL course. But it is important that the Vocational course builds on the grounding in the law obtained in undergraduate and postgraduate courses. Skills as they are acquired must be related to the developing knowledge and understanding of particular fields of law, and to ability in exposition of the law. That is one aim of the new ICSL course.

The summary in para. 5.17 of the main Green Paper puts the requirements of a vocational advocacy course at too rudimentary a level. For a barrister who aims to appear in every court from a Magistrates Court to the House of Lords, such a course would not provide a sufficient basic training. The Bar Council is certain that the year to be spent at the ICSL is not a day too long: ideally the ICSL course should be longer, but finance, both to run the course and to fund the living expenses of students, would not permit any further extension beyond the year.

COMMON VOCATIONAL TRAINING

19.10 The desirability of a common period of training for all practising lawyers has been expressed by a number of committees, including the Royal Commission on Legal Services (as the Government indicates in Annex C, para. 4, of the main Green Paper). This was considered afresh in 1987–8 by a joint committee of the two professions chaired by the Hon. Sir Leonard Hoffman and Mr. Richard Harvey. This committee came to the conclusion that, though in an ideal sense desirable, a common course is at present impractical. The experience of those responsible for the new ICSL course and syllabus reinforces this conclusion. The ICSL course, which those responsible for it consider the minimum required for the training of a barrister in advocacy, cannot be completed in less than a year. If a common course preceded the ICSL course, that would last 6–12 months, making a total period of vocational education of from 18–24 months. Finance is not available within the professions to fund courses of this length. Students find the funding of the fees for the existing ICSL and Solicitors courses lasting a year (as well as living expenses) very difficult. The local education authority (LEA) grant position (para. 19.14 below) is deteriorating. Furthermore students who wanted to specialise as barristers in advocacy, or as solicitors, would resent having to spend a period of 6–12 months learning what they do not need for their future specialisation: that has been clear from student consultation over a number of years. So there would probably be an adverse effect on the recruitment of graduates into the legal professions.

19.11 There is one argument for all aspiring lawyers to start with the same course, that it would enable them to delay their choice between the professions until a later time than is necessary at present. The Bar Council fully accepts the need to ensure that students are able to make an informed choice. The Bar Council and the Inns of Court appreciate the need for up to date knowledge of a career at the Bar among teachers of law, careers advisers and law students. Over the last 18–24 months strenuous efforts have been made to remedy this by, for example, (1) regular visits to universities and polytechnics; (2) a successful all-day conference with careers advisers organised by AGCAS, the Inns of Court, the Bar Council and the CLE; (3) a large expansion of mini-pupillages, in which students from schools, universities and polytechnics come to a barristers' chambers for a week or more and work with barristers in a similar way to actual pupils; (4) regular meetings with law teachers and law students in the Inns of Court; (5) conferences attended by sixth-formers organised by the Inns and the Bar Council; (6) one-to-one counselling by the Students Officers of the Inns of Court and by practising barristers.

19.12   This process of information and explanation has not yet gone far enough. But the Bar Council believes that if continued as strongly this will go a long way towards ensuring that every law student considering entry into the profession is fully aware of the alternatives before her or him. In addition, the Bar Council is committed to a policy of easy transfer from one profession to the other: see para. 5.20 above.

19.13   Because of these efforts to inform and explain the alternatives open to students, and because of the impracticalities of a combined vocational course, the Bar Council considers that it is better to continue with the existing pattern of courses but with improved syllabuses and teaching as is under way at the ICSL. If however further funds were to be made available by the Government, that would enable the future pattern of legal vocational education to be reconsidered. The Government already provides large sums for training under a variety of schemes, ranging from medical school teaching of future doctors and nurses to youth training and similar schemes. Is the Government prepared to devote to legal vocational training the substantial funds which would be necessary, on a long teɪɪn basis, to enable common training to be put in place? The Bar Council understands that the answer is "no".

STUDENT GRANTS AND OTHER FUNDING

19.14   Students at the ICSL are funded in part by LEA discretionary grants, in part by scholarships and studentships provided by the Inns of Court, to a small extent by barristers' chambers, and in too large a degree by parental contributions. The giving of LEA discretionary grants is arbitrary and uncertain. Some LEAs give no grants. Some give large grants to few students. Some give small grants to more students. All vary their grant policies according to political whim and financial pressure. The result is discriminatory and arbitrary. Funding of vocational education should not depend on the area in which parents live. Funding should be on a consistent basis and related to means. It is most regrettable that the Green Papers contain no reference to student funding and no assurance that the grants position will be improved.

19.15   The Bar is deeply concerned about the need to ensure that **anyone of ability**, whatever their means, can come into the profession. Para. 6.6 above shows how wide the net is now drawn. But unless the student grant position improves for those of little means, there is a danger that they would be unable to come to the Bar. The Bar Council and the Inns are trying to ensure that this does not happen. The policy of the Bar Council is that the scholarship funds of the Inns should be concentrated primarily on helping those who need help in the vocational year. The Inns will probably move in this direction as Chambers grants for the pupillage year increase. The Inns disbursed in total some £750,000 in 1988/89, the most that their limited funds could sustain; thus they cannot give sufficient help to every student who needs help.

PUPILLAGE: THE PRACTICAL STAGE

19.16   The Royal Commission on Legal Services considered (as did the Marre Committee) that pupillage was the best system for the practical stage of a barrister's education and training. Over the last 18 months the Bar Council and the Inns have been putting in place a new pupillage system, designed to ensure as effective a year of practical training as practicable. Pupil-masters have to be registered, as pupils have also. Each pupil has to complete a range of practical tasks in accordance with a "check-list" appropriate to the chambers in which she or he is a pupil. Each 6 months of the pupillage has to be certified either by the pupil-master or some other person entitled to do so under the Consolidated Regulations of the Inns of Court.

19.17   The proposals in paras. 5.18 and 5.19 of the main Green Paper follow the current requirements of the Bar Council and the Inns for pupillage in most respects, except two:-

(1) The Government suggests that the practical stage "is unlikely to last for less than six months". This period is apparently taken as the equivalent of the first 6 months of pupillage, during which a pupil has no right of audience and cannot accept any instructions (Consolidated Regulations, Reg. 56). The Bar Council would strongly oppose any proposal for a shorter period of practical

training before a barrister can be instructed or briefed. Ideally the period should be longer: but the pressures of finance make the ideal impractical. A year's pupillage is essential.

(2) It is proposed that students should keep "log books" during their practical training. The Bar Council agrees with this proposal, and will amend the requirements in the Code of Conduct of the Bar to incorporate this as an addition to the existing "check list" requirement.

However there is a danger that **form** (consisting of the filling in of check-lists and log-books) might become more important than **substance** (the reality of the training received and of the pupil-master's and chambers' assessment whether the pupil is able and ready to accept instructions or briefs). Throughout the main Green Paper too much regard is had to **form**, e.g. the completion of a "prescribed minimum amount of actual advocacy" as a qualification for "advocacy certificates". Minimum "flying hours" in court are not and should not be a substitute for informed assessments of ability. Similarly the completion of "log-books" is no substitute for the pupil-masters' and chambers' assessments of ability.

19.18 Pupillage (by whatever name it is described) is essential for the training of an "advocate" before she or he is allowed to accept briefs or instructions in the Courts unsupervised. Pupillage must be with an experienced practitioner as pupil-master, either a single pupil-master throughout, or pupil-masters within particular chambers. Suggestions have been made by the Law Society that solicitors might be "trained" as "advocates" without keeping a log-book of advocacy related experience and without being attached to an experienced advocate ("Striking the Balance", page 21). Such suggestions could seriously devalue the training of an advocate. One of the reasons why the Bar Council considers that rights of audience in the higher Courts should continue to be confined to those who have trained and practised as barristers or in the same way as barristers, is precisely that standards of training and performance would otherwise be devalued. The training and performance of barristers is not perfect. That is why the Bar Council, the Inns and the CLE have in train (and have had in train for nearly 2 years) major changes in the training of barristers (with the support of the present Lord Chancellor and his two predecessors) and a major revision of the Code of Conduct. But the changes already under way, and those indicated in this book, will meet the requirements proposed by the Government far better than the sort of training suggested by the Law Society in "Striking the Balance".

FINANCE IN PUPILLAGE

19.19 The Bar Council recognises that it is the obligation of the profession to ensure that all properly qualified pupils are adequately remunerated. The Bar Council has resolved to set a level of minimum income for pupils annually, so that each pupil will be in receipt during the 12 months of pupillage of that minimum income, and that it will be the professional obligation of all members of the Bar to ensure that this requirement is met. A working party of the Bar Council is to report by 20 May 1989 with detailed proposals for a scheme which could be implemented by the Bar to make provision for finance for pupils in accordance with this resolution of the Bar Council. The working party will consider what obligation to provide finance for pupils should be placed on the members of Chambers taking pupils, and what finance ought to be provided by the profession as a whole.

So far as concerns financing by Chambers at present, the funds made available by Chambers have doubled each year for four years running. For the coming year the funds available from Chambers will exceed £1.25 million. Chambers will be free to provide more than the minimum income to be specified, as many already do. Payments of £10,000 per annum and more will be made by some Chambers to their pupils in 1989/90.

19.20 One problem must here be mentioned. Many do pupillages with the independent Bar without any intention of practising at the independent Bar. They may wish to go after pupillage into commerce, finance or industry, the Government Legal Service, local government, the Crown Prosecution Service, or elsewhere. So the number of pupils in any event much exceeds the number wishing to practise (the problem raised by those who wish to practise but do not find places in Chambers is considered separately in Chapter 20 below). If every Chambers were required fully to fund all their pupils, this would be likely to lead to a substantial reduction in the number of pupillages on offer, to the detriment of many who need pupillage as a stepping-stone to another career. This problem will be addressed by the working party referred to in para. 19.19 above.

PUPILLAGE WITH EMPLOYED BARRISTERS

19.21 Pupillage has long been possible with barristers in commerce, finance and industry. Steps are being taken with a view to the first 6 months being at the independent Bar, but sponsored and paid for by the prospective employer. All barristers employed by the Crown Prosecution Service (CPS) from 1 January 1989, by agreement between the CPS and the Bar Council, will do their first 6 months of pupillage at the independent Bar and the second 6 months with an approved pupil-master in the CPS. It is understood that the CPS will fund their prospective employees during their first 6 months of pupillage. Similar arrangements are being discussed with the Government Legal Service, and with local government barristers.

CONTINUING EDUCATION

19.22 In October 1987 a working party of the Bar Council and the CLE proposed the introduction of a scheme of systematic continuing education of the Bar. Because of the major work on the new vocational course at the ICSL, this was held on ice for a while. It was taken forward with firm outline proposals in January 1989 which have received the approval of the Bar Council.

19.23 The main proposal in relation to advocacy skills is a week-long course on the lines of those pioneered by the National Institute of Trial Advocacy in the U.S.A. and also in Canada. This course is intended to be compulsory for all barristers once established in practice following the end of pupillage, and will be conducted by practising barristers and Judges. It will build on the practical advocacy teaching during the ICSL vocational course and the teaching and practice during pupillage. This is the type of course now proposed by the Government in para. 5.22 of the main Green Paper.

19.24 The other proposals relate to

(1) the acquisition of specialised knowledge of particular branches of law, by means of Open University-type courses, which will be examined, probably by open-book examination (the barrister will be able to make known her or his success in such examinations);
(2) up-dating courses of shorter length which will not be examined.

SPECIALISATION

19.25 The proposals in paras. 3.5 to 3.10 in relation to "specialisms" (other than advocacy) require careful consideration. They involve the creation of a potentially large number of new separate quasi-monopolies, by (1) creating "accredited specialists" in different fields of practice, and (2) barring anyone other than "accredited specialists" from holding themselves out to potential clients as specialists in particular fields. This proposal derives from the suggestions by the Royal Commission on Legal Services, the Government White Paper on Legal Aid in March 1987, and the Civil Justice Review that specialisation in the *solicitor* profession would be desirable.

19.26 The Bar of England and Wales is already specialised, and has been for many years. Areas of work such as criminal, patent, commercial, chancery, taxation, planning and local government, parliamentary and construction law are specialised in by barristers in particular chambers. They have their own specialist Bar Associations, of which some are directly represented on the Bar Council, and the representation of others is under consideration. Competent solicitors (and other professionals able to come direct to the Bar such as patent and trademark agents, chartered and certified accountants and chartered surveyors) are able to choose barristers with the appropriate specialised expertise (and the changes to date, and proposed, in the advertising rules will make this even easier). To impose on the Bar a compulsory pattern of "accredited specialists" and quasi-monopolies would give the lay public little or no advantage, and potentially considerable disadvantages of immobility, lack of cross-fertilisation of different areas of practice, and substantially increased fees.

19.27 As regards solicitors, in view of the size of the profession and the lack of any clear specialisation as is found at the Bar, there may be virtues in developing the kinds of specialist panels described in para 3.6 of the main Green paper. But the wise course will be to allow these specialist panels to develop organically and without the imposition of a rigid scheme. That is what has happened at the Bar of England and Wales, in contrast to the much smaller Bar of Scotland, and is likely to happen to the solicitors profession, due to the increasing complexity of society and commerce, and to the problems of recruitment already affecting that profession.

LORD CHANCELLOR'S ADVISORY COMMITTEE

19.28 This committee has been in existence since 1971, when it was formed as a result of the Ormrod Committee's recommendations. Until recently it was barren of achievements. It had failed even in its fundamental task of drawing together in harmonious collaboration teachers of law and law practitioners. Arrangements to this end have been made by the Bar Council and the CLE: see para. 19.6 above.

19.29 The need for education and training of barristers and solicitors to be independent of Government control has been dealt with in Chapter 14.

A LEGAL EDUCATION COMMITTEE

19.30 What is needed in relation to legal education and training is an active committee drawn from the Judges, teachers of law, barristers and solicitors to keep under review aspects of legal education and training, and to report annually to the Law Schools and the professions. Such a committee will command respect and successfully guide the Law Schools and the professions, **not** by the power of the Lord Chancellor to impose the Committee's or his views by statutory instrument, but by the excellence of its proposals. The Bar as a young profession, and the Law Schools, are responsive to good proposals for useful change. Above all, what should be avoided is the dead hand of yet another "quango" which does not command respect in the professions or the Law Schools.

19.31 Such committee (which might be called the "Legal Education Committee") should be composed on the following lines:

(1) A High Court Judge as chairman (preferably one who has had some responsibility for education or training);
(2) A representative of the Council of the Inns of Court;
(3) 3 barristers (the Chairman and Vice-Chairman of the relevant Bar Council Committee and a barrister of less than 4 years call);
(4) A representative of the CLE;
(5) 3 solicitors (the chairman and vice-chairman of the relevant Law Society committee and a solicitor with less than 3 years practise since completion of articles);
(6) A representative of the College of Law;
(7) 2 representatives of University Law Schools;
(8) 2 representatives of Polytechnic Law Schools;
(9) 2 representatives of barristers and solicitors employed in commerce, finance, industry, the Government Legal Service and public and local authorities;
(10) 5 non-lawyers, chosen for their knowledge and experience either in higher education or in the training of other professions.

It should be served by a joint secretariat provided by the Council of Inns of Court, the Bar Council and the Law Society (based on the good example of the joint secretariat for the Marre Committee).

Any funding required should be provided by the professions, and not by the taxpayer.

19.32 This Legal Education Committee should be separate from the Committee keeping professional standards in the legal professions under review (Chapter 18 above) for the obvious reason that teachers of law are not the right people for the Committee on standards, and a different mix of non-lawyers is required.

20

Barristers Practices and Advertising

20.1 The matters covered by Chapters 11 and 13 of the main Green Paper have for some years caused anxious concern to the Bar as a whole, and to the Bar Council and the Inns of Court. The appropriate structure of the profession and the financial and other support of the many young entrants in a time of unprecedented expansion have exercised many distinguished minds. It is here that the Bar Council feels most able to make a number of positive and constructive proposals for the future of the profession.

20.2 Matters such as partnership, incorporation and direct access by lay clients have already been dealt with and are not considered further in this Chapter.

RECRUITMENT

20.3 It is a central aim of the Bar to ensure that entry to the Bar is available to all women and men of ability whatever their means. Within the limit of the resources available to the Bar, there is determination that this aim should be met and continue to be met.

20.4 At the stage of the ICSL vocational course, the problems of funding of fees and living expenses have been dealt with in paras. 19.14 and 19.15 above. What the Government can do is to bring order to the present arbitrary and uncertain system of LEA discretionary grants. What the Bar can do is to pursue its policy (to which the Inns of Court will probably move as chambers grants in the pupillage year increase) that the scholarship funds of the Inns should be devoted primarily to helping students during their year on the ICSL vocational course. Chambers will be encouraged to do what they can to help, during the ICSL vocational course, those who will be coming to chambers the following year as pupils.

20.5 The Bar and the Inns will also continue their recruitment and information efforts described in para. 19.11 above, so as to ensure that as far as possible students at every university and polytechnic are made aware of what a career at the Bar offers. The success so far of these efforts is reflected by the facts set out in para. 6.6 above. But it must be appreciated that, as spelled out in Chapter 10 above, recruitment to the Bar is likely to be seriously damaged for the long term if the central proposals in the Green Papers are implemented.

PUPILLAGES

20.6 There are two particular problems which the Bar has had to address: (1) the allocation of pupillages; and (2) the financing of pupils.

ALLOCATION OF PUPILLAGES

20.7 The Bar Council accepts that there are potential unfairnesses in a system which depends on prospective pupils finding particular pupil-masters or particular chambers prepared to take them on as pupils. In a profession composed only of sole practitioners this is to some extent inevitable. But the Bar Council is keen to reduce unfairnesses to a minimum. The steps it has taken and will take are described in paras. 20.8 to 20.12 below.

20.8 Students find pupillages through a mixture of personal contacts (including sponsor Benchers and barristers in the Inns), help from the Student Officers of the Inns, and direct applications to chambers on the basis of the entries in the "Chambers' Pupillages and Awards" booklet issued by the Bar Council. Students of ability and energy, whatever their background, usually have little difficulty in finding suitable pupillages: they can turn to the Student Officers and their Inn sponsors who readily find them pupillages. But there are some students who have greater difficulty and need even more help.

20.9 The Bar Council and the Inns are taking steps to put in place by the summer of 1989 an information centre (to be called the "Pupillage and Tenancy Recruitment Information Centre" or "PATRIC") to act as a central point for providing information to prospective pupils and pupil-masters about the places available for pupils and the pupils looking for places. The aim will be to make it mandatory from 1990 for every chambers and every pupil-master to provide details of available pupillages to PATRIC and to keep PATRIC informed as pupillage places are filled.

20.10 Pupil masters are already required to be registered and approved: para. 11.4 of the main Green Paper is inaccurate in this respect.

20.11 So far as pupils from minority groups are concerned, it is part of the Code of Conduct that

(1) all pupillage applications must be considered fairly and without discrimination based on race, ethnic origin, sex or religion of the applicant;
(2) when considering applications the desirability of proper representation within chambers of persons of different race, ethnic origin, sex or religion is to be borne in mind;
(3) chambers are to keep records showing the manner in which applications are disposed of and where discernible, the race, ethnic origin, sex or religion of each applicant.

The Bar is in advance of most professions in having 5% of barristers from minority groups (only just over 1% of solicitors). But the Bar, as other professions, has not succeeded in ensuring that such barristers are widely distributed among existing chambers. Too many end up in chambers predominantly drawn from minority groups. The Bar Council commissioned in 1988 a professional survey of the position of barristers from minority groups. The report has been received, and is described in Chapter 25 below. The Bar Council will take whatever practical steps it can to bring barristers from minority groups into the mainstream of the profession. The proposals for a "library" system ancillary to chambers (paras. 20.26 to 20.29 below) will be one step towards this.

20.12 Pupillages with employed barristers already exist and are being actively developed (see para. 19.21 above). Para. 11.4 of the main Green Paper is inaccurate in this respect as well.

FINANCING OF PUPILS

20.13 The policy of the Bar Council and the steps being taken to implement that policy have been dealt with in paras. 19.19 to 19.21 above.

20.14 The Bar Council considers that by the application of the policy set out in para. 19.19 above it will be possible to ensure both that pupils receive adequate funds, and that the number of available pupillages remains adequate for those seeking pupillages.

ESTABLISHMENT IN PRACTICE AT THE BAR

TENANCIES

20.15 At present the only way in which a barrister can establish herself or himself in practice is by finding a "tenancy" in established chambers. Chambers usually give preference to their own pupils. A successful pupil in one chambers may not be as good as an unsuccessful pupil in another chambers. Not all pupils who wish and ought to be able to remain at the Bar find tenancies; they are lost to the Bar and find employment elsewhere or transfer to the solicitor profession.

20.16 The Bar has recognised the need to introduce a system which will enable available tenancies to be matched with available barristers more openly and more fairly, and so ensure that the most able do get taken on as tenants. The first step will be to use "PATRIC" (para. 20.9 above) as soon as possible to act as an information centre for those seeking tenancies and chambers offering tenancies, with the aim of making it mandatory

(1) for chambers to declare their policies on recruitment
(2) for chambers to register with PATRIC in advance tenancies which are available and the qualifications expected of tenants
(3) for chambers to consider for tenancies every applicant meeting those qualifications whether or not the applicant is a pupil in the chambers.

CHAMBERS

20.17 The present rules relating to chambers have served a useful purpose in the public interest in regulating (a) discipline; (b) efficiency of administration; (c) adequacy of access to library facilities; and (d) in encouraging and maintaining the availability of specialist expertise. But the Bar Council recognises that change is needed and that the rules should impose the minimum of restrictions necessary in the public interest.

20.18 The requirement of consent for the opening of chambers outside the Inns of Court or on the Circuits has been under consideration by a working party. That requirement will not be retained, and will be replaced by simple rules

(1) requiring registration with the Bar Council of all chambers and of those in chambers, whether as tenants, pupils or employees;
(2) preventing individual barristers from setting up in practice on

their own (i.e. otherwise than in existing chambers or in the Library system referred to in paras. 20.26 to 20.29 below) for 3 years after the end of pupillage (the Law Society has a similar rule);
(3) requiring competent and efficient management of barristers' work and of chambers including chambers' and individual barristers' finances (the Bar Council will strongly encourage bringing the management of all chambers up to the standard of the best, as the Binder Hamlyn report recommends);
(4) giving the Bar Council or accountants or others appointed by the Bar Council the right to inspect chambers and the management of chambers.

20.19 Accommodation has inevitably been a problem in a time of rapid expansion of the Bar, given that barristers practising in London wish to practise in the Inns or adjacent to the Inns. The Government apparently considers (para. 11.12 of the main Green Paper) that the Bar "should take active steps to find suitable accommodation for barristers outside the Inns". That is a sentiment with which the Bar Council (and the Inns) would entirely agree, if and only if continuing expansion of the Bar could be foreseen. But the changes proposed by the Government in the Green Papers would lead on the contrary to a marked contraction of the Bar. The effect on the Bar of some of the proposed changes has been set out in Chapter 10 and is not repeated here. Taking just one example, if all prosecutions in the Crown Court were to be conducted by the CPS that would take away the practice of some hundreds of barristers. The Bar Council and the Inns cannot plan for the expansion of the Inns' accommodation if the number of independent barristers is going to fall considerably, or if the future of the Bar is uncertain. If on the other hand the Government decides not to make the major and unwise changes it proposes, and the Bar can look ahead to a period of some stability, then the Bar Council and the Inns will be able to continue and to accelerate the existing processes of extending the Inns' accommodation to which reference is not made in the main Green Paper. Contrary to the impression given by para. 11.12 of the main Green Paper, active steps have been and are being taken to extend the accommodation considerably: see Annex 5.

20.20 In principle the Bar Council sees no objection to chambers opening in London away from the Inns of Court, or outside London away from the major centres where there are already established chambers. But there are two serious problems for any chambers or any barrister with offices distant from the Inns or one of the major centres: access to other barristers for help and guidance, and the provision of adequate library facilities. The Bar as a learned profession needs the major library facilities now available in London in the Inns of Court and the Royal Courts of Justice, supplemented by the libraries of the Institute of Advanced Legal Studies and of some of the constituent colleges of the University of London. It also needs the library facilities in the other major centres (some of which require improvement: see para. 20.21 below). If barristers were to set up in practice at a distance from these libraries, and were without ready access to adequate library facilities, that would be viewed with concern by the Bar Council. The cost of providing such facilities for one chambers or for a single barrister is so great as to be prohibitive for all but the most successful chambers. For the immediate future information technology cannot provide an adequate substitute for a well-stocked library.

20.21 The provision of library facilities is a major problem in some centres outside London, and the Bar Council wishes to work with the Lord Chancellor in ensuring that adequate library facilities are available in each of the main Court centres.

OTHER MEANS OF ESTABLISHMENT

20.22 The Bar Council fully recognises the need to ensure that the chambers system does not act as a restriction preventing the entry to independent practice of young barristers who can provide the further competition which is the life-blood of the Bar. Despite the large increases in numbers at the Bar there are some barristers of ability each year who fail to find tenancies and are lost to the profession.

20.23 The Bar intends to ensure that there is no bar to entry by the following means:-

(1) increasing accommodation for chambers (subject to the Government's intentions as to the adverse changes);
(2) encouraging chambers to keep pupils, to whom they have not offered tenancies, until the chambers and the pupils have made firm arrangements for the pupils' future careers, and actively to assist such pupils in making such arrangements;
(3) establishing a supplementary "library" system in London on the general lines long adopted by the Bars of Northern Ireland, Scotland and the Republic of Ireland.

20.24 If a pupil is not offered a tenancy by the chambers in which he or she is a pupil, other arrangements have to be made for the pupil's future career. Time will be needed to arrange either (1) a tenancy or a further pupillage in another chambers (2) for the pupils to enter the Library system (para. 20.26 below) (3) another career.

20.25 Chambers will be strongly encouraged to keep pupils who have not been offered tenancies until the necessary arrangements for the pupils' future have been made. Chambers will also be strongly encouraged to give their active help to their pupils in making those arrangements.

A LIBRARY SYSTEM

20.26 One of the great strengths of the chambers system (as contrasted with the library systems in Scotland, N. Ireland and Eire) is that it enables barristers to specialise in a particular field of law with the backing of the developed specialist expertise of colleagues in chambers. But not every barrister wishes to specialise to the same extent, and for those who prefer a more general practice a library system offers a simple basis for practice. Furthermore, there are always going to be barristers who do not find places in chambers as tenants, or who prefer to work alone. For all of these a library system may be desirable.

20.27 The essence of a library system is that barristers work in a central library or at home. Conferences take place wherever convenient, in rooms hired from the library, or at solicitors' offices, or at the Courts, or at the barristers' homes. At the library there are central office facilities, including (1) a barristers' clerk or clerks to help with diary and fee arrangements (2) a computerised fee accounting and collection system (3) telephone, fax and other communications (4) word processing and printing facilities supplemented by an agency when necessary.

20.28 It is the Bar Council's intention to carry out a detailed study of how a library system could be set up, with the cooperation of the Inns of Court. This study would examine the costs of setting up and running the library system and how far these costs would be likely to be recouped from charges to the barristers using the system. Subject to the results of this study, it is the Bar Council's intention to start a library system by 1990.

20.29 Within such a library system, there would be room for links between library barristers and chambers barristers. Indeed in the early stages of a library system such links would probably be essential to enable the library barristers to get started in practice, and desirable as a means of ensuring proper professional standards. The Bar Council proposes to encourage such links from the outset. It would also aim to establish further library systems outside London as soon as the need arises.

EMPLOYMENT OF OTHERS

20.30 If the independent Bar remains a profession of sole practitioners it will continue to be inappropriate for barristers to employ other barristers or solicitors who practise as barristers or solicitors. Barristers will obtain assistance from other barristers in chambers, or from barristers practising in the library system, without any employment. Employment of barristers in chambers would derogate from the independence of the Bar, from the requirement of the "cab-rank rule", and from the fundamental principle that each barrister competes on the sole basis of her or his talents, hard work and expertise. Barristers will continue to be able to employ researchers and administrative staff of all kinds.

20.31 If on the other hand the changes proposed by the Government were introduced such as partnerships and MDPs, then since the essential features of the independent Bar would in time disappear, no doubt employment of barristers and solicitors and others by barristers would develop.

FINANCING OF BARRISTERS IN EARLY YEARS OF PRACTICE

20.32 Following on from its policy for the financing of pupils, it is the Bar Council's policy that barristers in at least their first year of practice (and perhaps also their second year) should be guaranteed a sufficient income.

20.33 At present many chambers do ensure a sufficient income to new members until they have built up a practice and can earn enough for themselves (or have failed to achieve this and leave the Bar). Where chambers fail or are unable to do this, barristers tend to obtain bank or building society loans to tide themselves over the initial years of practice: but such loans can impose an undue burden of interest and capital repayment on a barrister whose start in practice is slow.

20.34 The Bar Council recognises the importance of ensuring that young barristers embarked on a career at the Bar have a guaranteed income until their receipts of fees reach a minimum level. A number of Chambers already ensure this. The working party referred to in para. 19.19 above is to report by 20 May 1989 with detailed proposals for achieving this.

20.35 Those barristers who join the library system will not have chambers to support them, but their overheads will be even less than the already low overheads of chambers. It will be the policy of the Bar

216

Council to give financial support to the barristers who have newly joined the library system and do not have support from chambers.

MANAGEMENT OF CHAMBERS

20.36 The functions of a barrister's clerk are those of an agent, business manager and office administrator on behalf of the barristers in chambers. As chambers have become larger, on average, the clerk's functions have moved further towards the administration of the office as a back-up to the work of the barristers. The role of the clerk is often misunderstood, and often criticised through ignorance, and unfairly. Whatever arrangements are made within a chambers there will always be a need for a person in charge of the office who knows the Courts, the Court administrators, the listing officers, the Judges and their clerks, other barristers and their clerks, who has at his fingertips an intimate working knowledge of every person and thing affecting the working life of the barristers whom he serves.

20.37 Changes have already been made in the Code of Conduct removing the specific requirement to employ a clerk. The Bar Council intends to remove from the Code the remaining requirements in respect of clerks. The simple rules outlined in para 20.18 above will impose a firm obligation on every barrister to ensure that her or his work and finances, and chambers organisation and finances, are managed competently and efficiently. Failure to meet this obligation will be a disciplinary offence.

20.38 Though clerks will no longer be compulsory, there can be no doubt that they will continue to be needed. The Bar Council is already working with the Barristers' Clerks Association to improve the training of clerks, so that they bring to their work the professional knowledge and skills they now require. The Bar Council's policy is that clerks of the highest calibre should be employed, including graduates from universities and polytechnics, and that clerks and other staff should be reasonably remunerated. The Bar Council fully supports the Barristers' Clerks in their aims for their profession as stated in their submission to the Lord Chancellor.

CIRCUITS

20.39 In para. 11.25(a) of the main Green Paper the Government questions whether barristers (other than those with chambers in London) should be required to be members of a Circuit or specialist association (section 14 of the Code of Conduct). For those barristers who practise regularly on a Circuit there is a public interest in imposing on such barristers the "peer group discipline" of the Circuit, on which depends the maintenance of high standards of professional conduct, not least as regards the duty owed to the Court. That was the view expressed by the Attorney-General (para. 13.41 above) and the Bar Council agrees with him. The Circuit system has in recent years worked well. The Bar Council considers that those who regularly practise on a Circuit should be strongly encouraged to contribute to the life of the Circuit by becoming members and paying a subscription to the relatively small costs of Circuit administration, collegiate life and discipline. The Bar Council intends to revise section 14 of the Code accordingly.

OTHER RESTRICTIONS

20.40 Holding conferences in barristers' chambers is not infrequently the most cost-effective method. The suggestion in para. 11.25(b) of the main Green Paper that this increases expense may be incorrect. But as already indicated in relation to barristers practising in the proposed library system, the Bar Council sees no need to continue to impose any restriction in this regard and will amend para. 23.2 of the Code of Conduct accordingly. In practice, convenience and cost will continue to tend towards the holding of conferences in chambers.

20.41 Other restrictions in the Bar's Code of Conduct are designed to ensure the independence and high standards of barristers. They have been under regular review, and a working party of the Bar Council is now considering them. Some will disappear in any event in the light of the changes set out above: others will change or disappear according to the recommendations of the working party. Only those which are central to the separate existence of the Bar as a consultant profession of independent sole practitioners operating under the "cab-rank" rule, and in the public interest, will be retained.

OVERSEAS PRACTICE

20.42 The comments on the Bar's overseas practice rules in paras. 11.26 and 11.27 of the main Green Paper are misconceived. It is there claimed that the Bar would not have made those rules if it thought that the "professional integrity" of barristers would suffer as a consequence. But the comparison is an unsound one, for the reasons indicated in para. 15.20 above.

ADVERTISING

20.43 The Monopolies and Mergers Commission (MMC) reported in 1976 upholding the Bar's total ban on advertising as being in the public interest. Nevertheless the Bar Council has made changes so as to allow information advertising and publicity consistent with the position of the Bar as a consultant profession. It is an essential feature of the Bar that direct access by lay clients is not permitted so that barristers can continue to practise independently, and at low cost, by avoiding the large overheads made necessary where such direct access occurs (as the level of solicitors' overheads shows). As a profession operating on a consultant basis it is inappropriate for barristers to advertise to the general public, but appropriate that detailed information should be available to assist solicitors and other professionals who consult the Bar to make an informed choice among the 6,000 barristers.

20.44 The role of advertising by a consultant profession has been recently considered by the MMC in their Report of March 1989 on the Advertising of Services of Medical Practitioners (Cm.582). With one minor exception (cosmetic plastic surgery) the MMC upheld the ban on medical specialists advertising to the public as being in the public interest, and accepted the view of the Department of Health that it would not be possible to devise watertight safeguards to avoid the effects adverse to the public interest of such advertising (para. 8.43 of the MMC Report). But the MMC held that bans on advertising to general practitioners were contrary to the public interest and tended to undermine the effectiveness of the system of referral by general practitioners to consultants (para. 8.46 of the MMC Report). The Bar Council agrees with the tenor of the MMC's conclusions which apply similarly to the Bar as a consultant profession.

20.45 The present rules on advertising by barristers are contained in Annex 8 to the Code of Conduct, the Code of Advertising and Publicity. Under this Code since December 1988 barristers have been permitted to advertise their charges if they wish: the contrary statement in para. 13.10 of the main Green Paper (that the Code "effectively prohibits barristers from publishing their charges") is wrong.

20.46 It is instructive to note briefly how this change in December 1988 came about. In the autumn of 1988, in the light of the Civil Justice Review, the Director-General of Fair Trading suggested to the Bar Council that the advertising of charges might be reconsidered. It was considered in detail. In November 1988 the Bar

Committee and the Professional Standards Committee approved the advertising of charges. This was approved by the Bar Council in December 1988. The Bar Council is able to and does act swiftly to make changes of this kind. On this occasion it acted too swiftly for the Lord Chancellor's Department!

ADVERTISING AND PUBLICITY IN THE FUTURE

20.47 The Bar Council has considered once again the principles which underlie its existing Code of Advertising and Publicity in the light of the MMC Report on the Advertising of Services of Medical Practitioners. The Bar Council's view is that it can largely rely on the good sense of barristers to ensure that wise use is made of advertising and publicity for the services of individual barristers and chambers for the benefit of solicitors and other professionals. The limitations can be reduced to the minimum needed to ensure that the general approach approved by the MMC is adopted. The existing rules for advertising and publicity for overseas practice (Code of Conduct, 4th edition, Annex 12) will suffice, subject to those changes necessary both to adapt those rules to practice within England and Wales, and to ensure that any limitations imposed are the minimum needed to comply with the MMC's approach.

CONTRACTS FOR FEES

20.48 As the law now stands in England and Wales a barrister cannot enter into a contract with an instructing solicitor or other professional in respect of the payment of fees or other matters. The Bar Council would welcome a change in the law to permit contracts with solicitors or other professionals who instruct barristers. Para. 8.3 misstates the position of the Bar in relation to overseas practice. What the Bar has done is to allow barristers to make contracts where the laws of other countries so permit. The Bar could not unilaterally change the law in England and Wales. A change so as to enable barristers to enter into contracts whether their work is to be done at home or abroad is desirable and welcomed.

21

The Foreign Dimension: The EEC, U.S.A. and Commonwealth

21.1 In this Chapter the following matters are considered:

(1) The Government's suggestion that their proposals would not damage the Bar because barristers have been able to gain large practices in Europe.
(2) The EEC problems raised by the Government's proposals.
(3) The lessons to be learned from the U.S.A.
(4) The lessons to be learned from the Commonwealth.

(1) WORK OF ENGLISH BARRISTERS IN EUROPE

21.2 In paragraph 8.7 of the main Green Paper the Government refer to the danger that, if the main Green Paper proposals go through, there could be a significant and serious contraction in the corps of independent barristers available to all solicitors, resulting in the choice of independent barristers available to all lay clients being substantially reduced.

21.3 As an argument for suggesting that there would not be such a reduction, the Government in paragraph 8.8 expresses its hope and expectation that a free market for the provision of independent advocacy services will flourish. It bases this hope and expectation in part on "the present success of English barristers in obtaining work abroad, especially in Europe".

21.4 Paras. 21.5 to 21.10 below answer this part of the Government's argument. These paragraphs are founded on the experience of English barristers with practices in Europe (led by Jeremy Lever Q.C. and David Vaughan Q.C.). They are all barristers with long involvement in practice in Europe, almost entirely in EEC law, have all practised at one time or another either exclusively or in part from Chambers in Brussels, and have very considerable experience of appearing as specialist advocates before the European Commission and the European Court of Justice.

21.5 English solicitors have in the past made substantial use of the Bar to provide specialist advocacy services in the EEC context (whether before the Commission or the Court). They have done this despite the fact that solicitors have the right of audience before the Commission and the Court in appeals from the Commission. But recently there has been a growing tendency for solicitors to conduct cases before the Commission, and then to instruct barristers only before the Court, and also for solicitors to conduct cases before the Court even though they are completely untrained and inexperienced in advocacy, and are not able properly to assist the Court and to present their client's case.

21.6 Lawyers from other EEC countries do not frequently come to the Bar for specialist advocacy services. When they do come, it is usually in one of the following circumstances:

(1) where the specialist advocate is regarded as "supreme" in the particular field, so that the decision to instruct him is virtually forced on the non-specialist lawyer;
(2) where the client insists (in the field of European law the client may be well informed on legal questions and legal personalities);
(3) where the non-specialist lawyer is prepared to accept that he is not equipped by training and experience to act as advocate in a case before the Commission or the Court.

The Bar is instructed by lawyers from outside the Community, for example, where U.S. lawyers instruct specialist advocates before the European Court of Justice.

21.7 The experience is that lawyers, however ill-equipped by training or experience to do so, frequently appear as advocates in their cases. This is so even though the client's chances of success would be very likely to be increased if a specialist advocate were instructed.

21.8 The evidence from the European experience of these barristers indicates that it is not possible to forecast to what extent specialist advocates will continue to flourish in the future in the European field, as the Government suggests in para. 8.8 of the main Green Paper. To the extent that the Bar has flourished in this field, this has been to a great extent due to the reputation of a few individual barristers, or to the existence of exclusive rights of audience in national Courts.

21.9   In the case of advisory services, the instructing lawyer may use the specialist lawyer to advise in fields in which the instructing lawyer either has no experience at all, or seeks a second opinion. However, the tendency in these circumstances will be for the instructing lawyer to send the work to a law firm or other lawyer with whom he has some reciprocal arrangement, or at least a solid expectation of receiving work in exchange. The independent lawyer will very rarely indeed be in a position to have work to offer in exchange.

21.10   It is the judgment of these leading English barristers, based on their long experience, that the hope and expectation expressed in para. 8.8 of the main Green Paper, to the extent that it is said to be based on European experience, cannot be said with any certainty to be either well founded or ill founded. Such confidence as they have in the future is based on the hope that, at least so far as their field of expertise is concerned, solicitors and their clients, brought up in the oral tradition of advocacy in the United Kingdom, will still feel that to be represented by a barrister as their specialist advocate will give them a real advantage. From discussions with Judges of the European Court of Justice, it is clear that the Court itself feels that there is such an advantage. The Court considers that barristers do not simply read prepared speeches, are more flexible in their presentation, and able to answer extempore the Court's questions.

(2)   EUROPEAN COMMUNITY: POTENTIAL PROBLEMS

21.11   The EC implications of the Government's proposals will be the subject of submissions from the Council of the Bars and Law Societies of the European Community, United Kingdom Delegation (CCBE). Accordingly the Bar Council includes here only some general observations in addition to the particular points already mentioned. The Bar of England and Wales has played a leading part in the discussions on the directives necessary to implement Articles 48 to 66 of the Rome Treaty in respect of rights of establishment of lawyers. With the other Bars and Law Societies of the United Kingdom it has worked closely with the Government until July 1988. It would be advantageous if the close collaboration between the Government and the U.K. Delegation of CCBE could now be resumed, in the interest of the public, the Government and the legal professions.

The leader of the U.K. Delegation of CCBE (John Toulmin Q.C.) is now involved in discussions on a directive to regulate rights of establishment for lawyers who wish to establish themselves in other member states under their own title, e.g. English barristers practising as such in Chambers in Brussels. The problems are difficult and underline the need for detailed and careful consideration before changes are made in the structure of the English profession which may affect other member states and the legal professions in those states.

21.12 The Government proposes (para. 1.8 of the main Green Paper) that the legal and other professions should be subject to the proposed U.K. competition legislation modelled on Article 85 of the Rome Treaty, and the jurisdiction of the new U.K. competition authority. At present EC competition law is not in practice applied to the rules of recognised professions, and in other member states national competition laws are not applied to such rules. Articles 48 to 66 of the Rome Treaty are the ones which principally apply. The impact of the proposals for U.K. competition legislation on the U.K. legal professions and on those of other member states will need further consideration, so as to ensure that (1) the U.K. professions are not adversely affected vis a vis the professions of other member states; and (2) the proposals do not lead to further measures being taken by other member states which would create barriers to the competitiveness of the U.K. professions. It may be wiser at this stage either to exclude the professions from the proposed U.K. legislation, or at least to provide in the legislation for power to include the professions at a later stage; and to take the opportunity in the meanwhile to negotiate with other governments for an agreed approach. The steps both proposed and contemplated by other governments could be adverse to the interests of the U.K. and of the U.K. professions, as the recent French and Luxembourg proposals have shown.

21.13 The proposals for the licensing of advocates within a framework imposed by the Government through secondary legislation, for the imposing of codes of conduct and for the recognition of specialisations have rather wide implications for the European Community and also other jurisdictions. Independence of the legal profession is a matter of importance in a number of the EC jurisdictions, and in the USA, the Commonwealth and other common law jurisdictions. The effect of the Government proposal to take away the independence of the legal professions, including the proposed power to give or to take away recognition of professional bodies, would be likely to be damaging, since this could lead to adverse reactions in other countries.

21.14 The Government's policy apparently is to encourage a proliferation of legal professional bodies with members able to provide legal services in advocacy. It is not clear what changes would be necessary to the Legal Services Directive of 22 March 1987 to accommodate this new policy, or what the consequences would be for the U.K. legal professions in terms of requests for changes by other member states. As regards advisory work, at present this is not a reserved area of work in the member states. The Government's proposal is to impose codes of conduct on professions offering legal advice for reward. It is not clear whether this would be regarded by other states as creating a new area of reserved work in the field of legal advice, and therefore would be used by other states in support of their attempts to create new areas of reserved work which the Government and the U.K. professions have previously resisted.

21.15 The Government proposes that non-lawyers would be licensed with rights of audience in Court in England and Wales. What would the effect of this be as regards other member states? Would non-lawyers from all the other members states have to be given the same rights in the Courts of England and Wales? The logic of the decisions of the European Court of Justice indicates that they would have to be given the same rights. This is a matter requiring further consideration.

21.16 The Government's proposals would create a new class of lawyer without the right to appear in any Court in England and Wales. Presumably this proposal would necessitate further alteration of the Legal Service Directive, and would lead to changes in the rights of English lawyers to appear in the courts of other member states and the Community courts. The consequences would have first to be considered carefully.

21.17 The proposals for limited and full certificates would have consequences for lawyers from other member states. At present they can appear in an English court in a particular case provided they are instructed in the case with an English lawyer having rights of audience in the Court. Under the Recognition Directive of 21 December 1988 they will be able to gain access to the English legal professions after undergoing an adaptation period or an aptitude test, according to the requirements laid down by the profession. Once they have entered the English profession it is unclear whether they will receive limited or full certificates. If they receive limited certificates, there will be the anomalous position that as foreign lawyers they can appear in any case in any English court (with an English barrister), but as English lawyers they can appear only in the lower courts. If on entry to the English profession they receive full certificates straightaway, there will be the different anomaly, that an English lawyer will have to complete the required "flying hours" before advancing to a full certificate whereas a foreign lawyer with no experience in England will be able to appear in the House of Lords, with no "flying hours" behind him.

The position of the employed barristers and solicitors will also be unclear, if the Government's proposals go through, having regard to the different treatment of employed lawyers by other member states.

21.18 These few observations indicate the need for the effect of the Government's proposals to be considered carefully and fully before they are implemented. It is the case that in the field of EC practice the consequences of changes, particularly a complicated set of changes, are liable to be complex and difficult to predict.

MULTI-DISCIPLINARY PRACTICES (MDPs)

21.19 The EC and foreign dimensions have already been touched on in paras. 15.29 to 15.31 above. Most member States of the EEC do not permit lawyers to join in MDPs. English lawyers have substantial rights of practice in other member states. So, if English lawyers were to be allowed to join in MDPs, that would no doubt have consequences for the recognition or non-recognition of English lawyers in other member States. Would English lawyers in MDPs be recognised as lawyers in States not permitting MDPs? If not, which English lawyers would still be recognised as lawyers in those States? Auditing firms of accountants must be controlled (at least 51%) by regulated auditors (the EC 8th Company Law Directive). If English lawyers formed less than 51% of an MDP composed of lawyers and auditors, what would be the position of such lawyers in other Member States? Would they only be recognised as lawyers if they were 51% or more of the MDP? None of these questions are addressed in the main Green Paper, and apparently have not been considered at all, though the consequences of the introduction of MDPs could seriously affect the ability of the U.K. legal professions to compete in Europe.

21.20 In the U.S.A. U.S. lawyers cannot join in MDPs. What would be the position of English lawyers in an MDP wishing to practice in the U.S.A. if the English lawyers formed (1) a majority or (2) a minority? This question is also not addressed in the main Green Paper.

21.21 In France avocats may not enter into MDPs. Conseils juridiques may, provided that they hold at least 51%. Significant links between conseils juridiques and the major international accountancy practices have already developed. These have seriously inhibited efforts to unite the professions of avocat and conseil juridique, because the links with the accountancy practices are regarded as inconsistent with the necessary independence of the avocat. Would France recognise an English barrister or solicitor, a minority partner or employee in an MDP dominated by accountants, as having the necessary independence to appear in the French Courts in competition with avocats? Presumably the answer is "no". But the question is not touched on by the Government, and apparently has not even been considered.

MULTI-NATIONAL PRACTICES (MNPs)

21.22 MNPs are permitted in some member States, but these are in a minority. MNPs in relation to English lawyers raise much the same problems and questions as MDPs.

21.23 In relation to the Bar, both MDPs and MNPs could affect the independence of barristers, as the Director-General of Fair Trading has advised: para. 10.5(4) above.

21.24 If MNPs are to be considered for solicitors, there is an obvious need to consult the other member States and to proceed in collaboration and not by unilateral measures.

CONTINGENCY FEES

21.25 The position of the European Community is not touched on at all in the Contingency Fees Green paper and has apparently not been considered. The contingency fee or "pactum de quota litis" is at present not allowed in the member States. This position is reflected in the CCBE Common Code of Conduct for Lawyers in the European Community, article 3.3, with an exception for agreements on an officially approved fee scale or under the control of the competent authority having jurisdiction over the lawyer concerned. The introduction of unregulated contingency fee arrangements would be inconsistent with the position in other States and with the requirements of the CCBE Code. No changes should be made in this regard without collaboration with the other member States as part of the programme of work on the protection of consumers.

CONVEYANCING

21.26 The main question as to the EC position relates to the position of employed lawyers employed by the large finance organisations, whom the Government in its Conveyancing Green Paper contemplates as providing legal services to customers of their **non-legal** employers. The position of employed lawyers has been touched on briefly in para. 21.17 above.

PAUSE FOR THOUGHT

21.27   It is apparent from the naive references to the EC position (in Chapter 1 and Annex A of the main Green Paper) that the authors were not aware of the complex questions raised by the inter-play of the laws of the Community and the laws of 12 member States and by the character of their legal professions. It would be wise, before any firm proposals are embarked on, which have major EC ramifications (as these proposals have), to proceed, first, by thinking through what those ramifications are, and secondly, by securing an agreed and collaborative approach with the other member states.

THE UNITED STATES OF AMERICA

21.28   All lawyers in the U.S.A. are, by training, generalists; there is no division of function between barristers and solicitors. The U.S.A. has the highest ratio of lawyers to population of any country in the world, and a far higher ratio than in the United Kingdom. In 1977 the Chief Justice of the United States (the Hon. Warren Burger) gave evidence to the Royal Commission that, after taking soundings in federal and state courts throughout the country, he concluded that only about a half or less of American lawyers appearing in the Courts were "really qualified to represent their client properly and to move the case along adequately" (22 July 1977, page 3–4). It followed in his judgment that the length of trials in the higher Courts was substantially greater in the U.S.A. than in England and Wales:

> "There is no way to make an accurate measure, but now, from well over 40 years of exposure both as a practitioner in the courts and as a judge in the intermediate court of appeal and on the Supreme Court, having reviewed thousands of records of trials of both civil and criminal cases, my intuitive judgment based on these comparative observations is that a case that is tried on our side generally taking 5 days or 10 days will be tried here in one day or a day and a half or 2 days at most, both civil and criminal" (22 July 1977, pages 4–5).

The Chief Justice accounted for this difference by pointing out that in England there are generally

> "three experts who have all been trained in the same tradition and in the same pattern. The judge almost by definition has been one of the leading members of the Bar, and the two advocates appearing before him are trained in the same way the judge was trained. That is not so on our side" (22 July 1977, page 5).

21.29   He went on to point out that inadequate trial lawyers affected the fairness of the trial, and even more the cost to the paying client or to the public paying the legal aid bill. The best studies in the U.S.A. indicated that in damages cases about half of the amount awarded was absorbed by the costs of the cases. In his view,

> "This is partly related to our contingent fee system; it is partly related to the fact that badly trained or untrained advocates just take too long to get the job done" (22 July 1977, page 6).

21.30 In 1986 a detailed report by the Institute for Civil Justice (R–3391–ICJ) concluded that in all U.S. tort litigation in 1985, of all the money paid in compensation and legal fees and related expenses of the tort litigation, injured plaintiffs received about 56% in net compensation. The litigation system consumed the rest. If the value of the time spent by the litigants was added to the costs, the injured plaintiffs received only 46% of the total expenditures. The ICJ estimates for 1985 were:

	$ billion
Total expenditures	29.2–35.6
Total compensation	20.7–25.1
Total litigation costs (including value of time lost)	15.5–19.2
Net compensation	13.7–16.4

21.31 The Chief Justice went on to criticise the American system for the lack of specialisation such as exists in England and Wales through barristers and solicitors (22 July 1977, page 8). For the United States he was "advocating an elite class of professionals" (page 9) as trial lawyers. "The technique of advocacy can be learned only by close observation and by participation . . . It cannot be taught in the way you can teach substantive law, and you cannot learn it out of a book" (page 10). He emphasised that lack of learning by regular practice in the Courts led to delay. The delays were unfair to plaintiffs and could be exploited by e.g. the large insurers (page 11).

21.32 Another report by the Institute for Civil Justice in 1984 (R–3165–ICJ) analysed in considerable detail the history of delays in civil cases in the Los Angeles Superior Court from about 1920 to 1981. Delay had throughout that period been a continuing and increasingly serious problem. Time-to-trial, i.e. time from the date the parties requested a trial (often months or years after the action started) to the date trial was scheduled to start, was shown to have increased from 6 months in 1940 to 40.5 months in 1981, despite large increases in the number of Judges. As the Bar Council has in England and Wales, so in Los Angeles the ICJ pointed to the failure by Court administrators to introduce up-to-date computer automated case handling to cope with the increasing case-load.

21.33 The Chief Justice emphasised again that lack of a specialised corps of barristers in regular practice was a defect of the American legal systems. He compared the position in medicine, where specialisation had developed, and where a specialist surgeon regularly performing a particular type of difficult operation achieved a higher degree of skill than one who performed that operation only intermittently (pages 12–13). He could not answer the question put by Lord Templeman, why such a specialist corps of advocates had not developed in the U.S.A. (pages 11–12), and could only regret that it had not developed.

21.34 At pages 16 to 17 the Chief Justice indicated his wish that future lawyers should decide after 2 years at law school "whether they want to be a litigation lawyer, a trial lawyer, or whether they want to be at large in the field of practising in what we would call the "office lawyer" on our side, the solicitor here". He rejected the suggestion that in England 2 lawyers had to be paid to do the work done by one lawyer in the U.S.A. (pages 17–18): in the U.S.A., it was often necessary to have 2 or more lawyers.

21.35 It was in response to the Chief Justice's concern about the increasing devotion of American lawyers to the making of money and their decreasing devotion to the principles of their profession, that the ABA Commission on Professionalism was formed: see paras. 4.6 to 4.7 above.

21.36 It is remarkable that the Government should wish to change the English legal profession towards the American profession, with its heavy weighting in favour of the large law firms and their ethics of high fees. Chief Justice Warren Burger's concern about the lack of competence of so many American advocates is reflected in

(1) the need for the Judges to do far more work out of Court than in Court, researching the facts and the law, rather than relying on the barristers before them as in England and Wales;
(2) the necessity for huge delays while everything is ponderously set down in writing;
(3) the short period allowed for oral argument which so often ensures that cases are inadequately decided and have to be appealed;
(4) the lack of good Judges especially in the State Courts which leads to a proliferation of applications and appeals, and causes trials to proceed too slowly.

The present Chief Justice, Rehnquist C.J., during his visit to Australia in 1988, expressed concern at the devouring of legal talent by the major law firms, with the result that access by ordinary people to competent practitioners is seriously reduced.

The former Chief Justice of Australia, Sir Owen Dixon, in "Jesting Pilate" at pages 130–131, stated in relation to the division between counsel and solicitors that

"it is wise, useful and desirable in a very high degree. . . . I think that the administration of justice in the United States has suffered from its absence. There is no completely independent body of men qualified by full forensic experience from which to recruit the Bench. . . . There is not the same confidence between Bench and Bar. Nor is it regularly possible for litigants to obtain the services of counsel who, in the common phrase, know their court".

U.S. AND DISTRICT ATTORNEYS

21.37 The office of the U.S. Attorney was created by Congress in 1789. The U.S. Attorneys represent the federal government in federal district courts, and each federal district contains a U.S. Attorney's office, under the overall central control of the Department of Justice through the Executive Office for U.S. Attorneys. The central control is wide-ranging, including a central body of regulations and instructions in the U.S. Attorneys Manual, and centralised expenditure authority.

21.38 "The need to win cases constitutes the strongest incentive in the work environment of assistants" working in U.S. Attorneys' offices: see "Counsel for the United States" by J. Eisenstein, page 152. The record of the assistant in gaining convictions determines his standing and reputation among his peers, the Judges and the members of the private bar, and affects the job opportunities available to him when he leaves. U.S. Attorneys use conviction rates to assess the work of their assistants. A U.S. Attorney's standing with the Judges depends in part on his ability to maintain a high rate of turnover of criminal cases, which in turn depends on maintaining a high rate of pleas of guilty. Without a high conviction rate, the guilty plea system is jeopardised because defendants are less ready to plead guilty. Conviction rates provide an obvious and convenient measure to compare the relative performance of various Attorneys' offices, and the concern of the Department of Justice with conviction rates is reinforced by pressure from Congress.

21.39 The need for high conviction rates reflects itself in

(1) regular exercise of the discretion not to bring charges so as to avoid bringing cases without a perceived certainty of conviction;
(2) extensive reliance on plea bargaining to secure the highest possible conviction rate;
(3) extensive reliance on multiple charges, especially the inclusion of

many stronger charges, so as to improve the U.S. Attorney's bargaining position in plea bargaining, including the unjustified inclusion of racketeering charges under the RICO Act with the aim of forcing defendants to settle for a plea of guilty to lesser charges;

(4) extensive reliance on plea bargaining to ensure quick convictions with minimal effort and anxiety;

(5) where plea bargaining fails, every effort in Court to secure a conviction.

21.40 Because plea bargaining plays so large a part, the relations between U.S. Attorneys' assistants and defence lawyers tend to be close. The assistants, if they are concerned about job prospects when they leave, shape their behaviour in dealing with defence lawyers so as to enhance their reputation for friendliness and cooperation. It is a major concern of the Department of Justice, and one of their justifications for maintaining control over decisions in U.S. Attorneys' offices, that assistants tend to try to curry favour with private lawyers. Similarly relations between U.S. Attorneys themselves and defence lawyers tend to be shaped by the U.S. Attorneys so as to improve their chances of appointment as federal judges.

21.41 The District Attorneys in the State legal systems show similar characteristics. Conviction rates and plea bargaining to ensure high conviction rates play a large part because of the need to secure re-election or other gainful employment when the term of office ends.

21.42 The lessons that examination of the U.S. prosecutors systems has for England and Wales seem to be these:-

(1) high conviction rates and league tables of conviction rates inevitably come to play a large role in the assessment of individual prosecutors employed by the state;

(2) though plea bargaining plays a much smaller part in English criminal justice, the ability to bargain is likely to be used by employed prosecutors to as full an extent as possible, and in conjunction with the ability to control what charges are made, to ensure a good record of convictions;

(3) the ability to decide whether or not to proceed with charges will be used as it is in the U.S.A. (and in Scotland: see Chapter 13 above) so as to improve conviction rates.

(4) LESSONS TO BE LEARNED FROM THE COMMONWEALTH

NEW ZEALAND

21.43 Students after a 3 year university law course, and a further part-time practical course for 1 year combined with work in a law firm, qualify as both barristers and solicitors. Most continue for their whole career to practise in a law firm, as an employee and then a partner, as both barristers and solicitors. On admission a barrister/ solicitor has full rights of audience in all Courts, having had virtually no training in advocacy.

21.44 Law firms attempt, regardless of their size, to provide a complete service to their clients. There is virtually no referral work between firms, primarily because of the fear of losing the client to another firm.

21.45 There is a small independent Bar which practises as sole practitioners taking work only on referral from law firms. This is based primarily in Auckland (the main commercial centre which is the financial centre of much of the South Pacific) and in Wellington (the capital).

21.46 Those who wish to work as independent barristers tend to move to the independent Bar after 10–15 years as a barrister/solicitor in a law firm. Independent Barristers work mostly on their own, though two embryo "chambers" exist in Auckland sharing common facilities. The independent junior Bar consists mainly of those who have not become partners in law firms or former partners who have left their firms to practise at the independent Bar with a view to becoming Queen's Counsel and subsequently Judges. Any barrister who wishes to become a Queen's Counsel must practise at the independent Bar, since that is a requirement of the status of Queen's Counsel. The High Court Bench is drawn almost exclusively from the ranks of Queen's Counsel. Usually appointment to the High Court Bench is within 3–5 years of becoming a Queen's Counsel.

21.47 Those who practise at the independent Bar receive much of their work from the smaller law firms, or in the case of the larger law firms from the firm where the independent barrister was previously a partner, since in that way the work can be seen to be kept effectively in-house. As far as possible the larger law firms like to keep their advocacy services for their clients in-house. The smaller law firms go to the independent Bar to fill gaps in their advocacy expertise or because the partners are too busy to go to Court. Queen's Counsel are instructed in large or difficult cases leading a partner or employee in the firm as the junior.

21.48 Because law firms prefer to keep work, especially "quality" work, in-house, there has not developed the size of Bar to be found in e.g. New South Wales or Victoria. The age at which juniors start at the Bar, and the quick promotion of Queen's Counsel to the Bench, are further factors tending to keep the independent Bar small in relation to the number of barristers/solicitors.

21.49 That Queen's Counsel are appointed only from the independent Bar and have to practise as Queen's Counsel independently, and that the Judiciary is appointed mainly from the independent Bar, are important factors in maintaining an independent Bar. If Queen's Counsel were appointed from and able to practise in the law firms, and if the Judiciary were drawn to a larger extent from the law firms, it is likely that the independent Bar would wither away.

21.50 In the past it was usual for particular law firms to be given the task of providing prosecuting barristers. Those from such law firms who prosecuted gained much Court experience and tended to find their way to the Bench. But there was a noticeable degree of polarisation between those who always prosecuted and those who always defended. This polarisation was criticised by Sir Robin Cooke, now President of the New Zealand Court of Appeal, in his oral evidence to the Royal Commission (21 July 1977, pages 10–11). The system is now in process of change, in the reverse direction to that proposed in the main Green Paper. Panels of prosecuting counsel are nominated, who are from time to time (and not the whole time) instructed to prosecute.

21.51 Sir Robin Cooke in his evidence to the Royal Commission commented on certain aspects of the legal profession in England and Wales:-

(1) **The existence of the independent Bar**

"I am one of those who does subscribe to this concept of a separate Bar; **and I make no secret of the fact that I think it one of the great British achievements to have evolved such a system or institution. One would be somewhat dismayed to find that in the country of its birth it was either abolished or radically altered.** I think that the idea of an independent body of men and women, specialist and skilled in their type of legal service, and not mere paid agents for the clients, but recognising that they owe some responsibility to the Court; and having the confidence of the Courts, and the standard of ethics and professional skills that tends to go with it, is an extremely valuable concept, and long may that continue". (21 July 1977, page 3: our emphasis).

(2) **The Inns of Court**

". . . we have unfortunately no institution at all analogous to the Inns of Court here. That is a great gap I think in New Zealand. Perhaps in time we will come to fill it; but we lack that sort of corporate life within the Bar, which must be a great help as well as training to young barristers; and partly because of that I think that there has been some suggestion that people are going out [to the independent Bar] without enough training, but they would be a very small number". (21 July 1977, page 7).

AUSTRALIA

21.52 The circumstances of the federal and state legal system in Australia differ to a considerable extent from those in England and Wales, and also as between the different Australian states.

21.53 New South Wales This State has a divided profession with solicitors and barristers admitted under the Legal Profession Act 1987. Solicitors have rights of audience in all courts in any matter in which they are instructed by or on behalf of any person whether or not instructed by that person or by a solicitor acting on behalf of that person (section 18). Transfer is possible but in some respects less easy than in England and Wales (see e.g. section 17 of the 1987 Act and paras. 5.19 and 5.20 above). Appointment to the High Court Bench is primarily from Queen's Counsel (who are all barristers), though some solicitors have been appointed mostly as Family Judges.

Only barristers practising at the independent Bar are made Queen's Counsel. Some Queen's Counsel have left the independent Bar and become solicitors, retaining their commission as Queen's Counsel. The present Attorney General of New South Wales is considering whether to require surrender of the commission by those who become solicitors. Selection of Queen's Counsel is made in this way: the first list is prepared by the New South Wales Bar Council after detailed consultation within the independent Bar and with the senior Judges. This list then goes to the Attorney General, who again carries out full consultation especially with the Judges, and then makes the final selection on behalf of the Government.

21.54 In 1976 the N.S.W. Law Reform Commission was asked to enquire into the legal profession. The Commission reported in 1982 as being, by a majority, in favour of common admission and practice on the lines of the Victoria profession (para. 21.57 below). That recommendation was strongly backed by the "mega" firms of solicitors in Sydney who wished to establish in-house chambers containing partners and associates specialising in advocacy. The NSW Government rejected the recommendation, and accepted the view that

(1) the proposal represented a definite threat to the continued existence of an independent Bar;

(2) there was a real public interest in continued access to such a Bar which could provide advice that was truly independent, not affected by unseen conflicts of interest, and not likely to be leaked to partners and associates;

(3) there was also a public interest in the provision of advocacy services at reasonable cost by an independent Bar, rather than at the much higher cost necessary to cover the overheads of the "mega" firms;

(4) the independent Bar was able to provide a more efficient and flexible advocacy service and better able to fit in with the efficient running of busy Courts.

The NSW Government decided that there should continue to be separate professions. The Law Profession Act 1987 maintained the separate professions with separate training and entry, as set out in para. 21.53 above.

21.55 Crown Prosecutors In New South Wales prosecuting in criminal cases is performed in all but the most serious cases by Crown Prosecutors employed within the department of the Director of Public Prosecutions (DPP). There is recognised to be a significant degree of polarisation between the prosecutors and the independent Bar who almost always appear for the defence. The newly born Criminal Law Association has been formed because of concern that the criminal barrister is undervalued and because of this unfortunate polarisation between those who always prosecute and those who always defend. The delays in criminal cases are very serious indeed, being measured in terms of years, not just months. The period between arrest and trial can be as long as 3–5 years. The position as regards prosecutions is different in the State of Victoria. There the DPP has deliberately fostered a practice of using the independent Bar in most prosecutions (about 70% of cases) so as to avoid the polarisation that has developed in New South Wales. There is some astonishment that the U.K. Government should be proposing to abandon representation by independent barristers (which has worked well in Victoria) and to move towards representation by employed Crown Prosecutors (a system which has not worked well in New South Wales).

21.56 Rights of Audience So far as concerns rights of audience, solicitors generally in all the States have rights of audience. It is of importance to note in what circumstances solicitors use these rights. In those States in which there is a formal division between barrister and solicitor (New South Wales and Queensland) or an informal but long standing division (Victoria) the main consideration governing the decisions by solicitors whether or not to do cases in-house, rather than to instruct independent barristers, is usually the cost to the solicitor. Except in very short cases solicitors are not able or prepared to bear the costs involved because their costs well exceed the charges they can make to their client or to the legal aid scheme, and well exceed the cost of instructing an independent barrister. However, if a case attracts a great deal of publicity, the potential financial loss to the solicitor may be outweighed by the publicity and the increased flow of work derived from the solicitors receiving that publicity. Too rarely is the test whether or not an experienced barrister would do the case better. The solicitor generally has the choice whether to do the case himself (and the choice is not left to the client) and exercises this choice too often on grounds of self-interest.

21.57 The Legal Profession in the other States Turning to the States other than New South Wales, apart from Queensland which has a divided profession similar to New South Wales, all the other States have fused professions but with independent Bars.

(1) **Victoria** has only a formally or nominally fused profession. Lawyers practise either purely as barristers, or purely as solicitors, or as both barristers and solicitors ("amalgams"). Queen's Counsel are required to practise only as barristers, and appointments to the High Court Bench are made from the ranks of Queen's Counsel. Queen's Counsel are not permitted to appear with a junior who is not an independent barrister. Probably the greatest change in recent years has been the development of "mega" firms of solicitors.

(2) In **Western Australia** a separate Bar has emerged from the fused profession since 1963. Queen's Counsel are drawn from the separate Bar, or from those practising as barristers and solicitors who are required to join the separate Bar after appointment. Judges of the High Court are drawn from the ranks of Queen's Counsel.

(3) **South Australia** has a fused profession with a small separate Bar which emerged in 1964. Much of the conveyancing work is done by land brokers, rather than solicitors. Since 1978 the Chief Justice has limited appointments of Queen's Counsel to those who undertake to practise at the independent Bar. Only one Queen's Counsel remains who practises within a firm of solicitors. The South Australian Bar sees the advantages of this rule in relation to Queen's Counsel as being:-
(a) the leaders of the bar are available to all solicitors, both "mega-firms" and small, and thus to a full range of lay clients;
(b) silks work in a more competitive environment;
(c) silks work in a more independent environment; independent, that is, from their instructing solicitors, their lay client, and financially;
(d) silks work with lower overheads than they would in conjunction with solicitors, so that junior silks can work for fees which would be uneconomic in a "mega-firm" (judging by the hourly rates of some solicitors).
The President of the South Australian Bar has said:-

"I disagree with the idea that silks should be able to join solicitors' firms. It seems to me it puts restraints on the proper role of a silk. Inevitably the cab rank rule would be eroded, the firms' clients getting preference to other clients. No doubt large firms of solicitors would seek to engage silks within their firm. This would be a loss to other litigants.

If, having taken silk, a barrister wishes to practise as a solicitor then it goes without saying he should forego his commission. . . . Silks 'sink or swim' at the Bar. I do not believe that would be the case if they worked from within solicitors' firms".

(4) **Northern Territory** has a single profession, but with a separate Bar which emerged following the Legal Practitioners Act 1973. Since 1979 Queen's Counsel have been appointed exclusively from the independent bar. Chief Justice Foster, now retired, said:

"I have practised as an amalgam and have had experience during 17 years on the bench of the appearance before me of amalgams and barristers whether belonging to a legally separate bar or a de facto separate bar. I have now no doubt that the Courts and the litigating public are, generally speaking, better served by cases being conducted by members of an independent bar."

(5) The **Australian Capital Territory** has had a small separate Bar since the early 1960's, with strong competition fron New South Wales and Victoria barristers.

(6) **Tasmania** has a fused profession, but a separate Bar has recently emerged.

21.58 It is difficult to draw many clear lessons from the Australian states because the circumstances are largely dissimilar. But these lessons at least can be drawn:-

(1) The large firms of solicitors many of which are based in Sydney would have rapidly expanded into advocacy work if they could have secured their object of being able to have barristers and Queen's Counsel within their own firms. This parallels the aims of the largest firms in London both of solicitors and of accountants: see Chapter 10 above. The consequences which would follow, if these large firms were permitted to do this, were succintly stated by the former Chief Justice of Australia, Sir Harry Gibbs, when commenting on the Green Papers:

"A recent phenomenon in Australia, and I believe also in the UK and elsewhere, is the formation of the mega-firm of solicitors. Now, in Australia, firms of solicitors, enormous in size, span the continent and seek to command the commercial work of the nation. Their aim, which is undisguised, is to be self-sufficient in all the specialties of the law. If a right of audience in the superior courts were given to a class of advocates who might be either barristers or solicitors (or neither), and barristers and solicitors were permitted to practise in partnership, the consequences would certainly be that each large firm would have, among its members, its own advocates. The choice of the smaller firms in briefing counsel would be reduced. In the end, the best men and women would be attracted by the security and other advantages which the large firms could offer. It would be optimistic to expect that the provision of independent services of advocacy would survive."

(2) The existence of a rank of Queen's Counsel drawn from the independent Bar, and forming the only source or the primary source for promotion to the High Court Bench is a significant factor in maintaining an independent Bar. The Government's proposals would remove this factor in England and Wales.

(3) The trend in Australia is at present towards specialisation, and towards practical recognition of the separate specialised functions of barrister and solicitor. The Government's proposals would represent a large stride in the opposite direction, towards generalism and away from separate specialised function, e.g. in the proposal for the effective fusion of the professions of barrister and solicitor, for direct lay access to barristers, and for the requirement that advocates do not specialise, and practise in both criminal and civil courts, if they are to be eligible for promotion as Queen's Counsel or as High Court Judges. The Australian experience demonstrates, as clearly as any, that these are steps in the wrong direction.

(4) The Australian experience does not support the Government's expectation or hope that, if it makes its revolutionary changes, the Bar will proceed as if nothing had happened. On the contrary, it shows how difficult it has been for a specialised advocacy profession to emerge from a generalist profession, and that the emergence of a specialised advocacy profession has depended on economic and other circumstances, and in particular on the economic power of the large firms. Where that power is not too great, emergence of the specialist profession has at last been possible. That is not the position in London, especially if the possibility of multi-disciplinary partnerships is to be contemplated.

(5) The experience with employed Crown Prosecutors in New South Wales has been an unhappy one, as compared with Victoria where 70% of prosecutions are conducted by the independent Bar.

CANADA

21.59 It is not proposed to deal at length with the position of the legal profession in Canada. In general, as a single profession, it follows much the same pattern as the U.S.A. The defects in the American system referred to above appear, though to a less marked extent in Canada. Contingency fees, in the Provinces in which they are permitted, lead for example to "ambulance chasing" but to a less extreme extent than in the U.S.A. The Queen's Counsel system is entirely different to that in the United Kingdom, Ireland, Australia or New Zealand, and has lost the mark of distinction which in these other countries it is intended to be. The polarisation between Crown Prosecutor and defending lawyer exists and is a phenomenon giving rise to concern, as is the problem of "success rates" of convictions.

21.60 The problems which affect barristers in the Canadian law firms, particularly in civil work include the following: They do not have enough practice in Court, because they have to spend so much time in the preparation of cases, doing the work which in England and Wales is done by solicitors. The result of having to do all the preparatory work is that barristers frequently have major back-logs of cases not ready for trial, which they cannot progress towards trial while engaged in court on another case. These back-logs are translated into serious delays in progressing cases to trial. Barristers are also exposed in their partnerships to pressures as to the way in which they conduct cases, pressures to satisfy clients' wishes, pressures to ensure that a large client does not move to another law firm, and pressures to protect the partnership. This is contrasted with the position in England and Wales where the independent barrister is insulated by the separation of the professions from these kinds of pressure.

21.61 So far as specialisation is concerned, barristers in Canada tend to have to be generalists, and to deal with the whole range of cases coming to their firms. Where they are specialists, their specialist services are available in practice only to clients of their own firm, and not generally as are the specialist services of an English barrister practising e.g. in the field of patents or trademarks. Barrister-only firms are non-existent. Litigation-only firms have not flourished. Law firms in Canada try always to keep cases in-house, even where the skills and experience available in-house are not adequate for the particular case.

21.62 As a distinguished lawyer, Mr. Rowland Williams, observed (after 13 years of practice as a litigator in a large law firm in a mid-Western city in Canada, and futher practice in England, mostly in commercial work as a partner in a firm of solicitors in the City of London):-

"Thus fusion, as applied to Canada's more de-centralized circumstances, has produced a firm-orientated legal system, with barristers generally overstretched, tending to be generalists rather than specialists in particular fields of law, not given enough courtroom time to develop their forensic skills early or fully enough, outnumbered, sometimes even dominated, by the solicitor members of their firms, obliged by their firm membership to give priority to their firms' largest clients, occasionally exposed to pressures from which they should obviously be free, semi-private rather than fully public figures." (Law Society Gazette, 30 March 1977).

It is apparent that, based on the Canadian experience, the likely developments if the Green Paper changes were made would include:

(1) Solicitors seeking to recruit from the Bar in competition with each other so as to gain the benefit of having leading barristers' names on their notepaper, as is "de rigueur" in Canada.
(2) Solicitors seeking to recruit advocates at the younger end, and to make arrangements with chambers leading to "closed shop" or "most-favoured nation" situations, by which a barrister's skills are available only or primarily to particular firms.
(3) A movement towards generalist barristers dealing with a range of cases within the solicitor firm so as to make best use of the barrister's skills in-house.
(4) The specialist skills of specialist barristers, which Mr. Rowland Williams regards as "the highest achievement of the independent Bar", over a period disappearing.

22

Probate

22.1 Under Section 23 of the Solicitors Act 1974 (as substituted by the Administration of Justice Act 1985) it is a criminal offence for any unqualified person, directly or indirectly, to draw or prepare any papers on which to found or oppose a grant of probate or letters of administration, unless he proves that the act was not done for or in expectation of any fee, gain or reward. Barristers and notaries, as well as solicitors, are not "unqualified persons" for this purpose: similarly an employee, fellow employee or partner of a solicitor or notary is not treated as an "unqualified person".

22.2 The Government proposes **either**

(1) to allow anyone to prepare documents for the purpose of obtaining a grant of probate (where there is a will) or letters of administration (where a person dies not having made a valid will): this is Option B; **or**
(2) to extend the classes of person who are treated as not being "unqualified persons" for the purposes of section 23: this is Option A.

As part of Option A it proposes that there should be no code of conduct and no control over charges for persons permitted to prepare the relevant documents, other than solicitors, barristers and notaries.

It is also proposed that the requirement to swear an oath (when making the affidavit necessary to support an application for grant of probate or letters of administration) might be abolished. These proposals are set out in paras. 14.11 to 14.33 of the main Green Paper.

22.3 These matters do not affect the Bar directly. The Bar does not at present exercise its rights under Section 23. The Bar's probate work is at present purely advisory.

22.4   The views of the Bar Council are that:-

(1) Option A should be followed.
(2) The classes of person allowed to do probate work for reward should be solicitors, barristers, notaries and trust corporations.
(3) The charges made by and standards of trust corporations should be subject to a measure of control.
(4) The requirement to swear an affidavit on oath should not be abolished, so long as it is retained generally for witnesses giving oral evidence in Courts and tribunals and for affidavits.

22.5   The general public needs protection from the unscrupulous and the incompetent. This is particularly important for the bereaved, who have, in addition to their inexperience in the law, the handicap of bereavement (which is often long-lasting).

FRAUD

22.6   The Bar is aware of not infrequent cases where a person has turned up at a funeral, or soon after, claiming to be a friend of the deceased and offering to assist the relatives in sorting out the deceased's estate. When the offer is accepted, the supposed "friend" then tries to trick and sometimes succeeds in tricking the relatives out of at least part of the estate. These cases by their nature do not always come to light. There is already a real risk of fraud, and this risk would be likely to increase if unqualified persons were allowed to prepare documents and apply for probate or letters of administration, and to make a charge for the services they purport to render.

INCOMPETENCE

22.7   The death of a person can give rise to a variety of difficult legal questions, of which three examples are:-

(1) the meaning of a will may be quite different from what on its face it appears to mean (the textbooks cite many such cases);
(2) the immediate family may well have claims against the deceased's estate, if not adequately provided for by the will, under the Inheritance (Provision for Family and Dependents) Act 1975;
(3) the tax burden may be capable of being mitigated (though there will be less opportunity for this if the 1989 Budget proposals become law).

By opening up probate work to unqualified persons who may have no knowledge or expertise at all in these matters, there would be the obvious risk of placing the general public at the mercy of incompetent unqualified persons.

WHO SHOULD DO PROBATE WORK FOR REWARD?

22.8   The classes of persons entitled to do probate work for reward should be limited to solicitors, barristers, notaries and trust corporations. These classes are by their professions, or in the case of trust corporations can be, subjected to the necessary controls on their standards. Such a restriction would both meet the difficulties now created for trust corporations (paras. 14.5 to 14.8 of the main Green Paper) and give to the general public sensible protection against the activities of the unqualified, the dishonest and the incompetent.

22.9   There has not been demand by chartered or certified accountants to do probate work. Those that wish to make a business of it (and therefore may be assumed to be prepared to acquire the necessary expertise over a broad field) will be prepared to form a trust corporation (as some have already) so that they can provide executorship facilities generally.

22.10   To allow licensed conveyancers (or the authorised practitioners proposed in the Conveyancing Green Paper) would be unwise. They do not have understanding of the whole field covered by probate work, but only of one small corner of it, namely title to and transfer of land and buildings.

EXTENSION OF SECTION 23

22.11   Consideration should be given to extending section 23 to cover any act done **for reward** as an executor or administrator of a deceased's estate (with an appropriate exemption for anyone given power to do so under the terms of a will). Section 23 at present only covers the formal act of preparing or drawing papers. If it is to give sensible protection it should cover all acts done **for reward**, at the same time as it is widened to include trust corporations.

THE OATH

22.12   The requirement that the value of an estate be sworn for grant of probate or letters of administration has two reasons:

(1)   a person's entitlement may depend on it, where for instance there

is an intestacy and a widow entitled to a statutory legacy, or the will gives legacies of a certain amount before a residuary gift;
(2) the tax liability will depend on it.

Reason (1) alone justifies the retention of the oath, since persons with potential interests in an estate rely on the truth of the value at which the estate is sworn, where, as is frequently the case, they do not have the knowledge or expertise to be able to value the estate.

CHARGES

22.13 Solicitors' charges are subject to the right of the client to have them taxed by the Court. The Royal Commission on Legal Services recommended that a trust corporation should be permitted to apply for probate of a will (para. 19.25) but that charges made by trust corporations should be subject to the same safeguards as are solicitors' charges (para. 19.27). As the Royal Commission pointed out, there is no check on the reasonableness of the charges of a trust corporation which

> "may be quite different from those prevailing when the will was signed. This is particularly important because the testator, who authorised the charge, will not be alive when the charges are made. In short, an interested party should have the right to require the charges to be taxed by the Court in the same way as solicitors' charges may be taxed at present. In cases where a bank, or a member of a banking group, acts as executor those safeguards should cover not only acceptance, administration and annual charges but also any associated bank charges and other financial advantages arising in the course of the administration" (para. 19.27).

22.14 It is no answer to the considered views of the Royal Commission to state, as the main Green Paper does (in para. 14.22), that market forces should set the prices. The choice of the trust corporation is made by the testator. Years, perhaps many years later, he or she dies, and the trust corporation exacts its charges at that time. There is no market, there are no market forces, and there is no setting of prices except the wish of the trust corporation at that time. It is common for trust corporations to charge a fee for renouncing probate in an estate where they are not prepared to act - a straightforward abuse of a dominant position. As for the assertion by banks that their charges are high "because they have had to pay solicitors to do work which they have virtually done already" (main Green Paper, para. 14.22), this is not a credible assertion. The true position is that trust corporations have often grossly overcharged, and there are insufficient safeguards for the inexperienced general public who do not have at their finger-tips a comparative chart of prices of different trust corporations and different solicitors.

Quality of Justice

22.15   The safeguard of a right to tax the costs of trust corporations should be adopted as the Royal Commission recommended. Such a safeguard would be in line with the policy of consumer protection adopted for example in the Consumer Credit Act 1974.

SHARE CAPITAL OF TRUST CORPORATIONS

22.16   The requirement that a trust corporation should have a paid up share capital of only £100,000 needs to be reviewed. This amount is too low by 1989 standards.

23

Conveyancing

23.1 "Conveyancing" involves the provision of specialist legal services in connection with the transfer of rights in or over land and buildings. These services are at present provided by solicitors, and by the small number of licensed conveyancers, a category established by the Administration of Justice Act 1985.

23.2 Solicitors who do conveyancing work are spread throughout England and Wales. 80% of their firms have 4 or fewer partners. Conveyancing work represents, on average, 30% of the fee income of solicitors' firms. In most of the smaller firms, conveyancing work represents much more than 30%, in some firms as much as 50–60%. Because of (1) the limitations on eligibility for legal aid; (2) the low level of fees paid for legal aid work; and (3) the delays in payment of legal aid fees, the loss of income from conveyancing work would have serious financial consequences for many solicitors' firms.

23.3 Solicitors' firms cannot be shielded from *fair* competition in the provision of conveyancing services, and the many letters sent to the Bar Council show that they are willing to meet any *fair* competition. At present there is strong competition between solicitors, and with licensed conveyancers, and this competition has shown itself in reduced fees and reduced margins.

23.4 The Government now proposes in its Conveyancing Green Paper that conveyancing services should be provided by banks, building societies, insurance companies, and other lending organisations (through employed solicitors or licensed conveyancers) to those who borrow from such organisations. It also proposes that any person, whether an individual, a partnership or a company, may provide conveyancing services to the public as an "authorised practitioner", provided that such person is within the regulation of an "authority" (e.g. as a surveyor, a valuer, an insurance broker, an

247

estate agent, or mortgage lending company) and meets certain stated "safeguards".

23.5 It is the Bar Council's view that these proposals

(1) would create wholly unacceptable conflicts of interest against which no nicely drafted code of conduct could provide any adequate safeguards;

(2) would create dangers, e.g. in the safeguarding of client's money, which similarly could not be safeguarded by any code of conduct;

(3) would introduce *unfair* competition likely to destroy the financial base of many independent solicitors' firms;

(4) by destroying the viability of independent solicitors' firms, would destroy the present benefit to the public of legal advice locally available through the large number of smaller independent firms (who in turn can consult any of the 6,000 independent barristers), without giving the public any real or equivalent advantage in place of this benefit;

(5) would be directly contrary to the scheme for the protection of the public when borrowing on the security of houses or flats under the Consumer Credit Act 1974.

THE AVERAGE HOUSE-BUYER

23.6 The buying of a house usually represents much the largest single transaction any person or couple or family ever undertakes. The mortgage payments which a family makes on the family home represent usually much the largest burden on the family budget, month by month. Ensuring that (1) the purchase proceeds without undue hitches, (2) finance is obtained on fair terms, and (3) there are no hidden problems which may affect the value of the home or cause expensive disputes in the future, is vital for every home-buyer.

23.7 The prospective home-buyer is usually unversed in the problems that may arise in connection with house purchase, occupation and ownership, in e.g. transfer of ownership, the grant or assignment of leases, multiple occupation of blocks of flats or converted houses, the terms of mortgages, loan transactions, linked life insurance policies, property insurance, or property owners or occupiers insurance. These are all matters in which home-buyers are likely to be dealing with organisations that have both far greater expertise and strong interests in making the maximum profits out of the home-buyer and the transaction. These are all matters in which the home-buyers are likely to need disinterested independent advice from an experienced professional, so as to guide the home-buyers through the pitfalls which may lie in their path.

THE "ONE-STOP-SHOP"

23.8 What the Government is proposing, put simply, is that a prospective home-buyer may go to a local finance organisation with a monopoly in the town or city area (i.e. at least 25% of the relevant business). In the organisation there may be

(1) an estate agency section persuading the home-buyer to buy a house or flat: the house or flat may be too expensive for the buyer, bad value for the price, or with disadvantages not apparent to the lay person: but the estate agency section would have a strong interest in selling the house or flat thereby gaining commission for the organisation, and securing the whole transaction for the organisation;

(2) a surveyor section reporting on the state and value of the house or flat: the house or flat may not be in an adequate state, or may perhaps need expensive repairs in the future, or be poor value at the price being paid: but the surveyor section would have a strong interest in ensuring that the transaction goes through, so that the organisation derives not only the estate agent commission and the survey fee but also all the other benefits from the transaction;

(3) a mortgage section arranging the terms of the loan and its repayment by the home-buyer: the terms of the mortgage may be disadvantageous to the home-buyer: but the mortgage section would have a strong interest in securing the best terms for the organisation and in ensuring that the transaction goes through, so that the organisation gains the benefit of those terms, and also all the other benefits from the transaction;

(4) a life insurance section arranging life insurance as security for the mortgage: the terms of the life insurance may be disadvantageous to the home-buyer, or less appropriate than the terms of the rival life insurances: but the life insurance section would have a strong interest in securing the best terms for the organisation (not the borrower) on the life insurance, and keeping the transaction all within the one organisation;

(5) a property insurance section arranging insurances for the home-buyer and the house or flat: the terms of those insurances may not be as good as they should be: but the property insurance section would have a strong interest in securing the best terms for the organisation (not for the home-buyer) on these insurances, as well as keeping the whole transaction within the one organisation;

(6) a solicitor or licensed conveyancer section, advising on the terms of the purchase and the terms of the mortgage: the terms may not be favourable to the home-buyer, especially the mortgage terms: but the solicitor section would have a strong interest not to advise

against the mortgage terms because they were in the interest of
the organisation;

(7) an accountant section, offering accountancy advice: the advice
may be in the interests of the organisation, and the cost may be
unduly high: the accountant section would have a strong interest
to advise in the organisation's interest, and to maximise the price.

23.9 It is obvious that in such a "one-stop-shop" financial
organisation the conflicts between the interests of the organisation
and the interest of the inexperienced and manipulable home-buyer
would be serious conflicts. That already such conflicts not only exist,
but also operate unfairly against home-buyers, can be seen in the
operations of the new chains of estate agents tied to banks or building
societies or insurance companies, which have strenuously "sold" to
home-buyers tied mortgage arrangements, tied life insurances and
tied property insurances, without any disclosure of the large financial
gains made by the estate agents and their owner banks, building
societies and insurance companies.

23.10 It is also clear that in such a "one-stop-shop" financial
organisation the ability to allocate costs to one section or another
would render a requirement to charge the "full cost" of solicitors'
services in conveyancing an inadequate safeguard. The allocation of
costs, especially overheads, between different parts of a business is an
art, not a science, and a frequent ground of dispute, e.g. in the time of
the Price Commission. Attempts by regulators to prevent cross-
subsidisation have been unsuccessful. The Monopolies and Mergers
Commission has had the greatest difficulty in identifying costs
applicable to particular services. Without external control, any
organisation required to show that it provides particular services at a
price not less than cost will build a costing system distributing items of
cost so as to achieve this objective. In theory the Government could
lay down a set of rules, but this would have to be complex and would
lead to economic inefficiencies as organisations altered their costings
to fit round the rules. The cost of checking compliance with the rules
would be excessively expensive. In practice there would be no
reasonably certain way of ensuring that cross-subsidisation of
conveyancing services was not taking place. The Director-General of
the Building Societies Association has confirmed that it would not be
possible to ensure a "level playing field".

THE ROYAL COMMISSION ON LEGAL SERVICES

23.11 The Royal Commission gave first priority to the protection of
the public as home-buyers. In para. 21.21 of their Report they

emphasised the importance to home-buyers of "the most expensive transaction of their lives", and of the need for the home-buyer to be "protected from:-

(a) dishonesty or carelessness with money;
(b) ignorance and incompetence;
(c) a level of charges higher than is fair and reasonable."

The Royal Commission were concerned merely with conveyancing as such, and did not have to consider the wider implications of tied transactions or "one-stop-shop" finance organisations.

23.12 The Royal Commission compared the position in the U.S.A. They found that in many parts of the U.S.A. there was no limitation on the right of any person to undertake conveyancing. So in theory there was full and free competition. But, in practice, the competition was not based on price, because the ultimate consumer had a small voice.

> "The competitive forces that do exist manifest themselves in an elaborate system of referral fees, kickbacks, rebates, commissions and the like. These practices are widely employed and have replaced effective price competition. These referrals or kickbacks paid by or to lawyers, lenders, title insurance companies, real estate brokers and others result in unnecessarily high costs".

The Royal Commission also quoted from an American Bar Association report which stated:-

> "In some sections of this country all parties are represented by lawyers from the beginning and the system works well. In England, in modern times, this has been the universal practice and *this system provides greater service at less cost than in America*". (our emphasis)

ADEQUATE SAFEGUARDS?

23.13 How could home-buyers be adequately protected if the Government's proposals went through? In December 1985 the present Government's view was declared in Parliament by the Attorney-General (Rt. Hon. Sir Patrick Mayhew Q.C. M.P.: then the Solicitor-General) to be as follows:-

> ". . . the Government are not satisfied that lending institutions could safely be permitted to offer both conveyancing and a loan in the same transaction. It is therefore proposed to prohibit lending institutions from providing conveyancing, either directly or through a subsidiary company in which they hold a majority stake, to those who are also borrowing from them".

23.14 But the Government has now concluded that it is safe to allow lending institutions to offer both conveyancing and a loan (and estate agency, life insurance, property insurance, accountancy and any other services) in the same transaction, and that it is safe to allow this without the safeguards written into the Building Societies Act 1986. At the same time the Government accepts how important it is for home-buyers to have an "informed choice" whether to employ a finance organisation or an independent solicitor or a licensed conveyancer to do their conveyancing.

23.15 The safeguards proposed and the reality of the "informed choice" must be considered in relation to what is likely to happen to home-buyers in practice. First-time buyers are vulnerable because largely inexperienced. Second-time buyers are in some respects even more vulnerable. They need to use the same lawyer to deal with the sale of their old home and the purchase of their new home, so that the two transactions can be coordinated, and so that they do not incur the expense of a bridging loan and the worry and expense of buying the new house before selling the old house.

23.16 The would-be home-buyers are likely to find the home they want to buy through an estate agency. The estate agency is likely to be part of a finance organisation. It will offer a "package deal". The safeguards suggested in the Green Paper will no doubt be set out in a document which the home-buyers will not have time to read, let alone understand. That is the experience after "Big Bang" in the City of London. The home-buyers are unlikely to appreciate the need to examine each part of the "package deal" separately, or to have the expertise to do this. They will not know whether or not the conveyancing services are being offered *at cost* (the safeguard suggested in the Green Paper against unfair competition), or, if that is so, whether that is being subsidised by another 1/4% on the loan, or a higher charge for life insurance, or for property insurance, or for accountancy services, or for the survey. It would be easy for any finance organisation to charge what is notionally cost price for conveyancing, and to make good their profits by higher charges on other aspects of the transaction.

23.17 It is hard to believe that a finance organisation's staff, remunerated in part by commission and bonuses, would be as concerned as would be an independent solicitor to see that the need for a bridging loan was avoided. They would be much more likely to persuade a second-time buyer to accept the need for a bridging loan, because they and the finance organisation employing them would benefit financially from a bridging loan: the independent solicitor would gain no such benefit and would, on the contrary, have every incentive to advise against incurring the cost of a bridging loan.

23.18 It is suggested in the Green Paper that it may be safe to provide that if one branch of a finance organisation acts for a buyer, and another for a seller, each branch might be treated as a separate practitioner (proposed code, para. 6). That naive suggestion ignores the fact that each branch has the same financial interest in maximising the profits of the finance organisation. "Chinese Walls" do not work in the City of London. They are even less likely to work where inexperienced home-buyers are involved, than in the City of London where the clients tend to be financially experienced. The suggested "Chinese Walls" approach would any way not work if seller and buyer dealt with the same branch, or if the two branches of the finance organisation used the same centralised conveyancing department of the finance organisation (such centralisation would be likely).

23.19 The Green Paper seems to be based on the assumption that a solicitor doing conveyancing is merely concerned with more-or-less routine paperwork. In some cases that can be true. But in most it is not true. The Royal Commission obtained a considerable body of evidence about this, and concluded:

> "In general, the evidence of those advocating abolition of the present restrictions tended to underestimate the number and frequency of difficulties which may be encountered unexpectedly in any conveyancing transaction, domestic or otherwise, and which require the advice and skills of a qualified practitioner. Among the difficulties we have in mind are those arising from planning and revenue law, the Matrimonial Homes Act 1967 [now 1983], the making of wills, and purchases by two or more persons. Problems of great complexity can arise when charities, limited companies, religious bodies and unincorporated associations appear in the abstract of title". (para. 21.34).

23.20 The solicitor's tasks in conveyancing are manifold. He has to coordinate purchases and sales. Couples need to be carefully advised about their beneficial interests in the home. Groups of young people joining together to buy a house or a flat need quite a sophisticated agreement defining their mutual rights and obligations. Points such as these are likely to emerge and be properly dealt with only after personal discussion with the solicitor. That is most unlikely to happen if the solicitor is in a centralised department of a finance organisation a long way away from the place where the house or flat is being bought. The unhappy experiences with the trustee departments of large banks, with their lack of understanding and contact with beneficiaries, show how inadequate remote departments of large finance organisations can be.

23.21 There are many unfortunate examples of large finance organisations making unreasonable demands of prospective borrowers which have been withdrawn only after strong representations by independent solicitors acting for the borrowers. In cases such as these the buyer-borrower has no likelihood of receiving strong independent advice, if his adviser is an in-house solicitor in the conveyancing department of the finance organisation making the demand.

23.22 Para. 3.2 of the Conveyancing Green Paper contains the extraordinary statement that

> "in the vast majority of cases, the interests of the borrower and the lender in the conveyancing transaction will be identical".

That statement is unfounded. There is no conflict of interest between borrower and lender in so far as both want to obtain valid title to a marketable property of a value sufficient to provide reasonable security for the loan. Thereafter their interests diverge. The lender wants the highest rate of interest, the borrower the lowest rate. The lender wants to provide a bridging loan, the borrower to avoid any bridging loan. The lender wants life insurance giving the lowest return for the premium, the borrower wants the highest return for the least premium: similarly with property insurance. The lender is interested in tying the borrower to the maximum number of the lender's services; the borrower's interest is in securing the best services at the lowest price from any source, not limited to the lender. It is regrettable that the Government should put forward proposals based to so large an extent on this incorrect assumption.

INCONSISTENCY WITH CONSUMER CREDIT PROTECTION

23.23 The Consumer Credit Act 1974 (the 1974 Act) is designed to protect the public as individuals when entering into agreements for the provision of credit not exceeding £15,000, other than agreements concerned with the buying of land or the provision of houses and flats. It covers second mortgages on houses or flats to secure credit agreements concerned with the provision of credit otherwise than for buying land or providing houses or flats. The detailed provisions of the 1974 Act are designed to distance the lender from the borrower, and to give the maximum incentive and opportunity for the borrower to reflect on the transaction and to obtain independent advice.

23.24 The Government's proposals in the Conveyancing Green Paper are a serious departure from the policy and practice laid down in the 1974 Act. The departure is the more serious because the buying of a house or flat is generally a much larger transaction and much more important to the home-buyer than the transactions covered by the 1974 Act.

23.25 Under the 1974 Act where a consumer credit agreement (a "regulated agreement") is to be secured on a house or flat (e.g. by second mortgage), the lender must send to the borrower drafts of the agreement, the mortgage and other documents, plus a statement of the borrower's right to withdraw. The lender must then wait at least 7 days before sending to the borrower the agreement, mortgage and other documents for the borrower to sign. The lender is precluded *from any other communication* with the borrower for a period which starts with the sending of the original drafts, and ends 7 days after the despatch of the agreement for signature or on the lender receiving the agreement signed by the borrower. Thus in practice for 14 days the lender must refrain from trying to persuade the borrower to go ahead. See sections 58 and 61 of the 1974 Act.

23.26 This elaborate system was devised specifically to minimise the opportunities for the lender to influence or pressurise the borrower. It was recognised by the Crowther Committee, whose Report led to the passing of the 1974 Act, that the ability of large and experienced finance organisations to influence inexperienced and unsophisticated borrowers needed to be counteracted. The reason why loans and mortgages for the buying of houses and flats were exempted from the stringent requirements of sections 58 and 61 of the 1974 Act was that it was assumed that the buyer-borrower would be using independent solicitors to carry out the necessary conveyancing, who could give independent advice on the terms put forward by the finance organisations offering mortgages.

23.27 If the Green Paper proposals are implemented, therefore, the anomalous position will be created whereby

(1) if the borrower is borrowing a large sum on mortgage to buy a house, he will be not only permitted but encouraged to place in the lending finance organisation all the trust and confidence which he would now place in his independent solicitor;

BUT (2) if he is borrowing a small amount of money for any other purpose and it is to be secured by a second mortgage on his home, the lender is compelled to treat the borrower with great care and is, at the most important time, barred from communicating with the borrower at all.

That such an absurd position could be suggested indicates that the authors of the Green Paper were unaware of the provisions of the 1974 Act and of the policy which underlies it.

23.28 The solution to this problem is *not* to place borrowers, in the most important transactions of their lives, under the influence of the proposed lenders, but rather to apply to conveyancing transactions principles at least as stringent as those contained in the 1974 Act, and therefore not to proceed with the Green Paper proposals.

SOCIAL NEEDS

23.29 If the Green Paper proposals were put through, finance organisations would be given a charter to destroy the economic base of local solicitors. They could charge for conveyancing services *at cost* (i.e. on a basis of cost determined subjectively by them) and could make up for lack of profit on conveyancing by charging a bit more on other services. If solicitors charged for conveyancing at cost, they would soon be out of business. They could not subsidise conveyancing out of legal aid fees, whether criminal or civil. Thus the large finance organisations would be specifically empowered by statute to compete unfairly. How it can be in the public interest to empower large organisations to compete unfairly is, not surprisingly, not explained in the Green Paper.

23.30 The effect of this unfair competition would be, over a period, to drive local solicitors out of business. No doubt some would be employed by the finance organisations, while others would gravitate to the large solicitor firms or the large multi-disciplinary practices which the Government proposes should be created. What the ordinary members of the public would lose would be the ability to seek quick and reasonably priced advice from a local solicitor with knowledge and experience of local needs. That would be a very serious loss to the public in matters which, though small in financial terms, are of great importance to the individuals affected. The matrimonial problems, the problems with children and with access to and custody of children, the small criminal charges, the small debts; on all of these it would be even harder for the individual to find legal advice at a price which he could afford, or with the benefit of legal aid, in his locality. Legal advice only available at higher cost from a large practice in a city 70 miles away may be useless to the individual who now can obtain cheaper advice in a small town 5 miles away from a solicitor whose reputation and experience is well-known and trusted.

23.31 Elementary matters such as these find no place in the Conveyancing Green Paper. In "Crossbow" for Winter 1989 the Secretary of State for Trade and Industry said that:

> "We know that unconstrained market forces can create monopolies, can lead to unfair agreements between companies and can create pricing

conditions which discriminate. That is why I prefer the phrase OPEN markets in describing what we have sought to achieve within our market economy over the last decade.

This government has intervened to ensure the openness of markets:

FIRST by acting against monopolies and cartels and to ensure that competition exists.

SECOND by providing ground rules which can give people confidence in the proper working or markets."

In relation to conveyancing the Green Paper proposals

(1) would give monopoly powers to the large finance organisations and ensure that less competition exists in this field by removing the economic base of the small local solicitor;

(2) fail to provide "a level playing field" which (as the Director General of the Building Societies Association has said) could not be achieved, whether by the proposal that the large finance organisations should not provide the service at less than cost, or in any other way.

CONCLUSION

23.32 In the Bar Council's view the correct conclusion is that it is not in the public interest for finance organisations to be permitted to provide conveyancing services. Serious conflicts of interest would arise. The public would not obtain from such organisations the independent advice which independent solicitors (with access to the entire Bar) can now offer. That was the conclusion of the Royal Commission based on a large quantity of evidence. The Green Paper proposals are based on no evidence, as the Lord Chancellor by his Permanent Secretary has acknowledged.

24

Contingency Fees

24.1 Shortly before the publication of the Contingency Fees Green Paper, the Bar Council published the Report of a Working Party led by Francis Ferris QC on contingency fees (which is at Annex 4). The detailed arguments are contained in that Report, and, except where the views of the Bar Council diverge from those of the Working Party, this Chapter contains only a summary of the principal points. Reference is made to the Report because it contains a much more carefully considered statement of the points and arguments than the Green Paper, in which no attempt is made at any study of the problems raised by the various possible types of contingency fee.

24.2 The Green Paper canvasses four possible ways in which a system of contingency fees might operate:

(1) A speculative basis similar to that presently permitted in Scotland;
(2) A speculative basis (as in Scotland) but with the additional feature that the lawyer would be entitled to an uplift in fees to reflect the risks he has undertaken;
(3) A restricted contingency basis;
(4) An unrestricted contingency basis.

THE SPECULATIVE BASIS

24.3 The speculative basis is that described in the Working Party Report as a "no win no fee" arrangement. The Working Party recommended that, as in Scotland, such arrangements should be permitted, for the reasons stated in the Report, which can be summarised as follows:-

(1) freedom of trade points in the direction of allowing such an arrangement;

258

(2) because a lawyer is unlikely to make a "no win no fee" arrangement unless the lawyer regards the chances of success as reasonably high, the risk of serious loss being suffered by the lay client, through having to pay the taxed costs of the action to the opposing party if he loses, can be regarded as in general not a major risk;

(3) though conflicts of interest would create problems when the question of compromise arose or the client wished to change lawyer, these would be unlikely to be serious problems in relation to "no win no fee" arrangements;

(4) the conduct of lawyers who enter into such arrangements could adequately be regulated by professional rules of conduct.

24.4 The Bar Council recognises that "no win no fee" arrangements do not give rise to dangers of the same magnitude as would occur if award-sharing fees were permitted. However, the Bar Council concludes, on balance, that it would not be right to permit "no win no fee" arrangements on three grounds of principle:

(1) A lawyer should not, in any circumstances, be permitted to have a direct financial stake in the outcome of his client's case.

(2) The conflicts of interest that would arise between lawyer and client when questions of settlement arose are inevitable and it is difficult to see how the rules of professional conduct could really provide any solution. When considering whether or not to accept an offer of settlement, the client is entitled to expect the lawyer to give disinterested advice based on his assessment of the case and the client's best interests. However, with a "no win no fee" arrangement another consideration comes into play. If the case is settled the lawyer can be sure of being paid; whereas if the case proceeds the lawyer risks receiving nothing. However scrupulous the lawyer, it is impossible for him to disregard these matters altogether.

(3) Such arrangements would tend to lower the ethical standards of the profession. The incentive to win and thus to receive remuneration for the case would inevitably tend to cloud the lawyer's judgment. It could also affect the bond of trust which should exist between the Judge and the barrister by virtue of the barrister's over-riding duty to the Court.

Furthermore, the Bar Council consider that any contingency fee arrangements including the simple "no win no fee" basis, would have little impact, if any, on the availability of legal services to persons of modest means.

24.5 Attention should be drawn to the fact that the Green Paper in para. 4.1 appears to be confused as to the circumstances in which a taxation of costs would be required. It is stated that:

> "It would not . . . be necessary to obtain a full taxation in every case
> funded on a speculative basis. Taxation would be required only where, as
> is the case now, there is a dispute between solicitor and client as to the
> amount that the solicitor can reasonably charge in his bill."

That is not a correct statement. It is important to understand that,
under the English costs rules, there are two systems of costs: (1) that
which applies between the parties to the proceedings; and (2) that
which applies as between the solicitor and his client.

24.6 *Costs between Parties* In the event that a party succeeds at
trial, he will usually be awarded his costs against the unsuccessful
party, to be taxed if not agreed. In the High Court, those costs are
ordinarily taxed on a "standard" basis, although the Court does have
a discretion to award costs on an "indemnity" basis (RSC Order 62
Rule 12). The difference between the two bases of taxation is in the
burden of proof. Where costs are taxed on the "standard" basis, the
burden of proof is on the claimant to establish that the costs were
reasonably incurred, whereas where costs are taxed on the
"indemnity" basis, the burden of proof is reversed. In practice,
taxations on an "indemnity" basis are rare.

24.7 *Costs between client and solicitor* As between a solicitor and
his client, costs are taxed on a quite different basis, the "solicitor and
own client" basis (RSC Order 62 Rule 15). In many cases, the result is
that the successful party recovers less from the unsuccessful party
than he is liable to pay to his own solicitor. For instance, under the
"solicitor and own client" basis, any costs incurred with the express
or implied approval of the client are presumed to be reasonable;
whereas, as between parties, the mere fact that one party has
approved the expenditure of costs by no means establishes that they
were reasonable. In the County Court where, particularly for smaller
cases, there are severe restrictions on what the successful party may
recover from the unsuccessful party, the difference between what the
client recovers from the other party and what he pays to his solicitor is
often very substantial.

24.8 Taxations are generally unnecessary where the parties agree
the costs. As between a solicitor and his client, taxations are not
frequently required. But as between parties, taxations are commonly
required. The number of taxations that might be required would
depend on the precise nature of the "no win no fee" arrangements
that might be permitted. If the Scottish system were strictly followed,
then, as we understand it, the lawyers would only receive such fees as
they could recover from the opposing party. In that case, there would
be no need for a solicitor and client taxation as between the successful
party and his solicitors, but there might have to be both a taxation

between the parties, and a solicitor and client taxation between the unsuccessful party and his solicitor. If this were all that was permitted, the solicitor who was engaged on a "no win no fee" basis could, even if his client was successful, often recover less than he would if he had been retained on the ordinary basis.

THE REVISED SPECULATIVE BASIS

24.9 The proposition (in the Green Paper) is that solicitors who enter into "no win no fee" arrangements should be entitled to fix an additional percentage by reference to the amount of taxed costs which the solicitor could recover from his client, to compensate the solicitor for the risk he has undertaken, by entering into the arrangement, that he might recover no fees at all. This proposal goes further than simply allowing the solicitor to recover his costs in the event of success on a "solicitor and own client" basis. This proposal apparently would entitle the solicitor to stipulate for, say, an additional 10% or 20% on top of the "solicitor and own client" costs which would be recoverable from the client in the event of success.

24.10 On a proper analysis there are grave objections to allowing solicitors to enter into such arrangements. The objections are, in essence, the same that are made in the Working Party Report in relation to award-sharing fees. Such arrangements would be offered to plaintiffs mainly in the personal injuries field though also perhaps in some debt and contract cases. To the lay client, such arrangements may seem attractive. But the solicitor advising the client would have a serious conflict of interest, between the client's interest in recovering what is due, and the solicitor's interest in making money. The ethical objections to this sort of arrangement are strong. In practice the solicitor is unlikely to offer such an arrangement unless he considers that there is a strong prospect of his client succeeding. In many personal injuries cases, it is virtually certain that the plaintiff will succeed, the real issue being the amount of damages. The client may well not obtain proper independent advice from his solicitor as to whether his interests are best served by entering into an arrangement of this kind with his solicitor. In practice we believe that to allow such arrangements would be to permit solicitors to increase their income at the expense of plaintiffs with strong cases, who would simply end up paying a larger bill than was justified.

24.11 Para. 3.12 of the Green Paper seems to contemplate that the main advantage of contingency fees is that they might give "small" plaintiffs the opportunity of bringing their claims to Court. In the case of small plaintiffs with small claims, the proposals could act particularly unfairly. In the County Court, "solicitor and own client" costs often account for a large proportion of the total claim, simply because the sum at stake does not reflect the amount of work involved for the solicitor. If these arrangements were permitted, the smaller the claim, the larger the proportion of it which would be taken by the solicitor in the form of his percentage uplift of costs.

THE RESTRICTED AND UNRESTRICTED AWARD-SHARING BASES

24.12 The Working Party's views on award-sharing contingency fees are set out in detail in their Report, and can be summarised as follows:

(1) Under an award-sharing arrangement, whether restricted or unrestricted, the lawyer would, if successful, gain much larger remuneration that he would under a conventional fee arrangement. The lawyer would be likely to be interested in award-sharing arrangements primarily in cases in which the client has a high chance of success. The interest of the lawyer in getting an award-sharing arrangement and the interest of the client in having an ordinary fee arrangement would be in direct conflict. But the client who would be likely to be poor, or suffering from physical or mental distress, and easily imposed upon, would be looking to the lawyer to advise the client in the client's best interests.

(2) Such conflicts of interest could not be avoided and could not be regulated.

(3) It has for centuries been the law of England that such a bargain between a client and his lawyer is presumed to have been made by undue influence, unless it is proved that the client made a free and fully informed choice, usually after obtaining wholly independent advice. To permit award-sharing arrangements would go against this elementary principle, and it is surprising that this finds no mention in the Green Paper.

(4) If an award-sharing arrangement were permitted, a stage in the case might well come when the lawyer's interests would be best served by spending no more money and accepting any compromise on offer, however inadequate from the client's point of view. Again the problem of conflict of interest would arise in an acute form.

(5) Similar problems would arise if the client wished to change his lawyer.

(6) The ethical standards of the profession would be lowered, since the lawyer would have a strong incentive to act unethically to secure his share in an award or settlement.

(7) The phenomenon of "ambulance chasing", which reached a nadir of cynicism after the Bhopal disaster and the Lockerbie crash, would become an inevitable feature of English life, as it has in the U.S.A.

(8) Award-sharing arrangements would lead to a greater number of unmeritorious claims the main purpose of which would be to "blackmail" defendants into settlements for the benefit of the lawyers. This is a well-known and much regretted feature in the U.S.A.

(9) Award-sharing arrangements would increase the cost of litigation.

24.13 The Bar Council agrees with all these reasons for opposing any form of award-sharing arrangement. To embark on allowing any such form of arrangement at a time when the United States are seeking to bring this kind of arrangement under control and to curb the serious abuses which result would not be wise.

CONTINGENCY LEGAL AID FUND

24.14 It is both surprising and disappointing that there is not even a mention of the proposal for a "Contingency Legal Aid Fund" (CLAF) in the Green Paper. It seems extraordinary that no consideration whatever is given to this important possibility which could, if introduced, operate strongly in the public interest. Presumably this was because the many reports including those by JUSTICE were not made available to the authors of the Green Paper.

24.15 CLAF was mooted by JUSTICE in 1966 and 1978 and has since been endorsed by other bodies. The essence of CLAF is a fund which would invite applications from prospective litigants. If an application was accepted, CLAF would undertake to pay the costs of the assisted litigant in the event of his failure including any award of costs in favour of the opposing party. If the action succeeded or were compromised, CLAF would have the right to a percentage of the amount recovered, the percentage being calculated at a rate sufficient to cover the costs payable out by CLAF in unsuccessful cases. So CLAF would be self-financing as a kind of mutual insurance fund.

24.16 The Bar Council considers that the viability of a CLAF fund should be tested by the introduction of a carefully controlled pilot scheme on the lines proposed by JUSTICE.

THE BALANCE OF BENEFIT AND DETRIMENT

24.17   At the heart of the discussion in the Working Party's Report is an attempt to balance the arguments for and against contingency fees by reference to the public interest. The Green Paper mentions some of the points in passing but makes no real attempt to analyse the problems.

24.18   *Conflict of Interest*   First, the risk of a conflict of interest arising if award-sharing contingency fees were allowed is discussed in two short paragraphs of the Green Paper. As stated in the Working Party Report (paras. 9.1–9.6), the conflicts of interest which would arise in practice would result in serious disadvantage to the client. It is naive to suppose that the client's interest can receive adequate protection from professional codes of conduct, especially when such codes, excellently drafted, exist in the United States, but have failed to prevent the grave abuses found there, as the Green Paper itself recognises.

24.19   *Fostering a litigious society*   Secondly, the Green Paper does not address adequately the potential for an increased volume of litigation arising from the introduction of award-sharing contingency fees. It is unrealistic to assume, as the Green Paper apparently does, that we would not follow behind the United States in becoming an excessively litigious society. It is illogical to assume that there would not be an increase in unjustified litigation if award sharing fees were permitted.

24.20   *Access to Justice*   Thirdly, as regards access to justice, the Green Paper takes a superficial and even doctrinaire stance. No one argument in favour of or against contingency fees is conclusive. It is quite wrong to state (para. 3.15 of the Green Paper) that

> ". . . allowing . . . freedom of choice could alone be regarded as grounds for lifting the ban on contingency fees."

The concept of clients "shopping around" lawyers to obtain the best contingency fee deal is illusory, especially if the client is "small". It is still more illusory for the poor, sick in mind or body, or disabled, or inexperienced in dealing with lawyers, as almost all lay clients are. It does not follow that the lawyer offering the cheapest contingency fee deal has the competence to do the case properly. Indeed it might be supposed that the least competent would be likely to offer the lowest rates to try and attract business which they could not otherwise obtain. But how is the lay client to judge whether the lawyer in fact has the necessary competence?

EXCLUDED PROCEEDINGS

24.21   In para. 4.14 of the Green Paper, comments are invited on whether there are types of proceedings in respect of which "no win no fee" or award-sharing arrangements would be inappropriate. The Bar Council considers that there are at least the following categories of case which require special consideration:

(1) *All Criminal Cases*   The Green Paper recognises that it would be inappropriate on the grounds of public policy to permit lawyers to act on a contingency basis in criminal proceedings. The Bar Council agrees.

(2) *Family Cases*   In the United States, contingency fees are largely prohibited in family cases. There are in essence three types of proceedings involved:

    (a) *Divorce, Nullity or Judicial Separation*: the "no win no fee" arrangement would be the only possible arrangement here, since there can be no award to share. On obvious ethical grounds it would not be in the public interest for a lawyer to have a direct personal and financial interest in the outcome of the suit.

    (b) *Custody of and access to children*: the only possible contingency arrangement would be a "no win no fee" arrangement. It would be wholly against the public interest if, in such already highly charged and fraught litigation, a lawyer had a direct personal interest in, for instance, obtaining custody of a child for his client.

    (c) *Financial provision*: here there is usually a sum of money on which an award-sharing arrangement could operate. But it would again be contrary to the public interest if the lawyer were entitled to a share of what had been awarded to his client by way of financial provision. Most divorces result in two households each much worse off in financial terms. Since the financial provision is calculated by reference to the *needs of the parties*, if the lawyer were to receive part of the provision, either that provision would be inadequate or the paying party would have to pay more. This could not be desirable.

(3) *Immigration cases*   It would not be in the public interest for the lawyer acting for the immigrant to have a direct personal interest in achieving success for that immigrant in securing the right to remain in the United Kingdom. The public would be disquieted in this sensitive area, if they felt that the lawyer might, for instance, be tempted to "improve" the evidence in order to

increase his chances of receiving a fee for the case. The objections are rather similar to the objections that the Green Paper accepts would arise if lawyers in criminal cases were to be remunerated on a contingency basis.

(4) *Other Administrative Law cases* Similar considerations would apply to all other cases in which an application for judicial review is made in respect of a decision by a person or body in the sphere of public law.

24.22 Finally, it must be stated that access to justice for all who need access to justice could not be affected more than minimally by any contingency fee arrangement. Even if CLAF were tried and proved successful, it could not handle the large proportion of cases which are not amenable to any sort of contingency arrangement. The choice is ultimately between making adequate provision to protect the legal rights of those who cannot afford to protect themselves, or leaving the poor, the disabled, the sick without effective legal rights.

25

Ethnic Minorities

25.1 "The Bar Council has, in recent years, taken positive steps to combat racial discrimination and disadvantage at the Bar." That is a quotation from the comments on the main Green Paper by the Race Relations Committee (RRC) of the Bar Council. The RRC is a large committee composed mainly of barristers from ethnic minority communities, with representatives of all the main minority communities, and chaired by a High Court Judge (the Hon. Mr. Justice Brooke).

25.2 In 1987 the Bar Council and the RRC decided that there was insufficient accurate information as to the numbers of barristers, pupils and applicants for pupillage from the minorities. Social and Community Planning Research with Coopers & Lybrand were commissioned to conduct a full survey. This achieved a remarkably high response rate from chambers of 88%. The survey report was received in March 1989. It is too detailed to be readily summarised. But a few statistics will show the nature of the contribution of the minorities and the problems they face ("EM" is used for "ethnic minorities"):-

(1) Proportions of EM barristers among all barristers and different types of barrister

All	–	5% EM
Q.C.s	–	1% EM
Juniors	–	6% EM
Pupils	–	12% EM

The proportions are lower among those in more senior positions. The survey team concluded that this may be a consequence of the differing age profiles of the positions, rather than a result of direct or indirect racial discrimination. The average age of economically active non-whites is considerably lower than the average age of senior barristers, so that in any event the team would expect to see fewer EM barristers in senior positions.

(2) Proportions of main ethnic groups among EM barristers

Asians	–	41%
West Indian	–	27%
Black African	–	19%

(3) 16 chambers with 4 or more EM barristers contained 53% of all EM barristers, but only 6% of all barristers. 46% of the barristers in these 16 chambers were EM barristers.

(4) Pupil applications, interviews and pupillages – EM as % of total

Applications	–	17%
Interviews	–	17%
Pupillages	–	12%

Many applicants made several applications and attended several interviews, and some had 2 or more pupillages. So the figures relate e.g. to applications rather than applicants. These figures appear to indicate that more EM applicants than white applicants are rejected for pupillages. But the survey team considered that EM applicants may, on average, have made more applications, had more interviews and turned down more pupillage offers than white applicants: if so, that would account for some at least of the difference.

25.3 The Bar Council and the RRC will now carefully consider the report and decide what steps are to be taken to remedy the problems especially those in recruitment. The Bar Council welcomes the fact that barristers from ethnic minorities are 5% of the Bar, a higher percentage it is believed than in most other professions. 4% of economically active people of working age are from ethnic minorities (Labour Force Survey). This figure is not directly comparable, but gives some indication of the Bar's achievement in recruiting from ethnic minorities. The statistics which cause the Bar Council most concern are those in para. 25.2(3) above. They show that EM barristers are much too heavily concentrated in a relatively small number of chambers. Policies to change this position will have to be devised with the help of the RRC.

25.4 It is against this background that the effect on ethnic minorities and barristers drawn from the minorities, of the Green Paper proposals has to be considered. The following points are made in the light of the RRC's comments on the main Green Paper:-

(1) There is no mention of race relations or the role of ethnic minorities in the Green Paper (except the passing mention in para. 11.4 of a criticism of the Bar's pupillage allocation system which the survey indicates may be an unfounded criticism). This is a serious lapse on the part of the Government and shows that it

did not give the role of ethnic minorities any priority in its overall thinking.

(2) The inadequate funding and restrictions on consumer choice envisaged under the new Legal Aid Act will mean that ethnic minorities will be the first to be adversely affected.

(3) The Green Paper proposals, if implemented, would probably bring about the end of the "cab-rank" rule. This would be against the interest of ethnic minorities, who would be the first to suffer in terms of choice and quality of representation in the courts.

(4) The proposals would be likely to lead to a curtailment of legal work done in non-specialist fields, and to result in a drastic reduction in the work done by most barristers from ethnic minorities. This would lead to a reduction in the number of ethnic minority barristers available to serve their communities.

(5) There is no reason to believe that the proposals on legal education, rights of audience and specialisation would make access to the legal profession by ethnic minorities any easier.

(6) Advocacy certificates would be a further obstacle for potential advocates from ethnic minorities, and would be seen as giving a potential opportunity to discriminate against able EM lawyers by those with the power to grant or withhold the certificates needed by EM lawyers to work on behalf of ethnic minorities.

26

Professional Bodies

26.1 This Chapter contains some proposals for the future of the bodies which control the Bar and the solicitors profession.

THE BAR

26.2 The present distribution of responsibilities between the General Council of the Bar (the Bar Council) and the four Inns of Court has virtues both of competition and collaborative joint venture:-

(1) The Inns are charitable bodies devoted to the education and welfare of students, pupils and other barristers. They carry out their educational functions through the Council of Legal Education (CLE) which runs the Inns of Court School of Law (ICSL). By delegation from the Judges the Inns call women and men to the Bar and exercise disciplinary powers over barristers and students (through the Council of the Inns of Court which appoints Disciplinary Tribunals for this purpose) subject always to the supervision of and appeals to the Judges as Visitors. The Inns compete with each other in the recruitment of students and in the provision of scholarships and other awards to students, pupils and other barristers, though the programme of visits to universities and polytechnics is coordinated by the Student Officers Committee of the four Inns. The Inns' main resource is their buildings, including a substantial number of chambers let to barristers. It is the policy of the Bar Council, as agreed with the four Inns, that chambers shall be let to barristers at market rents, so as to ensure that the Inns have reasonable funds for their charitable purposes including the upkeep of their present buildings, and for the building or acquisition of new buildings. The Inns are run by Benchers composed of Judges and senior practising barristers, both Queen's Counsel and Juniors.

(2) The Council of the Inns of Court provides an effective forum for joint decision-making by the four Inns on which both the Bar Council and the CLE are represented.

(3) The Bar Council is representative of all sections of the practising Bar. It is responsible for the professional standards of the Bar in accordance with a Code of Conduct laid down under the supervision of the Judges. It is responsible for the receipt or initiation and investigation of complaints against barristers and for the prosecution of disciplinary charges before Disciplinary Tribunals. It is responsible also for the formulation of policy matters affecting the Bar and for negotiations on behalf of the Bar in relation to all matters affecting the Bar including Legal Aid and other fees.

As appears above, the summary in Annex B, paras. 1 and 2, of the main Green Paper is not entirely accurate.

26.3 The long history of the Inns of Court would not justify their continued existence if they were not useful. They **are** useful. They form an important bridge between the Judges, the Bar as the advocates in the higher Courts, and the students wishing to become such advocates. In the ICSL they have an institution running the only course dedicated solely to the training of advocates for the higher Courts. They have a large body of experience and expertise in the development of qualified advocates and in the maintenance of high professional standards amongst advocates through "peer group discipline" and, where necessary, through effective use of disciplinary procedures.

26.4 It appears to be suggested by the Government that advocates would be licensed to appear in the higher Courts by other professional bodies, and would not have the benefits of control and encouragement by the Inns of Court. Such other professional bodies would have little or no accumulated knowledge or experience in training advocates, even for the lower courts, or in maintenance of the high standards of advocates which the Government expects and, much more, the public is entitled to expect.

26.5 The Bar Council considers that it would be the worst course of all to proceed, not only by destroying the basis of the independent Bar, but also by denying the public the benefit of training, control and encouragement of advocates by those with the most experience and expertise. Whatever changes the Government may decide to force through (over and above those changes which the Bar itself is making and will make: see especially Chapters 19 and 20 above) it is necessary and desirable that for the foreseeable future

(1) the CLE should continue to train the advocates who aspire to advocacy in the higher Courts;

(2) the Inns of Court should, under the continued supervision of the Judges, exercise "peer group discipline" and formal disciplinary control, subject to appeal to the Judges as Visitors, over all advocates who are to be permitted to appear in the higher Courts;

(3) the Inns should by delegation from the Judges exercise the power of deciding who may appear in the higher Courts, a power which could conveniently be exercised in conjunction with the running of a compulsory continuing education course on the lines indicated in para. 19.23 above.

26.6 Put simply, the Bar Council believes that it would be foolish to throw away, **destructively**, the benefits of the CLE course and of the Inns' role and expertise: the right course is to continue to build **constructively** on what is successful already and on the changes already in progress. There is a new spirit at work in the Inns and in the CLE, and it would be a waste of scarce human resources not to use them to the full.

SOLICITORS

26.7 The profession of "Solicitors of the Supreme Court" was created by the Supreme Court of Judicature Act 1873, bringing together the three professions of attorneys, proctors and solicitors. It is therefore a profession regulated to a large extent by statute (Solicitors Act 1974) though its main professional body, the Law Society, received a charter in 1831 and is still a body incorporated by Charter. Many of the statutory powers relating to solicitors are exercised by a senior Judge, the Master of the Rolls, who has extensive powers of supervision over the profession under the 1974 Act. Solicitors as officers of the Court are subject to the controlling jurisdiction of the Supreme court. Discipline is generally enforced by means of the Solicitors Disciplinary Tribunal appointed by the Master of the Rolls, though the Supreme Court retains disciplinary powers through its controlling jurisdiction.

26.8 The Bar Council makes the following observations arising out of experience in recent years, and the large number of responses received from solicitors firms all over the country to the Bar Council's Consultative Document (responses were received from over 1400 firms of solicitors).

26.9 There is a strong case for the solicitor profession to be under the supervision of the Judges to the same extent as the Bar. Recent cases for example involving major defalcations with clients' funds have been disturbing to the public and costly to the profession through the Compensation Fund maintained under the 1974 Act. They are only some examples of what needs fuller supervision by the Judges. If the task of supervising so large a profession (over 50,000 solicitors with practising certificates) were too onerous for the Master of Rolls, who also presides over the Court of Appeal, Civil Division, that task could be shared with the other Judges under the overall supervision of the Master of the Rolls.

26.10 The extensive evidence received by the Bar Council showed (1) a strong desire among many smaller firms of solicitors for greater representation in the Law Society; and (2) a wish for greater use in the Law Society of the talents of the best solicitors in the City of London. These are matters which the solicitors profession will no doubt wish to resolve themselves.

27

Epilogue

The public interest in the maintenance of a strong and independent Bar is stated most clearly and most simply in the following letter published in "The Times" in March 1989:

QUALITY OF JUSTICE

From Mr. Cyril Moseley

Sir,

The men and women of these mining valleys know pain and anguish only too well: Aberfan, the Lewis Merthyr Colliery explosion, men crippled and disfigured in accidents in the coal faces and in the tunnels underground. It is a melancholy chronicle, relieved only by stories of devotion and heroism. Those families needed first-class advocates. They got them: advocates of great skill and experience from Cardiff, Swansea and London.

At the Aberfan inquiry, at the end of the brilliant cross-examination of a prominant NCB witness by leading counsel for the parents and residents' association, one parent came up to me and said: "That was like balm to my soul". He had lost his wife, his two children, and his home. All he had left was what he stood up in.

I speak only of my own experience. I saw silks and junior counsel fighting on behalf of ordinary men and women and for powerful corporations. Most of all, I heard them in court on behalf of injured colliers and their stricken widows and children. My hope is that the Government will decide not to alter any part of the training and experience which moulded these advocates.

The delicate arrangements which produce the standards of excellence and spirit of independence should not be tampered with, lest we undermine or even destroy the very qualities which are crucial to us all in both judge and barrister.

The Inns of Court may seem mysterious places to most of us. But they produce the goods: a fearless judiciary and formidable advocates. As a retired solicitor, I believe that if the pool of counsel shrinks, if there is a suspicion that the appointment of the judge or the promotion of the advocate is tainted even remotely by prejudice, it is ordinary men and women who will suffer.

Yours faithfully,

CYRIL MOSELEY
Bryn-Onen,
Cefn-Coed-y-Cymmer,
Merthyr Tydfil, Mid Glamorgan.
March 21.